HELPING PEOPLE

The Task-Centered Approach
Second Edition

Laura Epstein
Professor Emeritus
School of Social Service Administration
The University of Chicago

MERRILL PUBLISHING COMPANY
A Bell & Howell Information Company
Columbus   Toronto   London   Melbourne

Cover art: Cathy Watterson
Published by Merrill Publishing Company
A Bell & Howell Information Company
Columbus, Ohio 43216

This book was set in Souvenir.
Administrative Editor: Vicki Knight
Production Coordinator: Anne Daly
Art Coordinator: Lorraine Woost
Cover Designer: Cathy Watterson
Text Designer: Connie Young

Photo credits: All photos copyrighted by individuals or companies listed. Merrill Publishing/**p. xiv; p. 143** (Jean Greenwald); **pp. 46, 212** (Mary Hagler); **p. 222** (Jan Hall); and **pp. 22, 172** (Bruce Johnson). Student Support Services Publication Center, University of Minnesota/**pp. 84, 103.**

Library of Congress Catalog Card Number: 87-061413
International Standard Book Number: 0-675-20834-3
Printed in the United States of America

1 2 3 4 5 6 7 8 9—92 91 90 89 88

PREFACE

Practitioners and students in human service occupations have some dominant concerns, among them how to make plans of action specific enough to guide their cases and how to provide service that is client-oriented and also in harmony with the operations of complex organizations. The most urgent question practitioners ask is *What do I do?*

This book offers guidelines for deciding what to do in many of the usual circumstances of general practice. It attempts to explain how characteristics of agencies, belief patterns of the professions, and social sanctions and expectations of the public affect the results of direct work with clients.

The task-centered model of practice is the base on which this book is built. Presently, the term *task-centered* is affixed to many different ideas about intervention, but when the Task-Centered Project was established in 1970, it was only coming into professional usage. The Project was sponsored by the School of Social Service Administration at the University of Chicago, originally through a small start up grant from a private foundation. The development of the task-centered model was aided by a grant from the Federal Department of Health and Human Services (SRS Grant 18–P–57774/5–03). The work began and continued through the collaboration of William J. Reid and myself, with valuable support from Dean Harold A. Richman and Associate Dean John R. Schuerman.

Research on the model at the University of Chicago occurred between 1970–1978. During those years the Project enrolled about 125 graduate students. They suffered through the trials of the model, testing and refining the work. Doctoral students were exceptionally helpful in conducting studies, supervising students, and developing the task-centered model in new, ingenious ways. Thirteen social agencies in Chicago collaborated by affording fieldwork placements for students and research case material. These agencies included medical and psychiatric hospitals and clinics, school social work departments in public elementary and high schools, child welfare agencies, and others. The Project tests of the task-centered model included approximately 1300 cases handled by students in Chicago agencies between 1970 and 1977. Of this entire group, a smaller number became the sample for the research on processes and outcomes. The practitioners in the American project were nearly all graduate social work students. A number of studies were undertaken in England, using experienced practitioners.

The mission of the Task-Centered Project was to develop technologies that could be learned efficiently, increase the effectiveness of direct services, and increase the ability to conduct research on treatment practices. The first three years of the project, roughly from 1970 to 1973, saw the designing of the basic task-centered model. Its processes and effects were studied in actual case practice. With the publication of *Task-Centered Casework* (W. J. Reid and L. Epstein, New York: Columbia University Press) in 1972, the model attracted interest in agencies throughout the country and abroad. Practitioners and researchers from many settings began to test and develop the model. A specialized literature began to appear. References can be found at the end of each chapter in this book.

Many of the case examples I have used have come from actual cases handled in the Project. Others are from practice supervised by former doctoral students. All cases have been disguised; the names of the agencies have been withheld to prevent improper disclosures.

The technical guidelines described in this book are my attempt to distill and arrange the product of years of model building and practice. Wherever possible guidelines are derived from practice research conducted in the Project and from published practice research conducted elsewhere. Since the end of the Project in 1978, it has been necessary to rely upon personal contacts and published reports from numerous sources to obtain new information. A good deal of practice experience and innovation occurs in day to day work and is not published. Sometimes, it is possible to get such information by word of mouth.

The origins of the task-centered model are varied and represent selections and revisions from a host of ideas and practices that preceded it. Although many questions about the task-centered model remain, years of research-based practice and evaluations of that practice support the conclusion that task-centered practice is effective in reducing many of the problems encountered in a range of agencies.

Many central ideas of the task-centered model have combined with ideas of practice that have other origins. The task-centered model has been adapted to coexist within an eclectic practice framework. This second edition of the book explains how the task-centered approach can be used flexibly. This means considering more settings than originally conceived, and harmonizing the task-centered model with additions and rearrangements by mixing and matching other compatible approaches.

The many clients, students, and agencies who cooperated by giving their effort and resources to this endeavor have been indispensable in making the work possible. Helen Mansfield, The Department of Health, Education, and Welfare (predecessor of The Department of Health and Human Services), aided in shaping the early presentation of this model.

I am indebted to colleagues from the original Project: Professor William J. Reid of The State University of New York at Albany; Associate Professor Lester B. Brown, Wayne State University; Associate Professor Ronald Rooney, University of Minnesota at Minneapolis; Associate Professor Anne E. Fortune, Virginia Commonwealth University; Associate Professor Eleanor R. Tolson, University of Illinois (at Chicago); and Assistant Professor Robert Basso at the Wilfrid Laurier University in Waterloo, Ontario, Canada. To Gwendolynn Graham, who put the original manuscript into readable form, my very great thanks. Also, I sincerely appreciate the constructive comments and suggestions I received from reviewers at different stages in the development of this text: Ronald H. Rooney, University of Minnesota; Craig W. LeCroy, Arizona State University; Jack F. Finley, Portland State University; and Debbie D. Hoffman, Belmont College. I am extremely grateful to Dean Laurence Lynn, and Associate Deans Jeanne Marsh and William Pollack for the resources they provided so that I could carry on this revision.

LAURA EPSTEIN
The University of Chicago

CONTENTS

The indeterminate quality of personal problems | *The relativity of problem definitions* | *Complexity of defining social and personal problems*

CHAPTER **4**
STARTING UP
Receiving Referrals and Applications   **85**

CHAPTER **5**
FIRST STEP
Target Problem Identification   **103**

CHAPTER 6
SECOND STEP
Contracting: Plans, Goals, Tasks, Time Limits, and Other Agreements   143

CHAPTER 7
THIRD STEP
Problem Solving, Assessment, Task Achievement, and Problem Reduction   173

CHAPTER 8

FOURTH STEP
Termination, Extension, Monitoring   213

CHAPTER 9
USING THE TASK-CENTERED MODEL FLEXIBLY   223

CHAPTER

THE TASK-CENTERED MODEL

What It Is; How It Is Applied

Task-centered Practice as a Set of Procedures
Scope of the Task-centered Model: Where Should it be Used?
Basic Procedures: In Brief and In General
Case planning
Implementation
Tasks
Assessment
Summary

THE TASK-CENTERED PRACTICE
──────────── AS A SET OF PROCEDURES ────────────

Task-centered practice is a technology for alleviating specific *target problems* perceived by clients, that is, particular problems clients recognize, understand, acknowledge, and want to attend to. Important other people who care about the clients or put pressure on them influence and shape the target problems. Sometimes authorities require clients to work on problems; in other words, some problems are mandated.

Task-centered practice has a particular way of unfolding. It consists of a start-up and four sequential but overlapping steps. (See Figure 1–1.) The regularity of the steps is important because orderly, systematic processes are most likely to result in good outcomes. Under the pressure of problem solving, these steps tend to occur out of sequence; nonetheless, the practitioner should return to the normal procedure as soon as possible.

The steps in the task-centered approach are methodical and systematic. To the extent that practice is systematized, it tends to be as thorough as circumstances permit. Being systematic can protect clients and practitioners from extremes of bewilderment, frustration, and irrelevancy. Systematic practice minimizes waste of time, effort, and money and encourages effective practice. The influence of structured practice on good outcomes has been demonstrated in studies that cut across various fields of practice and various helping occupations (Reid & Epstein, 1972; Reid & Hanrahan, 1982; Rubin, 1985). Task-centered practice will take a lot of weight and still produce reasonable results. Take a look at Lester's case, which reflects one type of task-centered practice.

Start-up	Client referred by an agency source	Client applies, independently and voluntarily
Chapter 4	**Find out** • Source's goals **Negotiate** • Source's specific goals • Source's resources to achieve goals	Not needed

FIGURE 1–1   Detailed map of the task-centered model

Step 1	**Client target problems identified**
Chapter 5	**Find out** • Problems defined by client • Client priorities (hold to three) • Referral source priorities (mandated problems) • Preliminary rapid early assessment

Step 2	**Contract**
Chapter 6	**Cover** • Priority target problems (three maximum) • Client's specific goals (accepted by practitioner) • Client's general tasks • Practitioner's general tasks • Duration of intervention sequence (time limits) • Schedule for interviews • Schedule for interventions • Parties to be included

Step 3	**Problem solving: task achievement, problem reduction. Select as needed**
Chapter 7	**DEFINE AND SPECIFY TARGET PROBLEM (THREE MAXIMUM)** **Restate and name the problem:** the particular conditions and behaviors to be changed **Assess** (related to target problem and goal) • Target problem How often it occurs (frequency) Where it occurs (site) With whom (participants) What immediate antecedents (forerunners) What consequences (effects) What meaning (importance)

FIGURE 1–1, *continued*

• Social context (social conditions precipitating and maintaining the problem)
Work-school circumstances
Economic status
Family organization
Peer group organization
Housing state
Cultural/ethnic background
• Cognitive-affective circumstances
Client characteristics
Mode of functioning
Personal resources
• Other assessments

GENERATE ALTERNATIVES
• Find out and identify a feasible range of possible problem solving actions

NEGOTIATE SUPPORTIVE AND COLLABORATIVE ACTIONS OF OTHER PERSONS AND AGENCIES

DECISION MAKING (confirm goals, select what will be done, and design details of the intervention strategy)
• Re-affirm contract and goals
• Determine basic interventions
• Plan timing and sequence
• Select participants
• Get client agreement and understanding (informed consent)
• Get agreement and understanding of others

IMPLEMENT (carry out strategy)
Develop tasks
• Formulate tasks
• Get client understanding and agreement to tasks
• Get client understanding of rationale and incentives for tasks
• Summarize tasks
• Review expected difficulties
• Devise plans for client task performance
• Summarize tasks
• Devise plans for client task performance

Support task performance
• Review number of sessions outstanding
• Obtain and use resources
• Find out obstacles to resource provision
• Give instruction

FIGURE 1–1, *continued*

• Give guidance
• Do simulations
• Do role plays, simulation, and guided practice
• Accompany client for modeling and/or advocacy
• Other
• Find out obstacles to task performance
  In the social environment: lack of resources, stress,
     discrimination, structural problems
  In the interpersonal transactions: deficit and conflict, lack of
     cooperation
  In the psychological state: fears, suspicions, lack of knowledge
• Plan actions to remove, reduce, alter obstacles
• Remedy practical barriers to task performance, e.g., lack of
  skills, lack of cooperation and support from others, and lack of
  resources
• Alleviate cognitive barriers to task performance: discuss fears,
  suspicions, lack of knowledge, adverse beliefs
• Plan and state practitioner tasks: inform client of practitioner
  tasks, review implementation of practitioner tasks, review
  problem state

Verify (check, test, confirm, substantiate probable effects of
interventions) and
Monitor (record problem status regularly—use structured
notations, charts, graphs, plus brief, succinct narrative comments)
Revise contract, or some parts of it, if:
• Progress unsatisfactory
• Progress exceeds expectations
• New problems emerge
• Problem takes on different characteristics
• Tasks not performed, or poorly performed
• Supports and resources ineffective
• Practitioner tasks ineffective or not feasible

Step 4	Termination
Chapter 8	**End** **Extend** on evidence of client commitment **Monitor** when mandated by law, court order, or formal agency requirements

FIGURE 1–1, *continued*

CASE 1–1: _____

Lester

Lester is 30. Family, friends, residential care personnel, and social workers say, "He looks mentally retarded." Pushed to explain what such a look is, they say he is thin, has buck teeth, squints often, and has a silly grin. We often rely on such stereotypes to form a commonsense appraisal of others, but it is deplorable if such stereotypes are exalted as "diagnosis."

Lester comes from an average family with a complicated life. His father is a truck driver. His mother died when he was 15. The father was left with Lester, his twin brother, and a small child of 4 years with cerebral palsy. As children, both twins seemed stupid. Shortly after their mother died, their father married a divorced woman who had custody of her two young children.

The stepmother could not care for the teenaged twins as well as the handi-capped son and her own children. Looking for a way to take care of the twins, the father and stepmother had them evaluated at the local psychiatric clinic. Tests showed that both had IQs in the fifties. They were committed to a state residential facility for the mentally retarded; that is, they were sequestered in a place where they could be educated and cared for.

As such places go, the institution was good. The twins attended school. They were to be prepared for "independent living"—meaning self-support. They received vocational training in ceramics, sawmill work, and dairy farming in a western state with lots of tourists (who might buy ceramics), lots of trees (which can be sawed in mills), and lots of cows (for milking). The cost of this care and training for 15 years was estimated at roughly $50,000. What did Lester and his brother get out of it? A 20-point jump in IQ. The twins learned a lot of the things tested on IQ examinations, and that is obviously all to the good. With IQs raised to the 70s, they were no longer so stupid.

When the twins entered the institution, their state had not yet implemented a deinstitutionalization program. But in the first wave of deinstitutionalization pro-grams that occurred in the 1970s, Lester's brother was released first. He fared satisfactorily. Lester stayed inside for another two years. Fifteen years after his admission, Lester was sent to his father, and this started a huge contretemps. The other twin was supporting himself on odd jobs and living in a rooming house, where his father visited him occasionally. But Lester was home, just sit-ting around, a strange, helpless 30-year-old man—in the way, scary, disrupting the home. His father and stepmother were in a panic, furious, and over-whelmed. They demanded that the local welfare office take Lester off their hands—at once!

But should an agency intervene and in what way? Parents are supposed to like and want their children and to offer them care and protection. When the parents came to the welfare office to be interviewed, they defined two and only two target problems: they did not want Lester at home, and they could not afford to pay his rent, feed, and clothe him elsewhere.

Could Lester's parents accept counseling to think about how to adjust their style and habits with Lester at home? To think about how they could make him self-supporting? No. The father's income was too high for him to be eligible for counseling at no cost; he would have to pay a fee. Lester's father was of no mind to receive counseling, let alone pay for it.

What did Lester think was his problem? He had no job, and he did not know his way around the city to look for one. The regulations of that state prohibited cash benefits to able-bodied, single men (Lester was "ineligible"), and Lester's IQ was now too high to qualify him for disability benefits, one category of income-maintenance program.

What was the practitioner's judgment?

There are all kinds of possibilities. It could be stated that the father was a narrow-minded bully or a selfish, opinionated, passive-aggressive personality; that the stepmother was a rigid, obsessive personality, and so forth. Taking such positions would box the practitioner into a corner. As soon as these labels are attached to persons and problems, current logic often holds that counseling is needed to alter the personalities, attitudes, and behaviors involved. In this case, that change would probably mean that the people would need to change part of their personal make-up in a way to achieve their adaptation to the new person in the home; after all, he was a son. This particular practitioner suggested that work be done to decrease the problems targeted by the parents and son, using about eight interviews with the son. Lester was eligible for free counseling because he had no income, and the agency was responsible by administrative regulations for counseling those recently deinstitutionalized. The father would be consulted by telephone (to get around the fee charge). Lester's father said this sounded good: "We'll do what you want; you're the boss."

At the end of that first and only in-person interview with the parents, the father added another target problem: Lester's worrisome conduct. He was lethargic and unhelpful around the house. He had been home one month, had not gone out, and had not lifted a finger (target problem specification). Operating on the general assumption that people do what they know how to do and avoid what they do not know how to do (i.e., they have or lack particular cognitive and/or social skills), the practitioner advised the parents to teach Lester how to do things in the home, as long as he was there, and to treat him as if he had a reasonable amount of brains. At the same time, Lester was advised to come for a series of eight interviews, once weekly.

Meanwhile the practitioner took on his own tasks. He phoned a halfway house to find out if that agency could provide Lester job-finding services. The agency was willing but, as it turned out, not able to find him a low-skilled job. The practitioner phoned the vocational rehabilitation office. It was willing to accept Lester for job training but could not accomplish anything because he was erratic about workshop attendance. The practitioner consulted a public psychological testing service for a retest for Lester. If his IQ was lower on a retest, he might be eligible for financial support. This idea was dropped. In truth, Lester's was not a problem of low intelligence anymore. His problem was lack of knowledge about the city map, streets, and how to talk to ordinary people about the ordinary things people talk about daily. No one rescued the practitioner. Other agencies were reasonable but ineffective. Each had a particular work focus and style; they all did what they thought they were supposed to do and what they could. The practitioner should have understood this but did not. He thought the official job-placement services ought to take over and do whatever was necessary to get Lester placed. His expertise was not in finding jobs for clients but in general counseling and in making and monitoring appropriate referrals for specialized services.

Feeling stymied, he nevertheless did what needed to be done, but he felt let down by the other agencies. In interviews with Lester the practitioner worked out tasks designed to get him a job and a room in a boarding house. The start-up tasks were to make a list of possible places where he might ask for work and to make a list of possible rooming houses where he might live. These are ordinary and unexciting things, yet for Lester they made the difference between knowing and not knowing, doing and sitting around, having tolerable circumstances and intolerable circumstances. Self-actualization and fulfillment of one's potentialities comes down to tolerable versus intolerable circumstances. When solving problems, no neon signs light up; no cymbals clash. Problems get solved and life looks better after a hundred ordinary and unexciting details are taken care of.

To help Lester get his tasks done, the practitioner sat down with him and looked over the want ads and notices from the public employment service about vacancies as well as the rent ads and lists from real estate firms. He taught Lester first how to make the lists, then how to approach a businessman and a landlord: what to say, what to expect, what to do, think, feel. Interview after interview Lester tried, and his results were nil at first. The worker and Lester drudged on.

Meanwhile at home the parents were teaching Lester to use the dishwasher and vacuum, to make his bed, and so forth. They made the effort to talk straight to him and have reasonable expectations. From time to time they felt defeated (depressed), afraid, and enraged. They called up the practitioner and complained loudly. He suggested things they could do and described how they could do them.

SCOPE OF THE TASK-CENTERED MODEL
Where Should It Be Used?

The task-centered model can be used with a variety of personal, interpersonal, and situational problems and with many different types of clients and settings. Published reports concerning use of the model have come from those who work with the aging (Cormican, 1977; Dierking, Brown, & Fortune, 1980; Rathbone-McCuan, 1985); families and groups (Fortune, 1985; Garvin, 1974, Reid &

Epstein, 1977; Reid, 1981, 1985); children in foster care (Rooney, 1981, Rzepnicki, 1985); children and adults (Fortune, 1979; Reid, 1978; Reid & Epstein, 1977); corrections (Larsen & Mitchell, 1980; Goldberg, Gibbons, & Sinclair, 1984), mental health (Reid & Epstein, 1977; Goldberg, Gibbons, & Sinclair, 1984). The task-centered model can be used with difficult cases, easy cases, and all the cases that fall between those two categories. Obviously, the most important problems and the most involved conditions will probably need the most complex applications of the model.

Most troubles have two components: the person lacks resources for alleviating a problem and the person lacks skills for alleviating a problem. By configuring for these two problem sections, the practitioner should be able to plan workable interventions.

There are serious and exceptional problem circumstances, to be sure. Occasions arise when a client may be in danger or when he or she may be dangerous to others. Human service practitioners are not commonly involved with violent or dangerous clients or clients whose conditions are truly rare. However, when the need is there, organizations employ security personnel trained to handle dangerous situations. Organizations of good standards have experienced supervisors and access to specialized consultants. They also provide specialized training to staff when necessary. Counselors can manage dangerous or novel situations by using available resources to protect clients and staff and to shed light on the obscure situation. The task-centered approach has much to offer in serious situations; it is a distinct aid in focusing and holding to a focus. Thus it helps the therapist organize ameliorating interventions rapidly and prevent the escalation of a crisis situation. (See Chapter 9.)

BASIC PROCEDURES
In Brief and in General

Ordinarily a client has a target problem; that is, she is in a state of distress, uneasiness, upset, turbulence, malfunction, handicap, or perplexity, or perceives a threat to goals and expectations; she knows or believes that a particular event or occurrence is the center of the trouble. The target problem is what the client thinks is the problem, what she thinks should be alleviated, and what she thinks should be worked on. People are generally able to make a coherent statement defining, or at least describing, their target problem. When they cannot do so, practitioners can help in various ways to develop a target problem statement. Practitioners can sometimes usefully consult important other people to identify these problems. In task-centered practice, everything begins and may end with the client's target problem.

The target problem is embedded in a *target problem context*, that is, the real conditions shaping the problem. These include important interpersonal relations, role performance difficulties, economic and financial difficulties, and other features of the social environment. Influential other people, including professionals, agencies, or other social institutions, may also have opinions about the client's situation.

In the task-centered model, the target problem becomes operational only upon the explicit willingness of the practitioner to focus upon that defined problem. If the practitioner judges that the client's selected target problem is wrong, or that it is not feasible to work on that problem, then he is obligated and is responsible for giving his professional opinion and helping the client explore other options. (Chapters 2 and 5 discuss working with target problem definitions and focusing in greater detail.)

Task-centered intervention is a set of procedures for alleviating the specific target problem decided upon for the focus of the work. (See Figure 1–2.) When people are referred to or obliged to use a service, that is, when they are *involuntary clients,* a start-up sequence draws out the client's problems and draws out the problems identified by the referral agencies. To alleviate target problems, we depend on problem-solving processes. Goals are as specific and tangible as possible. Stretching out a client's motivation is normally not necessary and rarely succeeds. What is necessary is that the client obtain the resources and skills for problem-solving work.

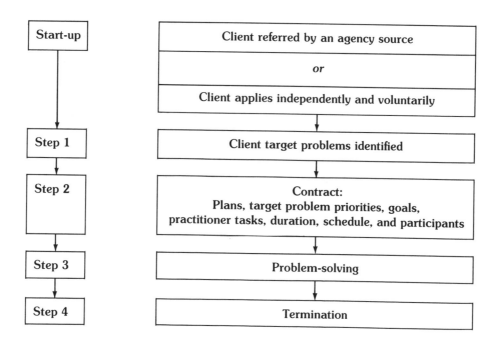

FIGURE 1–2 Basic steps

Case Planning

The general strategy for a case plan consists of assessment and a problem-reduction program of action. The focus is on client target problems. The assessment is elaborate about the details of the problem occurrences in the present, and is narrowed to the boundaries of the target problem and its immediate context.

The practitioner constructs a program by making judgments about what changes can be expected to reduce the problem. To make this judgment he considers the substance and direction of action the client is willing to undertake, the available formal information (i.e., published, reported in official channels, communicated in official supervision and consultation) indicating actions expected to have greatest impact on the problem, and the resources and rules of the particular agency responsible for the case.

Implementation

A *contract* is made to shape and organize the problem-solving work. *Tasks* state exactly what the client and practitioner are to do. To overcome obstacles to the client's task performance, the practitioner concentrates on providing clients with the resources for getting the tasks done. The client is also instructed in the skills needed for accomplishing the stipulated tasks. Goals, problems, and tasks are set firmly but with reserve flexibility. The practitioner's responsibility is to create a favorable climate for task performance. The practitioner procures resources, instructs the client in relevant social skills, negotiates resources and favorable attitudes (with other agencies and with the family, peers, and important others), reviews progress on problem alleviation, and arranges to terminate, extend, or follow up (monitor) the original contract.

Tasks

Tasks state what the client is to do. A task may state a general direction for the client's action, but general tasks are broken down into more specific task specifications. Tasks change form and content as intervention proceeds. Some tasks are dropped out; others are added. Target problems change sometimes. The practitioner's tasks are commitments to clients for actions to be taken on their behalf by a representative of the agency.

Assessment

In the initial phase (the first two sessions with a client), the practitioner makes a rapid early assessment. (See Chapter 5.) However, throughout the case, he continues to obtain information and refines his assessment. (See Chapter 7.) Assessment consists of finding out the problems (also called exploration) as well as classifying and specifying the problems. The practitioner also identifies the influential conditions in the environment, the problem context, and should note the client's special traits, talents, abilities, and problem behaviors as well. Assessment is confined to the logical boundaries of the target problems. A target problem can be classified according to its best fit into a typology that defines the scope of the assessment (Chapter 5). Assessment does not extend beyond problems that can be subsumed under the target problem classification or the logic of the target problem. Reassessment occurs if and when the target problem has to be changed; the practitioner may decide to alter the treatment plan and strategy in those circumstances.

Psychiatric classifications and assessment
The task-centered model does not usually require the therapist to formulate a psychiatric diagnosis of the client. However, that information, if available, adds a useful dimension to the assessment. The psychiatric classification is always made if the client is in treatment in a psychiatric hospital or clinic, or is being considered for that type of intervention. The psychiatric classification is useful in other settings, but may not be essential, as an additional way to describe the client and to aid in understanding his traits and abilities.

Since 1980, the standard guidelines for making a psychiatric classification are found in the *Diagnostic and Statistical Manual of Mental Disorders,* third edition, known as the *DSM III.* These guidelines attempt to provide clear descriptions of diagnostic categories to enable clinicians and investigators to diagnose, communicate about, study, and treat various mental disorders. The psychiatric classification is never adequate for prescribing treatment; it is an initial step. Practitioners need specialized training to use the *DSM III* competently. Persons without this training should work under the supervision of or in collaboration with a professional trained in the use of the system.

The *DSM III* classification is required in psychiatric treatment facilities because they are under the hegemony of the medical profession and governmental regulations. The classification is one way of controlling quality of care, and it also provides necessary statistical information. In other types of helping organizations, these classification processes are optional and their use depends on custom and agency styles. There is no conflict between use of the *DSM III* classifications and the task-centered model although the model needs to be adapted to fit into the usual clinic setting. (See Chapter 9.) Regardless of setting, the psychiatric classification is invariably useful when the target problem is, or is affected in important ways by, a physical or neurological disease, when drugs or other biological interventions are being administered, or when the client is suffering from delusions, hallucinations, or thought disorders.

Life history, problem history, and assessment

In normal task-centered work it is not useful to obtain extensive life history data. Such information can reveal a good deal about how a person is thought to have developed and how her character seems to have evolved. However, personal histories seldom need to be used in interventions to reduce the client's target problem. In fact, accumulating substantial past history is inefficient and may mislead the client about the intentions of the practitioner; that is, the client may infer that he is to be an unwilling participant in a "deep" psychotherapy process. Long duration of a problem may or may not color its meaning in the present. Although information about a problem's duration and how it has changed or remained constant over time is sometimes an aid to clear understanding, identifying minimal demographic and historical characteristics is usually enough. Research evidence suggests that such minimal data is surprisingly powerful in describing clinical situations and helping therapists make predictive judgments (Sundberg, 1977, p. 107). These facts pin down and clarify the problem, especially if attention is given to the immediate personal and social context, and to what the problem means in the present time. However, past history may be explored if the emphasis on the present does not shed enough light on the assessment. (See also Chapter 5.)

Personality and behavior theories and assessment

Personality and behavior theories deal with the characteristics and tendencies believed to determine a person's thoughts, feelings, and actions (Maddi, 1980). A practitioner trying to assess a client and her situation will find that an understanding of personality and behavior factors is valuable. There are many theories and each has its adherents, but at this stage in the development of psychology, it is not known what theory is best. Efforts to create some unifying framework have proved elusive. Each of the important theoretical positions is informative and often helpful.

The framework of the task-centered model primarily offers guidelines for problem-solving actions, but task-centered intervention calls for practical eclecticism so far as personality and behavior theory is concerned. Practitioners, of course, bring to practice their own beliefs and preferences in the area of personality theory. The flexibility built into the model generally allows it to accommodate different opinions about personality and behavior functioning although it is a poor fit with personality and behavior theories addressed to deep intrapsychic characteristics and the assessment and treatment of widespread psychological dysfunctions thought to reside primarily inside a person's mind. The task-centered approach *is* adaptable to theories that attend to interpersonal transactions and transactions between the person and environment and to theories that view thought, feeling, and action as a linked pattern of being. The task-centered model is compatible with explanatory theories of behavior derived from ecological, cognitive, behavioral, and psychodynamic approaches.

CASE 1–2

Joseph and Rita

Joseph is 11; his sister Rita is 8. They are black children living in a deteriorated neighborhood. Before Joseph and Rita were born, this neighborhood was crowded. Two main business streets were heavily trafficked and noisy. There were lots of shops. The merchandise was overpriced. Bright, ugly signs grabbed you. The "El" train ran on top of one of the main streets. Every block had some variant of tavern, gyp joint, greasy spoon, welfare office, bank, gambling and drug joint, or mental health clinic. Gangs fought. For ten years the neighborhood burned; today, empty lots are cluttered with bricks. Buildings are shells; here and there a block or a building stands in the rubble. The streets are dangerous. The two main streets are deserted. Urban renewal high rises and town houses show up strangely. The real estate speculators are there. The urban renewal experts are there. The school attended by Joseph and Rita used to be a loud, teeming place. Now it has empty rooms and lots of special education classes.

Joseph and Rita live in an apartment with their 31-year-old mother and two younger sisters. Their mother is on welfare. She came to this northern city from the South twelve years ago. She has never had any paid employment; she has been on welfare during most of her years in the city.

Joseph and Rita were referred to the school social worker because they were dirty. This is a mandated problem but of relatively low power: that is, no one is likely to be deprived of liberty or subjected to police action for poor body hygiene. But this problem raises potentially more important ones: the mother might be labeled "neglectful" and become subject to investigatory procedures; the children and mother might be pressured by school officials, reported to the welfare department, and so forth. Since cleanliness is a high priority in our society, it is sometimes believed that a parent who fails to keep children clean may be doing worse things, may be guilty of neglect, even abuse, for instance.

The teacher who referred Joseph and Rita for a dirtiness problem had both children in her room, an ungraded learning disability (LD) class. The two children were first interviewed by a social worker. Joseph was a spontaneous, lively, talkative child; Rita was his follower, quiet, shy, and depending on big brother to talk for her and fight for her. When Rita wanted to add something or change something Joseph was telling the social worker, the girl would gesture to Joseph and whisper.

The social worker told the children the reason for the referral. They denied the accusation. They were only dirty from being on the playground. They had different woes (target problems): the teacher was unfair to them, singling them out for criticism when they acted no differently from the other children; they did not know why they had been put in a LD class; and they did not know what to do to get out of the class.

The children agreed that the social worker visit their mother. She did and found the apartment clean, the laundry facilities adequate, the quantity of clothing adequate. The mother showed the social worker her things to defend herself against the false accusation of uncleanliness. The mother's target problems were that she had never been informed her children were to be placed in an LD class (a violation of law in that state if true) and that the white teacher was prejudiced against black kids.

The practitioner's judgment was that Joseph and Rita were, in his experience, average in cleanliness and in their mother's attention to cleanliness. What came through was the family's distress and indignation at the children's being labeled LD—dumb. The family blamed the school officials; they thought the teacher was prejudiced and generally unfair.

Discussion: The Case of Joseph and Rita

Start-up and Steps 1 and 2, Combined

The information just summarized in the case of Rita and Joseph came out in the first two interviews, one with the children in school and the other with the mother in her home. No case is "perfect." This one is no exception. The good points are that the social worker involved the mother immediately and obtained her opinions; he observed the children's home to get a direct impression; and he paid attention to concentrating on the problem as viewed by the clients. Unfortunately, he did not confer and negotiate with the referral source (teacher) to find out how often, when, and to what degree the children were dirty; why they were in an LD classroom; what their learning disabilities were; what they could be expected to learn, how fast, with what educational program; what the teacher wanted to change and why; and what the teacher could do to help change along.

In the case of Rita and Joseph, then, the start-up step was bypassed, Steps 1 and 2 were done simultaneously, and Step 3 was begun all in the first two interviews. (And yet, in real practice the steps tend to run into one another in just this way and the task-centered model is adapted to fit real-world circumstances. However, in combining steps, the practitioner should nonetheless not overlook the necessary parts of the steps even though he adjusts their order and priority.)

The content from Steps 1 through 3 was that the target problems were identified and general tasks were stated as follows:

1. Joseph and Rita were to obtain an understanding of why they were in LD.
2. Joseph and Rita were to get along better with the teacher.
3. Intervention was to last six weeks; the children were to be seen twice a week for 30-minute sessions, together or separately.
4. Their mother was to be seen as needed, alone or with the children.

Step 2: Contract

This contract is on the right track but lacks enough specifics to move things along. The errors follow:

1. Target problems not sufficiently congruent with clients' viewpoints. The target problems have been given a practitioner's twist, or bias, altering the way the children and mother want to go. The clients want information and redress of grievances. They could be expected to have high motivation to get action on those problems. However, when the practitioner influences the children to think about ways to cut down on conflict with the teacher, the children's motivation will not be high. The children are too powerless to put themselves in the position the practitioner is suggesting.

2. Mother's participation not sufficiently structured into the work plan. Work with the mother, who has certainly been interested, exists somewhere out on the sidelines. The contract is really only with the children. The practitioner should have pinned down how often the mother would be seen and for what, and whether the children would be seen separately or together. The most efficient way to get action may well have been to see all three together.

3. Practitioner tasks not developed on time. From the start, there should have been practitioner tasks to find out from the school officials why the children were in LD, whether their rights had been violated, what the teacher recommended regarding uncleanliness and school program, what the teacher could do to get the desired changes, and if the charges of unfairness and prejudice had any observable basis.

Step 3: Problem Solving

Interviews 3 through 12 took place over five weeks. These interviews were with the children together and with their mother by phone. There was virtually no assessment. The practitioner developed one client task only and with the children only: the children were to ask their teacher why they were in LD. This task was steady and unchanged in interviews 3 through 8, six 30-minute sessions. The children did not do the task.

The immediate obstacle was that the children did not know what to say to the teacher. This obstacle was worked at by discussion, instruction, simulation, and role playing. They did not do it anyway. The children said that on some days they had no opportunity because the teacher was absent due to illness. On other days—all the days she was in school—she was in a bad mood.

The problem context was fuzzy. The children acted as if they liked the sessions. They recited for the practitioner what the task was and rehearsed repeatedly, but they never did it in real life. The practitioner urged them on, mentioning that the sessions had a time limit. Also, during the sessions the children became lively when talking spontaneously about their "Dad," but information they gave about their father or about problems related to him was not recorded, if it was obtained—not even who he was. Possibly the practitioner was trying not to be intrusive; but it would seem that if the children talked about this man spontaneously, they would not object to having the practitioner ask a relevant question or two. Perhaps they were even inviting the inquiry. At the end of the eighth session, the practitioner decided to take on the tasks of conferring with school officials and involving the mother with school officials to work on the target problems.

Why were these errors made? It seems that the practitioner made a judgment: to give the children maximum independence in solving their own problems. This judgment has a certain moral attractiveness but is unrealistic for an 11- and 8-year old in these circumstances. These children and their mother do not have enough clout and self-assertiveness to take on successfully a formal bureaucracy such as a school system. They need a mediator and possibly an advocate. Those are the roles the practitioner should have taken on at once.

Due to the slow start of focused work, the bulk of the interventions were bunched together at the end of the sequence. By interviews 9 and 10 the children were telling the practitioner that they felt smarter than kids in the regular classrooms, that they did their work conscientiously, and that no one had explained to them or their mother why they were in an LD classroom. The target problem surfaced again. The practitioner-imposed task is not even being attempted by the children. Belatedly, the practitioner hears. He contracts himself for several tasks: to arrange for an appointment for Joseph and Rita with the teacher; to accompany the children to that appointment; to request a staff meeting with appropriate school officials to explain to the children and their mother what the LD placement is all about; and to obtain exact and detailed information about the laws and regulations dealing with LD placement procedures and rights of the parents and children.

The staff meeting took place. Present with the family and practitioner were the teacher, the adjustment teacher, and the principal. The school people produced from their files a signed form showing that a parent gave permission for LD placement. At first the mother did not recognize the signature. It then came out that the children had been taken for psychological tests (the basis of the LD placement) by the mother's boyfriend (the "Dad") and he had signed the papers. The civil rights mystery was solved. The staff recommended that Joseph be provided with a typewriter so he could practice fine motor skills at home, that he keep a notebook to identify words he did not know, and that he be relieved of a baby-sitting job (it was just now discovered that he had one) that kept him up every night until midnight. Rita (the follower) was not mentioned in the staffing, an important oversight, probably due to time pressure and insufficient planning for the conduct of the conference.

Step 4: Terminating
By session 13 the target problem disappeared. Everyone now knew why the children were in an LD classroom. The children and their mother were satisfied. Joseph and Rita agreed the teacher was not so bad. Joseph was going to move into a regular classroom soon. Rita would be left behind. The mother was to pay special attention to Rita.

Conclusion

What was done in sessions 9 through 13 could have been done in sessions 1 through 4. A plan for Rita should not have been overlooked. Such a plan could have been worked into the intervention if so much time had not elapsed before the practitioner corrected the strategy. The focus would have been more correct if the problem context had been assessed and if the logic of the client's target problem had been more painstakingly adhered to.

There are many loose ends to this case. It should be said at once, however, that *every* case does *not* have to finish in a state of neat completeness, since life does not allow such a nirvana. But certain loose ends really stand out here. For example: what accounts for the wide difference in interpretation between the practitioner and the teacher as to whether or not the children were dirty? It seems likely that the teacher's reason for referral was more complicated than a simple concern about surface cleanliness. Again, what exactly was the extent and type of learning problems that had originally caused the school to call in the psychological testers and what exactly did those tests reveal? There should have been a more robust recommendation about these children's learning needs besides the somewhat unrealistic advice to buy Joseph a typewriter and teach him to type. Who was going to buy the typewriter and do the teaching? What should he type? Maybe a computer would be better! And maybe the school would have one. How can we account for *everyone's* almost complete disregard of Rita ? What might that portend? And was it the job of the practitioner to explore the family composition to find out if that disregard was a problem and if it could be helped? There was enough room in this timed sequence to look into these problems if the case had been better planned and focused. Furthermore if focused exploration suggested an extension of time, and if the clients and referral source wanted it, there is no barrier in the model for maximizing service if the time and effort are used productively and by mutual agreement.

SUMMARY

Task-centered practice is a set of articulated actions designed to be put into effect in an organized and planned manner for the purpose of alleviating client target problems. The heart of the task-centered model is close congruence between the practitioner and the client on the problem that is to be the focus of work, the *target problem*. The model provides for an agreed upon plan in the form of a contract that describes the nature of the actions to be embarked upon with the client's informed consent and provides for a time plan to mark off the duration of the intervention sequence. The model can be used in dealing with a variety of personal, interpersonal, and situational problems, and with many different types of clients and settings.

The basic procedures of the model concentrate on case planning ad-dressed to the specific features of the target problem and aimed at its alleviation.

Implementation of the model concentrates on achieving performance of a variety of specific tasks designed to reduce the problem. Assessment is important to define and describe the problem to be addressed, to sketch in the social context, and to evaluate the personal, interpersonal, and environmental resources and deficits that will influence what can and should be done. Assessment should be for immediate use in planning and restricted to understanding the target problem in detail in its present form and obtaining an overview of the client's personality, family, work or school circumstances, health, finances, and ethnic and cultural background.

REFERENCES

American Psychiatric Association. (1980). *Diagnostic and Statistical Manual of Mental Disorders* (3rd ed.). Washington, DC: Author.

Budman, S. H. (1981). Looking toward the future. In S. H. Budman, *Forms of brief therapy*. (pp. 461–462). New York: The Guilford Press.

Cormican, E. (1977). Task-centered model for work with the aged. *Social Casework, 58*(October), 490–494.

Dierking, B., Brown, M., & Fortune, A. E. (1980). Task-centered treatment in a residential facility for the elderly: A clinical trial. *Journal of Gerontological Social Work, 2* (Spring), 225–240.

Fortune, A. E. (1979). Problem-solving process in task-centered treatment with adults and children. *Journal of Social Service Research, 2*(Summer), 357–371.

Fortune, A. E. (1985). *Task-centered practice with families and groups.* New York: Springer.

Garvin, C. D. (1974). Task-centered group work. *Social Service Review, 48*(December), 494–507.

Goldberg, E. M., Gibbons, J., & Sinclair, I. (1984). *Problems, tasks and outcomes.* Winchester, MA.: Allen and Unwin.

Larsen, J. A., & Mitchell, C. T. (1980). Task-centered, strength-oriented group work with delinquents. *Social Casework, 61*(March), 154–163.

Maddi, S. R. (1980). *Personality theories: A comparative analysis*, (p. 10). Homewood, IL: Dorsey Press.

Rathbone-McCuan, E. (1985). Intergenerational family practice with older families. In A. E. Fortune (Ed.), *Task-centered practice with families and groups* (pp. 149–160). New York: Springer.

Reid, W. J. (1978). *The task-centered system.* New York: Columbia University Press.

Reid, W. J. (1981). Family treatment within a task-centered framework. In E. R. Tolson & W. J. Reid (Eds.), *Models of family treatment* (pp. 306–331). New York: Columbia University Press.

Reid, W. J. (1984). Treatments of choice or choice of treatments: An essay review. *Social Work, 29*(January), 33–38.

Reid, W. J. (1985). *Family problem solving.* New York: Columbia University Press.

Reid, W. J., & Epstein, L. (1972). *Task-centered casework.* New York: Columbia University Press.

Reid, W. J., & Epstein, L. (Eds.). (1977). *Task-centered practice.* New York: Columbia University Press.

Reid, W. J., & Hanrahan, P. (1982). Recent evaluations of social work: Grounds for optimism. *Social Work, 27* (no. 4), 328–340.

Rooney, R. H. (1981). A Task-centered reunification model for foster care. In A. N. Maluccio & P. A. Sinanoglu (Eds.), *The challenge of partnership: Working with parents of children in foster care* (pp. 135–150). New York: Child Welfare League of America.

Rubin, A. (1985). Practice effectiveness: More grounds for optimism. *Social Work, 30*(November), 469–476.

Rzepnicki, T. (1985). Task-centered intervention in foster care services: Working with families who have children in placement. In A. E. Fortune (Ed.), *Task-centered practice with families and groups* (pp. 172–184). New York: Springer.

Schulberg, H. C., & Killilea, M. (1982). Community mental health in transition. In H. C. Schulberg & Killilea, M. (Eds.), *The modern practice of community mental health* (pp. 40–94). San Francisco: Jossey-Bass.

Sundberg, N. D. (1977). *Assessment of persons* (p. 107). Englewood Cliffs, NJ: Prentice-Hall.

Wells, R. A. (1982). *Planned short-term treatment.* New York: Free Press.

CHAPTER
2

PROBLEMS

Where Services Start

THE IMPORTANCE OF PROBLEM DEFINITION
—————— IN THE TASK-CENTERED MODEL ——————

The guidelines of the task-centered model call for concentration on the *target problem,* which is defined as the problem perceived by the client that is acceptable in the professional judgment of the practitioner. Target problem concentration is intended to minimize deadlocks when clients are resistant or reluctant to accepting the practitioner's problem focus, and to maximize the client's motivation by adhering to what he wants and is willing to do. The client's focus may be, and often is, changed in the course of the client-practitioner dialogue.

The main criterion for defining the focus is that it be congruent with the client's interests. Attention to the problem in the client's own terms is also an ethical consideration. The task-centered model's position is based on respect for the client's independence, rights of choice about what is going to happen to her, and as much control over her own fate as possible. The problem formulation defines the condition or state that is to be affected by the intervention program. In other words, in the terms of the model, the problem is the target of change.

The task-centered model is addressed to the problems in everyday living. These constantly encountered psychological, environmental, and social interaction problems become the subject of professional intervention when people request help voluntarily, are referred by an agency ,or are required by courts or other authoritative bodies to take help, and when they cannot carry out effective problem-reducing actions on their own or through informal helpers. The purpose of the task-centered model is to enable clients to solve or ameliorate their problems by assuming appropriately formulated tasks with proper support. How the problem is formulated influences the focus selected and the treatment plan. Hence, formulation of the problem is of the highest importance in designing the whole treatment program.

DILEMMAS OF PROBLEM
—————————— IDENTIFICATION ——————————

Which problems do I work on? Who decides? How is it decided? What is the rationale for a particular choice? How much change is necessary? According to what criteria? How much change is sufficient? What are the consequences of failing to solve a problem? These questions are uppermost in the minds of practitioners as they approach each helping situation. Answering these questions requires that they make judgments about possible goals, priorities of interventions, relevant assessment, and feasible focus. Realistically, practitioners need to pursue several trains of thought to make an appropriate judgment that suggests a focus. This chapter and Chapter 3, "Intervention," will discuss the basis for deciding on a focus and planning the implementation of task-centered approach. Most dilemmas of problem identification may be perceived as falling into three areas: the indeterminate quality of personal problems, the relativity of problem definitions, and the complexity in the process of problem defining.

The Indeterminate Quality of Personal Problems

The type of personal problems that arrive in the offices of human service practitioners are associated with multiples of lack of resources or skills (the results of real deficits or deprivation), unhappiness in personal feelings and interpersonal relationships, disturbing consequences of ineffectiveness and failure in major and important life tasks (such as work, love, friendships, and self-respect), and deviance (which places the person in conflict with himself or with family, peers, and authorities).

Personal problems can be viewed in varying ways. They can be thought of as being (predominately) the result of unfairness and insensitivity of social institutions, for example, social stratification or inequality in the distribution of opportunities and wealth. Problems also can be viewed as the result of poor schools, racial prejudice, stigma, and discrimination. Unhappiness and ineffectiveness may be attributed to emotional disturbances, cognitive disturbances, poor performance behaviors, current threats and challenges to a more or less steady state in life.

Personal problems may result from or be associated with *deviance*, behavior that departs markedly from accepted norms and that has a public character calling for intervention by societal agents. Deviants significantly depart from approved behaviors and life styles. They develop conflicted interactions with those around them, especially families, teachers, and employers, and also with organizations and staffs authorized to help and control them. The etiology of deviance, however, is subject to considerable controversy, and it has been attributed to all of the types of problems and events that result in an individual being labeled as a wrongdoer. However, the labeling of deviant individuals or groups is relative. Not everyone agrees on particular designations. Furthermore, conditions deplored at one period of time become less important under other historical circumstances; and conditions that have been dormant for long periods of time later emerge as crises for the society (Kitsuse & Spector, 1973; Merton, Robert K., 1971; Piven, 1981; Spector & Kitsuse, 1974).

When persons with problems are widely spread out in a neighborhood, region, or society, their individual conditions may become aggregated into discernible patterns of social life, for example, "the underclass." These conditions may be publicly recognized as social problems. To acquire such public recognition, the community has to be ready and prepared to understand the condition. That is likely to be the case if the public perceives the problem as being intrinsically real, observable, having some understandable cause, and if they are willing to act collectively to protect themselves or the problem bearers. In addition the public has to believe, or have faith that it is possible to correct the problem now or in the near future (Thio, 1978).

Individual problems experienced by a single person or by a small group are aspects of wider social problems. Individual problems are affected by and, in turn, influence, members in a family and peers in formal or informal organizations. Individual problems (for example, depressions, anxiety, or low self-esteem) have common features that make it possible to classify or at least label them descriptively and communicate about them. However, individual problems also have distinctively particular aspects, leading to the perception of a high degree of uniqueness in problem experiences. No two persons experience depression, for example, in identical ways; it is always an individual experience that partakes of many common elements.

One group of sociologists prominent in the study of social problems who adopt the social reactions perspective (Becker, 1966) consider opinion to be the essence of a social problem. They believe that conditions become defined as problems by a complex and fluid process. The process of problem definition centers on the issue of who defines the problems, and how the problem definers decide on the definition. Problem definers are those who give voice to an issue and who exercise power to declare the existence and parameters of a problem. Problem defining takes place in social interactions. Decisions that identify some condition as a problem emerge in a family interaction; between peers; in a community, labor, or special interest organization; between the readers and writers of newspapers and magazines; between the viewers and producers and commentators of television accounts; between teachers and students, workers and supervisors, management and labor; within professional organizations; among scholars and researchers and their various publics; and among politicians or between politicians and constituents. In other words, throughout all the varied and multiple social interactions, the nature of and the opinion about some behaviors and conditions produce the perception that a condition is a problem.

The Relativity of Problem Definitions

Defining problems is a continuous and changing process. Who defines and what is defined are reflections of how a social order is functioning at a particular time. Social problems are defined and redefined in the process in which individuals, families, groups, and organizations experience the stresses produced by modern living with its industrialization, urbanization, and political and ideological movements. This process produces changes in the ways that agencies organize services and methods for the control, treatment, and alleviation of individual and family problems. Over time there develop varying emphases by government, research, and practice organizations to change and develop content of treatment methodologies and their applications (Allen, 1981). Even particular individuals change the way they perceive their own problems.

A recently and highly publicized social and individual problem is "child abuse," a subject formerly given so little public attention that it did not appear

(handwritten annotation in top margin: "Probs defined, redefined & ways of dealing w. them. i.e. of Social Wo")

in the *Reader's Guide to Periodical Literature* until 1968. Before that "cruelty to children" was indexed intermittently. The Library of Congress changed its primary entry to "child abuse" in 1968 and most of the major indexes followed suit (Nelson, 1984). Similarly, recent additions to the roster of important social terms noting problems are the "feminization of poverty," and "single mother" (earlier labeled as "unmarried mother," with a different set of beliefs about causes and treatment). Other fairly recently identified problems, or problems identified differently from their earlier versions, are homelessness (formerly regarded as mainly the problem of skid row alcoholics, or "stranded men" as they were known), and "battering" (what used to be known as "wife beating"). Having an abortion was once considered a problem; today, for many it is a solution. Abortion legislation has become a problem for some people—a new problem. Homosexuality is a condition that has and has not been considered a problem, depending on the historical era being considered.

The changing nature of problem defining is, in part, a result of a constantly increasing and improving quality of social science knowledge about the human condition in the modern world. It is also the result of fads that rapidly infiltrate professional thought and behavior and spread by effective dissemination in the media. The perception and importance of problems also change under different political, ideological, and cultural conditions. Furthermore, the wide dissemination and approval of therapeutic intervention offers the expectation of problem reduction for problems when they are conceived as individually rooted psychological or emotional disturbance or illness.

Reporting on a recent study of the process of problem formulation, Proctor and Rosen (1983) state: "In nearly every approach to systematic treatment, thorough and accurate problem formulation, or the assessment of what constitutes the client's problem, is a basic component of planning the overall intervention and is considered central to the success of treatment" (p. 22). Nevertheless, clinical judgments are not sufficiently reliable, and problem formulations vary widely among practitioners. Considering the issue of variability in problem formulation, the researchers suggest it may stem from the widely held practice assumption that:

> . . . change in one type or domain of behavior will lead to other changes in behavior. As a consequence, therapeutic interventions are often directed at what is viewed as the covert, basic, or core elements of the person, with the assumption that such changes will permeate to or result in overt and observable changes in everyday behavior (p. 26).

However, the empirical evidence available fails to support beliefs about the significance of particular underlying causes (such as specific family environment, dramatic or traumatic experiences, or constitutional abnormality) thought to give rise to a particular pattern of disordered behavior (Kanfer & Saslow, 1969, p. 423). There is also no evidence in the empirical literature of a direct link between insight and symptom relief (Fisher & Greenberg, 1977, p. 412).

Complexity of Defining Social and Personal Problems

Defining the target problem calls for exercising informed and discriminating judgment about persons and the important features of their social context. The physical and social environment and surroundings, cultural, ethnic, age, socioeconomic, and status considerations, and sometimes the politics of the community may together produce a context that decisively shapes the appearance, content, and meaning of a client's problems.

The context may also figure in the practitioner's deciding what interventions to use. For example, the problem may be defined in such a way as to make a good fit with a known and preferred intervention program already organized and supported by some elements among the public or within the helping professions. Some interventions may have better reputations than others at various times, and, accordingly, will tend to be preferred, and so the problems tend to be defined to fit the capabilities of the preferred intervention program. Some problems are of greater interest to the public, clients, the media, and professionals having some inherent interest. Naming the problem, describing and specifying it, attributing importance, deciding on goals to shoot for, making realistic plans, selecting interventions with a good track record—all these call for judgments that are difficult to make. So many things have to be considered, and often there is insufficient information or knowledge to underpin firm decision making. At the same time, there is almost always pressure to make fast judgments decisively.

The tension that exists in making judgments about problem definition is between focusing primarily on the individual person (his traits, attributes, character, personality, psychopathology), and focussing primarily on concrete changes in the environment and/or in the habitual patterns of social interaction. It is not uncommon to view a problem as being primarily within the general social structure that provides work, health, education, housing, opportunity, and so forth, and yet find that professional preference and style concentrate on a portion of an individual's dysfunctional behavior or attitudes and feelings. It is also common to take a global approach to personal dysfunction, that is, to define a problem with excessive breadth. These tensions always exist and are based on the nature of the helping disciplines. Attempting to tackle these issues makes counseling difficult, challenging, and important and develops the background of experience and professional thinking that is the distinction of the helping disciplines.

To illustrate the dilemmas facing the professional attempting to define a problem, three major social problems are briefly described in Boxes 2–1, 2–2, and 2–3. They reveal vividly the kinds of issues that typically appear as one attempts to define problems that fall into the broad categories of poverty, child abuse, and mental illness. Some general guidelines will be suggested; the balance of this book develops these and other techniques in greater detail.

BOX 2–1

Poverty: Prominent Facts and Opinions

The vast majority of poor people in the United States are women and children (Sidel, 1986). In 1984, 14.4 percent of all Americans—33.7 million people— lived below the poverty line. From 1980 to 1984 the number of poor people increased by 4½ million. For female-headed households in 1984, the poverty rate was 34.5 percent, five times that of married-couple families.

Despite improvements in the labor market for professional women, most working women remain in low-paid jobs, receiving on the average 64 percent of the wages earned by men (Sidel, 1986). The poverty rate for white female-headed families was 27.1 percent, for black female-headed families 51.7 percent, and for Hispanic families headed by women, 53.4 percent. The poverty rate for the elderly, most of whom are women, was 12.4 percent in 1984. Two out of every three poor adults are women, and the economic status of families headed by women is declining.

Many children are poor (U. S. House of Representatives, 1985; Institute for Research on Poverty, 1985; Sidel, 1986). The poverty rate for children under six was 24 percent in 1984. This means that nearly one out of every four preschool children lived in poverty. Of all children living in female-headed households, 53.9 percent are poor. The poverty rate for black children in female-headed families was 66.6 percent, for Hispanic children 70.5 percent.

Nationally, the number of persons needing general income maintenance is increasing (Stagner & Richman, 1986). General Assistance programs help persons not eligible for federally funded social welfare. This is a group of welfare recipients in which men predominate, especially black men. A recent study in Chicago revealed that 45 percent of GA recipients had some high school education, and 27 percent some college. These are largely persons who are the fallout of unemployment generated by the economic downturn of the early 1980's.

People use welfare for relatively short periods of time, but patterns of use vary with household categories (Rank, 1985). Persons who receive welfare do so typically for one to two years. Longer-term welfare users are the female- and elderly-headed households. Women are hindered in the labor market because of child care responsibilities, lack of adequate day care, and earnings likely to be lower than those of male counterparts. The elderly are at a disadvantage due to the disabilities of age, ill health, and the stigma of being depreciated.

With these opinions and facts in mind, what dilemmas does the practitioner face in defining the problem when the client is poor? If the client is poor, the practitioner is confronted with assessing how the socioeconomic and other environmental background factors are shaping the problems. For example, is the client's problem being precipitated and maintained by socioeconomic status, the school, the neighborhood, the character of discrimination he experiences, conflicts between her culture and philosophy and the values, customs, and beliefs of the dominant culture? In addition, the counselor must decide where to locate the target problem—primarily in the environmental realm, the interpersonal realm, the personal area, in social relationships and role performances, or in a combination of these areas.

Using the case described earlier (see p. 14), we can review it having in mind issues that might have confronted a task-centered practitioner.

☐ ☐ ☐

Rita and Joseph—Again

Presenting Problems
Rita and Joseph were children of a welfare mother. Public assistance benefits (cash payments plus food stamps and Medicaid) maintained the family, but at a level below the poverty line. The mother was faced with an investigation of her cleanliness and her child care, with the implication of possibly inadequate performance as a mother. She was indignant at the insult and went to great pains to convince the practitioner that she was clean and so were her children.

She readily asserted that a problem existed. Mother and children were anxious and angry at the children's having been stigmatized by the placement in an LD classroom. The mother believed that Rita and Joseph were being shortchanged in their education. The children were upset, afraid of the authorities, and felt that they were caught among powers they could not control. Then the children spoke about their dad whose presence had not been known to the school authorities. Perhaps he was a boyfriend, a companion, a husband.

Environmental Context
Rita and Joseph are poor and black. The combination of ethnic minority status with poverty is a powerful conditioner. "To be poor in America is to let America down—to let that Pepsi image down; to let the American dream down; to not do your share, carry your weight, lift up your corner of the flag" (Sidel, 1986, p. 9).

Low-income and minority clients are not a homogeneous group. Minority populations are represented at all economic levels, but whites outnumber non-whites among the poor. Life in poverty and minority status is not stereotypically bleak, disadvantaged, deficit-ridden, or meager. It *is* different from the lifestyle ordinarily pursued by the majority, and it *is* unfair and over-stressed. It is sometimes full of justified fear, anxiety, and suspicion. It is generally understood among scholars that observing, acquiring knowledge about, and resisting stereotypical thinking are among the most important conditions for making accurate and fair assessments of minorities and poor people (Lorion & Parron, 1985; Solomon, 1976).

It takes immense effort, planning, and resourcefulness to provide for oneself and a family on food stamps, welfare, unemployment insurance, or minimum wages. Poverty is an endless series of unpredictable crises, calling for shifting meager resources from one necessity to another. Everything needs repair. Credit at stores is rarely available. Borrowed funds have to be taken out at exorbitant rates and no money can be saved because it is all spent on current necessities. Daily decisions are necessary to survive the reality of economic hardship. One can often see the resourcefulness, or at least the rationale, behind apparent "impulsiveness' and short-term planning.

In the case of Rita and Joseph, neither the family nor the school raised any problems having to do with financial matters, housing, health, employment, or other conditions related to socio-economic status. Nor was adequacy of the children's education dealt with directly. We are left with a number of unanswered questions: Was there prejudicial intent in perceiving these children as dirty and possibly neglected? Was there lack of sensitivity to the stress the mother was under, managing on her welfare grant? How did that stress affect the children? Did the fact that the family was black lead to an assumption that the children were not clean enough and were mentally inferior?

These questions were not thoroughly explored. Should they have been, or how might they have been, explored since at no time did the mother raise any question about her economic circumstances? The practitioner needed to rely on observations and sensitivity. The economic facts, the low-grade housing, the unattractive, dangerous neighborhood, all suggest that many of the stresses described earlier existed to some extent and that, if they did not actively produce or exacerbate the presenting problem, they created tensions that added weight to the problem.

Interpersonal and Personal Features: Are Poor People Special?

Contemporary scholarly research and theory in the specialized psychological and interpersonal characteristics of ethnic minorities and the poor are not well developed. Interculturally skilled counseling is a priority of the National Institute of Mental Health, the American Psychological Association, the National Association of Social Workers, and other professional and public organizations. The governing ideas about personality theories and human development represent core values of the Western industrialized world of Europe and North America and are middle-class values at that. The available ethnic-sensitive literature, although voluminous, is widely distributed among many sources, some of them not well-known, and much of it has been criticized as being of poor quality (Pedersen, 1985).

Are Joseph and Rita Special?

Joseph and Rita are black, and some distinctive psychosocial features of black culture noted by contemporary observers are seen in their case. For example, the majority of black children have never been able to have a protected childhood, and black children know and understand this. Black children early confront a reality that contains racism, illegal, and violent events in their immediate neighborhoods and perhaps even in their own homes. Exposure to harsh conditions often speeds the development of adaptive behaviors that enable them to survive in a hostile environment. And there is among blacks a tradition of older children caring for younger siblings and being given jobs and chores as a way of preparing for an adult work life (Jones, 1985). Elmer (1981) has graphically detailed the association of poverty conditions with problem attitudes and behaviors of children, such as chronic fearfulness and sadness, apathy, and lack of energy.

Joseph and Rita's mother seems a strong person, able to fend off official criticism about her child care and personal hygiene. She probably approved of Joseph's baby-sitting job, wanting to help him grow independent in a society that will not make things easy. She probably encourages Joseph and Rita to stick together and encourages the older boy to take care of and protect his more vulnerable sister.

However, when the mother was summoned to school to confer about the children's academic problems, her strength may have failed her, and she may have turned to her manfriend to take care of something she feared to confront. Or, perhaps she thought a man would be more respected by the school authorities than a woman. Perhaps her manfriend tried to protect her by not telling her all that had transpired at the school when he authorized the children to be placed in the LD classroom. Perhaps he told her and she forgot. Still, why had the school accepted approval of the transfer to an LD classroom by a person not known to be the children's guardian? The tenor of the case referral from the school suggests rather strong disapproval of the mother. She must have been suspicious of the school authorities and revealed her situation only in the smallest bits absolutely necessary without volunteering much. All these behaviors and interpersonal transactions can be understood as normal reactions to real and perceived threats in the situation and as careful attempts to deal with a threatening bureaucracy.

The school may have misinterpreted the children's home life because of inadequate perception of adaptive or normal behaviors common among some, or perhaps many, black families. Problems may have been perceived where there were none, or the problems of concern to the family may have been different from the ones identified. Tensions about contradictory views of the problem were understood by the practitioner in this case. She eventually used a conference of all parties to separate facts from supposition and accusation.

☐ ☐ ☐

Summary
Defining the Problem When the Client is Poor
Poverty exerts strong influence on lifestyle and is a condition impossible to ignore. Problem definitions must take it into account in every instance. The practitioner's framework of thought should taken into account the influence on behavior, attitudes, and lifestyle of poverty and its associated conditions, such as

poor housing, poor schooling, and limited neighborhood childcare and recreational facilities. This framework needs to include numerous elements:

1. A specialized knowledge about poverty and its consequences
2. An attitude of openness in order to observe and understand, without condescension, the realities of low-income and minority lifestyles and culture
3. A special attentiveness to the conditions of many women with children but without spouses, of working women earning unfair and inadequate wages and salaries, lacking adequate affordable day care, and of elderly women, never married or widowed.
4. A sensitivity to clues about the client's attitudes and feelings, such as suspiciousness resulting from experiences with hostile authorities, including other professionals; resistance, reluctance, caution, or protectiveness about making disclosures for fear of being misunderstood, criticized, humiliated, frustrated; mistrustfulness of the professional relationship leading to denial, misstatements, and similar distortions; readiness to be angry and respond quickly or suddenly out of experiencing unbearable frustration or humiliation that may have been accumulating over hours or days; a dependent and demanding attitude, often a strategy for minimizing resentment or appealing to the practitioner.

In addition, women, single mothers, and members of ethnic minorities have unique patterns of response to discriminatory and impoverished conditions, to personal relationships, and in the way they view themselves. These patterns are related to their particular status and stereotypes about them. In such complex circumstances, the problem definition has to be simplified. If not, the problem exploration will go on interminably, or may result in a stereotypical evaluation that is useless or harmful.

The key to formulating a problem definition that takes account of poverty, race, gender, and ethnic factors is to avoid scrupulously any prepackaged definition. Instead, having general knowledge about poverty and the other relevant conditions, carefully and thoroughly explore in detail just how it is that the client defines the problem, that is, what the client thinks the problem is. Once the client's perception has been established, it is possible to shape a useful problem definition. Professional knowledge guides the process through specific steps to clarify the problem, make sure it has been stated accurately, make sure the definition takes into account the way the problem reflects poverty (and race or gender), sifting through the information to identify, explain, and make some judgments about the problem's nature. (See Chapter 5.)

This means, for example, that poor clients ought to be provided not only with material resources but also with needed and wanted counseling, planning, support, and social services. It means that poverty will not be misinterpreted as psychosocial pathology and treated as an illness. It means that pychosocial maladjustments should be treated in ways that are acceptable to the clients and that reflect the best available professional knowledge.

BOX 2–2

Child Abuse: Prominent Facts and Opinions

Protective services are the basic means for intervening in cases of abuse. Family problems that result in the neglect, abuse, or exploitation of children normally are channeled into *protective services,* that is, services sanctioned by law in state and federal statutes, requiring investigation and interventions, including services to persons who do not want intervention and are involved involuntarily. In fact, services are often initiated by a third party report, that is, a complaint coming in over a hotline operated by officially designated public child welfare organizations. The obligation to protect is in conflict with a basic theme of the task-centered model, namely to legitimate client voluntarism. This is a conflict that cannot be easily reconciled; it can be glossed over, or in some circumstances, ignored, but it will not go away.

Child abuse is a public issue. A study sponsored by the National Center on Child Abuse and Neglect reported 652,000 maltreated children out of a child population of children under 18 of 61,900,000, or an incidence rate of 10.5 per 1000 children. Sexual abuse, which receives high publicity, accounts for a small number of abuse cases involving 44,700 children, or an incidence of 0.7 per 1000 children (Gelles & Cornell, 1984).

Child abuse is now accepted by the political, legislative, and administrative apparatus of government as a social problem about which public consensus has been developed. The press and television regularly disseminate information, some of it oversimplified or melodramatic. Keen public interest has linked child abuse to public issues of violence and personal autonomy (e.g., rape, wife battering, incest, sexual abuse, pornography, and attacks on the elderly, for example). The policy-making process has turned toward the social-psychosocial underlying problems (Nelson, 1984).

The intense media and legislative attention to child abuse creates its own dilemmas. Aware of the limitations of treatment technology to reduce or eliminate child abuse within the short time span often demanded by public demands, professional practitioners develop harried, defensive, or evasive tactics. The task-centered approach is not a solution to problems of social and public policy that erupt into public consciousness. The task-centered approach is a set of techniques that guide case practice. The public atmosphere in which case practice involving child abuse often takes place may shape practice in ways not in tune with the sense of the model.

Intervention in child abuse is multidisciplinary. Because child abuse is a medical, legal, and social problem, protective service workers work with judicial, police, medical, and legal personnel, as well as with professionals from social service agencies and community representatives. It has become common for protective services to be organized by a team of personnel, and to consist of packages of services put together to fit the individual characteristics of each case.

Teams have broader access to numerous types of knowledge about interventions and consequently are thought to have access to comprehensive evaluations perceived to increase the validity of assessments and problem definitions.

Because there are so many actors involved in most child abuse cases, and because of the participation of several disciplines, there easily develop differences of opinion about how treatment should be designed. Professional jealousies and struggles over turf push and pull the decisions on problem definition, assessment, and intervention strategy in different directions. These differences must be compromised. Prudence suggests that as much of the task-centered approach as possible be preserved, which is usually quite possible to do. A cooperative intervention calls for an eclectic posture (see Chapter 9).

Numerous social, environmental, and psychological factors are involved in child abuse problems. There are no simple generalizations about types, signs, and patterns of social, individual, and family problems involved in child abuse. Kadushin (1980, pp. 178–222), in his review of the literature, concluded that

> . . . There is some low-level consistency in the configuration of factors frequently associated with abuse. These include a history of abuse and/or rejection in childhood; low self-esteem; a rigid, domineering, impulsive personality; social isolation; a record of inadequate coping behavior; poor interpersonal relationships; high, unrealistic expectations of children; and lack of ability to empathize with children. . . . Abuse appears to be a response to psychological stress. The parent is reacting to internal conflicts, selects one child in the family as a victim, and responds to his misbehavior in a disproportionate manner. Families referred for protective service are generally living under socially stressful situations.

There are several types of explanations of family violence, but none of them are conclusive.

☐ *The psychiatric explanation* holds that the abusing parent is mentally disturbed, even though the prevailing impression is that only a small portion of family violence is attributable solely to personality traits, mental illness, or psychopathology.

☐ *The social-situational explanation* proposes that the personal problems of violent parents arise from interpersonal conflict, unemployment, isolation, unwanted pregnancy, and stress.

☐ *Social learning theory* suggests that people learn to be violent by growing up in violent homes.

☐ *Resource theory* suggests that persons of low status who lack resources may become violent as a way to assert power and dominance.

☐ *Ecological perspectives* explain family violence by society's support for the use of physical force to discipline children and the absence of public and private resources for family supports (Gelles & Cornell, 1984).

Some authorities hold that, despite the appearance of child abuse in middle-class and upper-class families, the problem is largely found among impoverished and deprived families. Their circumstances are thought to make them vulnerable to the stresses and deprivations that provide the necessary conditions to develop patterns of child abuse. Still, poverty in itself does not explain child abuse without mediating conditions such as individual particularities that create unusual vulnerability to stress and recourse to violent behavior (Pelton, 1981).

What are the recommended interventions? Currently the theory and research available do not provide firm conclusions about what kinds of interventions are most likely to achieve desired results in cases of child abuse. Involuntary cases taken on to protect children and families are characterized by only modest success. The most successful approach may be one that is directed to situational changes. Parents seem to be helped by learning homemaking and parenting skills, developing regular routines, accepting a firm, supporting attitude from the practitioner, receiving highly structured statements of unambiguous expectations, with the practitioner demonstrating willingness to effect some concrete improvements in the client's living situation (Kadushin, 1980). Task-centered casework is recommended by Horowitz and Wolock (1981). There would seem to be a good case for the using the task-centered approach because of its emphasis on providing resources and enhancing social skills.

Gelles and Cornell assert that intervention must protect the victim while preventing further violence, if possible, by strengthening the family (1984, p. 134). It would follow that immediate crisis intervention is called for when children are at risk. Beyond crisis abatement, interventions that could be expected to protect victims or predicted victims should include homemaker services to augment the role of a poorly functioning or nonfunctioning mother, a hot line for on the spot aid in parent-child crises, transportation, child care, counseling, health care, clothing and shelter, access to self-help groups, and other resources to ease the burdens of children and parents involved in such critical situations (Gelles & Cornell, 1985; Stein, 1981).

Defining the Problem When Child Abuse is Confirmed: The Task-centered Approach

The problem definition in a protective case where the client is involuntary or semivoluntary has two parts.

☐ The *target problem*, i.e., the problem exactly as it is perceived by the client, and modified by the practitioner to the extent agreed by the client. Mandated problems should be defined according to the general task-centered rules for pinning down the individualized interests and concerns of the client. (See chapter 5.)

☐ The *mandated problem*, i.e., the problem specifically as it is perceived by the governing authority, agency, court, law enforcement, or other duly sanctioned organization. Mandated problems are formulated according to the style and preferences of the authority responsible for stopping or preventing abuse. (See Chapter 5 for further discussion.)

In most instances the two parts of the problem definition will contain the same or similar issues but probably in different form. To obtain the most impact, the target problem should contain as exactly as possible what the client sees as the feature or condition most troublesome. Often the client's problem will be lack of resources and the negative or harmful actions of others. The mandated problem must be kept in place by the practitioner's authority. The likelihood is that improvement in the target problem will either spill over into improvement in the mandated problems or will release some motivation for the client to work on the mandated problem.

☐ ☐ ☐

BOX 2–3 _____

Mental Disorder

Mental disorder is a psycho-social-medical problem and is revealed in personal behaviors that deviate substantially from consensually understood norms. When deviations are channeled into the medical classification and treatment system, they are defined as disease. The disease formulation of mental disorder has two essential components: a given symptom or syndrome that is a recognized pattern of cognitive-affective-behavioral abnormalities, and an actual biological abnormality or belief that biological causation is a distinct possibility to be eventually confirmed or refuted by research.

However, mental disorder is more than a disease in the narrow medical sense. It is a set of ideas and personal-social actions that are presently unacceptable or incomprehensible. The presence of a known biological abnormality may or may not be discerned. Mental disorder is part of the whole social-psychological context in which a person lives (Wing, 1978).

Problems of mental illness are distributed throughout the human services service system and can be dealt with in a wide variety of settings. They are often handled without the direct intervention of a psychiatrist when the problem is minor. If the problem is more severe or is chronic, the patient may need social supports, resources, and skill enhancement, instead of, or in addition to psychiatric treatment.

Mental illness is often treated in specialized clinics, particularly in community mental health clinics where the chief authorities are psychiatrists although they are the fewest in number. Professionals from the other helping disciplines carry most of the day-to-day treatment. It is becoming common for psychologists, social workers, and nurses to acquire major responsibility for psychotherapy, short of prescribing and dispensing drugs.

Special Features of Defining Target Problems in Instances of Mental Disorder

Particular considerations arise when defining a problem where mental disorder is part of the condition. These considerations are discussed in detail in Chapter 9 but are briefly outlined here.

If medical personnel are in charge, the diagnostic and treatment processes will normally follow a medical model. The central client will be viewed as a patient afflicted with an identifiable symptom or syndrome having a known or suspected underlying biological abnormality. The medical organization will define the problem in accordance with the classification system approved by the American Psychiatric Association (1980). The standard procedures advocated in the *DSM* III provide for appraisal of the client's pathology, physical condition, and the social-environmental stress. These procedures legitimate the formulation of a problem definition that will include the relevant aspects of the problem besides the focus on psychopathology. Nevertheless, the usual procedure results in a strong focus on the disease aspects of the problem. The *DSM* III is firmly oriented to the medical disease approach to psychopathology.

If nonmedical personnel are in charge, the style of work may nevertheless be dominated by the medical model that is influential throughout all the helping disciplines. There is no set of consensually approved rules for classification of psychosocial problems, making it likely that the *DSM* III will be used even though not entirely applicable, if at all. However, the principle of making a problem definition that reflects the relationship between people and environments, the person-in-situation context, is well accepted. The individualized target problem definition recommended in the task-centered model, concentrating on what the client perceives, how he perceives it, and what people want to and can do about their problems, can be made perfectly clear. Even if the dominant practice preferences put high value on attending to theoretically determined underlying problems or classified psychopathology, practical professional common sense usually prevails.

Conflicts of opinion often develop when disputes arise between disciplines about how cases should be processed. Professional practitioners, colleagues, and supervisors may differ about how the client problem is to be defined and how the work is to be focused. Differences of opinion come about because of differences in professional education, contending value systems, and differentials of status, power, and authority.

The exception to emphasis on the target problem occurs when the client is incompetent, incapable, homicidal, or suicidal, and when action must be taken at once on his behalf to prevent clear and present harm.

The crucial decision about problem definition is to answer these questions: Which problem of major concern to the client, if ameliorated, would make the most difference in quality of life, and what are the feasible solutions to the problem?

_____ PREPARING THE PROBLEMS FOR WORK _____

Defining the Problem: Describing, Specifying, and Naming

The problem definition delimits and succinctly explains the problematic issue at hand. The statement should describe, specify, and name the problem. To construct the problem definition is to make decisions, to the extent possible, about what is to be included or excluded and why.

Problems should be described clearly and specifically, and in sharp, exact, and vivid detail so it will be comprehensible to the client and to other professionals and collateral persons. Everybody involved should be able to comprehend what is being talked about and meant. It should be possible for another similarly trained professional observer to duplicate or repeat the same processes and extract the same or a similar description. Ambiguity is expected because of the complexities described and discussed earlier, but the practitioner's aim is to minimize ambiguity and to be clear about the uncertainty that does exist. Clarity pays off by making interventions better and more efficient. Though it is possible to leave some questions open, working closure is needed to implement an intervention program. If an inappropriate target has been decided upon, the plan will change.

There are yet other reasons for achieving closure, even though tentative, on the problem definition. We want to construct interventions to fit the problem, and we want to perceive the problem in sufficient detail to see at intervals whether it is abating, getting worse, or staying the same. Clarity and detail provide points of reference for comparing where we began and where we are now in the intervention and help us determine whether or not the intervention is working. To perceive a change in the situation over the time of the intervention sequence encourages the client, collaterals, and professionals. Monitoring the ongoing process is an early warning system for ascertaining that all is not well and that the plan needs to be revised.

The specification component of the problem definition is a relatively small selection from the description. It defines the essential characteristic or quality of the problem that pinpoints the focus. Specifying the problem helps client and practitioner convert the larger problem into pieces or bits that can then be utilized to fit into the concentrated work to reduce the problem.

Naming a problem is a communication device. The name is shorthand for a longer problem description and refers to some key distinguishing feature of the problem. The name of the problem is *not* the same as the problem classification adapted from the task-centered or any other typology but rather is an individual characterization that comes from the particulars of the client and the client's situation.

Locating the Focus

The *focus* of the intervention work is the concentration point. If we review the case of Joseph and Rita, we can see the relationship between problem definition and focus.

First, the problem definition will *describe, specify and name* the problem. Then the focus picks out a distinct image that captures the chief site of the problem. This site should conform to the client's perception and should generate specific tasks that can be worked on with a reasonable expectation of success and a reasonable amount of client motivation. The focus is obtained directly from the problem specification. The focus may be the same as the specification, but if it is different, it will vary in convenience of expression or style of the formulation, not in substance.

☐ *Problem described.* Joseph and Rita, and their mother, are seriously distressed and troubled. They all believe the school is unfair and discriminatory and has thus deprived the children of proper education (because the children have been placed in the learning disabled class). They think the teacher is unfair, singling the children out for criticism when they act no differently than other children. They do not know why they were put in the learning disabled class; and they do not know how to get out of it and into a regular class. Note is made of the school's view that the children may be neglected because they come to school dirty.

☐ *Problem specified.* The children fear the teacher and are shamed by their placement. Children and mother want this wrong rectified by placement in a regular class.

☐ *Problem named.* Conflict with school authorities.

☐ *Focus.* Clearing up why the children are in LD.

Problem Definition and Focus

As we have seen, the focus is drawn out of the problem definition and is actually the problem definition put into operational terms. It is the problem in the way it is understood to be ready for or in condition to be affected by problem reducing work. For example, the focus with Joseph and Rita is *clearing up why the children are in LD.* When this is done, it is expected that the focus will change to *making an educational plan that is proper and satisfactory.*

The term *focus* is used in this book to refer to the concentration of the whole intervention. (Sometimes we speak of the focus of a single interview, but that is a temporary matter and a convenient expression.) At times it refers to the concentration point of a single interview or portion of an interview. The focus of intervention should be stable until the problem definition alters. An unstable case focus will lead to an inefficient drift in the work and may jeopardize effectiveness.

Managing Client-Practitioner Disagreement

Disagreement on focus can create an impasse that slows or stops the work. Avoiding the impasse or arriving at a compromise can minimize the obstacles. Disagreement can be avoided or reduced satisfactorily by achieving congruence between client and practitioner on the focus. Achieving congruence is more complicated if client and practitioner have very different perspectives or ideas and a struggle starts about whose ideas will prevail. The likelihood is that the practitioner will prevail in a straight power struggle because the practitioner has more power. However, the client may ultimately win by handling the practitioner skillfully, artfully, possibly deviously, and by discontinuing contact. Compromise is the best way to ensure that the client's interests are genuinely attended to and the practitioner's professional judgments and recommendations are clearly given along with adequate opportunity for the client to give them proper consideration.

Identifying Mandated Problems

Mandated problems must be attended to by law, court order, or public sanction and should be placed in a focal position. Doing this often means that the case situation will be worked on with two foci: the client target problem and the mandated problem.

Problem Definition and Assessment

Problem definition and assessment are related concepts. The assessment is a set of observations, explanations, and interpretations that places the problem definition within an understandable context. General information about the client's life circumstances and major interpersonal relations compose the context.

The relationship between assessment, problem definition, and focus can be thought of as one of increasing specificity. The assessment is the most comprehensive and inclusive and attempts to formulate an answer to the question: What is the trouble, the whole trouble? The problem definition proceeds to narrow the terrain by answering the question, "What exactly is the trouble here and now?" The problem definition attempts to say, "The trouble here is this." The focus makes a statement, saying, "Here is what we concentrate on." (See Chapter 5 for more about assessment and focus.)

Problem Definition and Practical Judgment

Practitioners in the human services professions need to be broadly knowledgeable about human conditions and the social contexts of living. No one ever knows enough, but an individual can have sufficient knowledge to take beneficial action. All instances require a practical judgment, and in defining problems, a practical judgment means deciding what problem to put in focus and what is the problem definition for the work at hand.

Knowing what to do is specific and particular—not general. Specific knowledge for doing purposes is set within the context of a whole, concrete situation. The act of taking professional action, "doing treatment," as they say, has no theory in and of itself and cannot have a theory. That is because the professional act itself is not explaining anything, analyzing anything, or hypothesizing. Applying a theory, doing something suggested by knowledge and theory, is not simply making some clear and logical jump from the theory to practice, like making some kind of calculation. Application is not simply derivative. Application involves making a decision based on judgment.

> There is no science of judgment (as little as there is of decision); that is, judgment cannot be replaced by, or transformed into, science, even though it can avail itself of the findings and even of the intellectual discipline of science and is itself a kind of knowledge, a cognitive faculty. Judgment, says Kant, is the faculty of subsuming the particular under the universal . . . . Judgment is . . . the bridge between the abstractions of the understanding and the concreteness of life. (Jonas, 1966, p. 340).

Practical judgment is a reliable mode of balancing out a variety of observations, information, intuition, and pressure to arrive at an individualized conclusion about problem definition, focus, and treatment. It is based on experience of many sorts, but particularly on experience with similar types of conditions. Parts of that experience can be adapted and applied to new and novel circumstances. Almost always, in the human service organizations, there are colleagues, supervisors, and consultants whose wider knowledge can be obtained to bear on a particular judgment. Texts, such as this one, contain a quantity of guidelines, both general and specific, that are based on empirical knowledge to the extent it exists and on the practice wisdom of the author or the group of practitioners with whom the author identifies. What remains to be put into effect is the practitioner equation, namely the work the practitioner does within his or her own mind to think about what is best and what is rational and logical, and what is relevant and makes sense.

SUMMARY

Two features in the task-centered model make it distinctive: the central importance of defining the problem to be congruent with the client's own interests and in the terms of the client's own perception and its attention to proceeding to work in as structured and systematic a fashion as possible under unruly real life conditions.

This chapter addressed the issues arising out of adherence to the target problem principle. Questions having to do with the techniques of carrying out this principle are discussed in chapter 5. It is valuable, however, to review the issues before proceeding to the techniques. Uncertainty occurring from the issues can be troublesome; in this instance facing up to the issues helps the practitioner to make judgments needed to apply the model.

The dilemmas of problem identification occur for three reasons. First, personal problems are indeterminate. They are associated with multiples of lack of resources or skills, unhappiness, ineffectiveness and failure, and/or deviance. Just exactly what components constitute the problem is a matter of what observations happen to be made and what viewpoint is applied in interpreting those observations. Secondly, personal problems are relative and there are no absolute criteria for establishing their presence. Problem defining is a continuous and changing process. Finally, problem defining itself is a complex process, relating to the state of knowledge about social problems and varying public and professional views about them. These complexities are illustrated by the number and quality of factors that have to be considered in problems involving poverty, child abuse, and mental disorder.

After a practitioner makes a judgment on the problem definition, she must find the focus within that definition. Client-practitioner disagreement about focus has to be negotiated. Mandated problems have to be considered and fitted into the focus. The problem definition process is best considered as a part of focusing and assessment. In the end, the problem definition is a matter of judgment, that feature of practice that is the vehicle by which decisions get made and action occurs.

REFERENCES

Allen, F. A. (1981). *The decline of the rehabilitative ideal: Penal policy and social purpose.* New Haven, CN: Yale University Press.

American Psychiatric Association. (1980). *Diagnostic and statistical manual of mental disorders* (3rd ed.). Washington, DC: Author.

Becker, H. S. (1966). *Social problems: A modern approach.* New York: Wiley.

Brown, L. B. (1980). *Client problem solving in task-centered social treatment* (Doctoral dissertation, University of Chicago).

Dewey, J. (1933). *How we think.* Lexington, MA: D. C. Heath.

D'Zurilla, T. J., & Goldfried, M. R. (1971). Problem solving and behavior modification. *Journal of Abnormal Psychology, 78*(August), 107–126.

Elmer, E. (1981). Traumatized children, chronic illness, and poverty. In L. H. Pelton (Ed.), *The social context of child abuse and neglect* (pp. 185–227). New York: Human Sciences Press.

Fisher, S., & Greenberg, R. P. (1977). *The scientific credibility of Freud's theories and therapy.* New York: Basic Books.

Gelles, R. J., & Cornell, C. P. (1985). *Intimate violence in families.* Beverly Hills, CA: Sage Publications.

Hartman, A. (1983). Theories for producing change. In A. Rosenblatt & D. Waldfogel (Eds.), *Handbook of clinical social work.* San Francisco: Jossey-Bass.

Horowitz, B, & Wolock, I. (1981). Maternal deprivation, child maltreatment, and agency intervention among poor families. In L. H. Pelton (Ed.), *The social context of child abuse and neglect* (pp. 137–184). New York: Human Sciences Press.

Institute for Research on Poverty, University of Wisconsin-Madison. (1985, Summer). Special issue: Conference at Williamsburg. *Focus, 8*(2).

Jonas, H. (1966). *The phenomenon of life.* New York: Harper & Row.

Jones, D. L. (1985). African-American clients: Clinical practice issues. In J. Oliver, & L. B. Brown (Eds.), *Sociocultural and service issues in working with Afro-American clients.* Albany, NY: Rockefeller College Press, State University of New York at Albany.

Kadushin, A. (1980). *Child welfare services* (3rd ed.). New York: Macmillan.

Kanfer, F. K., & Saslow, G. (1969). Behavioral diagnosis. In C. M. Franks (Ed.), *Behavior Therapy: Appraisal and status.* McGraw-Hill.

Kitsuse, J. I., & Spector, M. (1973). Toward a sociology of social problems: Social conditions, value judgments, and social problems. *Social Problems, 20*(4), 407–419.

Lorian, R. P., & Parron, D. L. (1985). Countering the countertransference: A strategy for treating the untreatable. In P. Pedersen (Ed.), *Handbook of cross-cultural counseling and therapy.* Westport, CT: Greenwood Press.

Merton, R. K. (1971). Social problems and sociological theory. In R. K. Merton, & R. Nisbet (Eds.), *Contemporary Social Problems* (pp. 793–845). NY: Harcourt, Brace, Jovanovich.

Mouzakitis, C. M., & Varghese, R. (1985). *Social work treatment with abused and neglected children.* Springfield, IL: Charles C. Thomas.

Nelson, B. J. (1984). *Making an issue of child abuse: Political agenda setting for social problems.* Chicago: University of Chicago Press.

Pedersen, P. (1985). Preface. In P. Pedersen (Ed.), *Handbook of cross-cultural counseling and therapy.* Westport, CT: Greenwood Press.

Pelton, L. H. (1981). Child abuse and neglect and protective intervention in Mercer County, New Jersey. In L. H. Pelton (Ed.), *The social context of child abuse and neglect* (pp. 90–136). New York: Human Sciences Press.

Perlman, H. H. (1957). *Social casework: A problem-solving process.* Chicago: University of Chicago Press.

Piven, F. F. (1981). Deviant behavior and the remaking of the world. *Social Problems, 28*(5), 489–508.

Proctor, E. K., & Rosen, A. (1983). Problem formulation and its relation to treatment planning. *Social Work Research and Abstracts, 19*(3), 22–27.

Rank, M. R. (September, 1985). Exiting from welfare. *Social Service Review, 59*(3).

Reid, W. J., & Epstein, L. (1972). *Task-centered casework.* New York: Columbia University Press.

Sidel, R. (1986). *Women and children last: The plight of poor women in affluent America.* New York: Viking.

Simon, N. (1985). Artificial-intelligence approaches to problem solving and clinical diagnosis. In K. F. Schaffner (Ed.), *Logic of discovery and diagnosis in medicine.* Berkeley: University of California Press.

Solomon, B. (1976). *Black empowerment: Social work in oppressed communities.* New York: Columbia University Press.

Spector, M., & Kitsuse, J. I. (1974). Social problems: A reformulation. *Social Problems, 21*(2), 145–159.

Stagner, M., & Richman, H. (1986). Reexamining the role of general assistance. *Public Welfare, 44*(2), 26–32.

Stein, T. J. (1981). *Social work practice in child welfare.* New Jersey: Prentice-Hall.

Tallman, I. (1976). *Passion, action, and politics: A perspective on social problems, and social problem solving.* San Francisco: W. H. Freeman.

Thio, A. (1978). *Deviant behavior.* Boston: Houghton Mifflin.

United States House of Representatives, Committee on Ways and Means (1985). *Children in poverty.* Washington, DC: U. S. Government Printing Office.

Urban, H. B., & Ford, D. (1971). Some historical and conceptual perspectives on psychotherapy and behavior change. In A. E. Bergin & S. L. Garfield (Eds.), *Handbook of psychotherapy and behavior change: An empirical analysis* (pp. 3–35). New York: John Wiley & Sons.

Wing, J. K. (1978). *Reasoning about madness.* Oxford: Oxford University Press.

CHAPTER
3

INTERVENTION

Frameworks and Technology

Purpose
Types and Models
Goals
What are goals in social welfare services?
Goals are not a panacea
Why goal-oriented interventions?
Types of goals
From Goals to Results: Developing a Plan
Elements of a plan
Exercising choice
General types of interventions
Sequencing
Contracting
The Issue of Effectiveness
The effectiveness of the task-centered model
From Goals to Results: Problem-Solving Methods
The task-centered approach
Psychodynamic approaches
Cognitive behavioral approaches
Planned brief treatment and crisis intervention
Family approaches
Group approaches
Blending approaches: eclecticism
Professional relationships
Problem Solving in Complex, Natural Circumstances
The influence of helping organizations
The role of organized professional judgment
Effects of environment
Effects of the the personal characteristics of the client and practitioner
Summary

The term *treatment* is usually associated with practicing medicine, and ordinarily refers to curing, healing, medicating, and similar activities. However, treatment also refers to acting upon something with an agent for the purpose of improvement or alteration. It is the latter, nonmedical meaning that applies to the services nonmedical staff perform to help people with problems in living.

Intervention means "coming between." Providing a social welfare resource such as residential care for a child or financial assistance to a single mother comes between the child's lacking proper care and having proper care or between eviction and being at home. Psychotherapy in any of its varieties comes between (for example) drinking oneself out of a job and keeping that job, or between depressed loneliness and a modicum of reasonable companionship. Intervention is an interference in a state of affairs.

PURPOSE

Interventions have purpose, objectives, and goals. These three ideas have similar meanings and are often used interchangeably; all refer to intentions. In this book we tend to say "purpose" when we mean a broad, general, far-reaching intent or expectation; we tend to say "objective" when we mean an end to which our effort is directed; we use "goal" as a technical term to mean specific and particular behaviors, conditions, thoughts and feelings (cognitions) that are actively sought to be the end product of the intervention sequence. The main purpose, or objective, of intervention is to cause desired actions to occur. Other purposes are to restrain, control, or hold back certain actions; to maintain or alter a condition; or to permit or encourage actions. These purposes are viewed within a matrix of principal or grand purposes determined by history and social-political forces, namely, *social control and therapy.*

When performing *social control functions*, practitioners are attempting to help people attain normative functioning on the grounds that the individual is better off if she can fit in with the generally accepted modes of acting in society and will be happier personally and less difficult to deal with in society. Basic social control is the accepted role of police, but human service professionals are often responsible for meeting society's needs to reduce conflict and ensure that the general welfare is not endangered by harmful acts. Protective services in cases of child abuse and neglect is an important instance where human service practitioners, especially social workers, have a major responsibility for social control.

Therapeutic functions include remedial treatment of emotional disease or disorder and of dysfunctional interpersonal relationships in families or among peers and other important people. Therapeutic functions include a wide variety of activities, organized according to numerous models of practice. Their purpose is to correct personal disturbances of many sorts, to enhance the individual's ability to engage in satisfactory interpersonal relations, to enhance self-esteem appropriately, to increase skills for personal problem solving, and, generally, to reduce unhappiness and dissatisfaction and to improve the quality of personal relationships. Therapeutic functions may also include resources and educational counseling to enhance social skills.

TYPES AND MODELS

The terms *types*, *models*, and *approaches* are somewhat interchangeable. *Types* and *approaches* refer to broad categories of technical guidelines that have strong similarities or are based upon similar intellectual grounds. We speak of cognitive-behavioral types or approaches, psychodyanamic types or approaches, group treatment types or approaches, task-centered types, brief treatment and crisis intervention, and so forth.

Model is a more contemporary term that refers to collections of practice guidelines, derived from a specified body of knowledge and often from a specified research work. Models offer organized sets of related interventions that are identified and described with a high degree of specificity. They do not displace professional judgment and they cannot account for all possible occurrences. They guide the practitioner through a process that is in harmony with the real practice conditions, cutting down on some drift and trial and error. They depend on sensible professional judgment to adapt the model as necessary and encourage flexible use. Models are a product of the development of technologies in the helping occupations and help organize input, and identify results that are specific and possibly measurable, capable of being described, and replicated.

GOALS

Goals are powerful instruments for determining intervention. The present and particular interests of a single client and groups of clients shape intervention goals. By themselves, however, a client's goals are not the only factors that determine the substance of intervention programs such as, for example, those found in a mental hospital, a juvenile court, or a welfare agency. Public outcry in the newspapers and on television shape the goals of intervention by establishing the public, or society in general, as influences that decide what goals should be. Decisions at a professional conference and the information and opinions expressed in professional books, journals, and training programs also shape intervention goals. Because all these influences come from different directions, goals become tangled, complex, and ambiguous. Some of the influences shaping goals are in conflict. The conflict may be muted; that is, the operational goal may be a compromise among contending factors. For practical purposes a practitioner may focus on one or two aspects of the whole goal situation, yet uncertainty and ambiguity will remain a natural condition of the goal setting process. To reduce the ambiguity, goals should be explicit. *Unstated, vague, hidden goals are powerful and elusive and may often work against the overt goals, complicating intervention unnecessarily.*

What are Goals in Social Welfare Services?

The idea of a goal is straightforward. It is the end toward which effort is directed; it is a point beyond which something does not or cannot go. A goal is *not* a practitioner's, agency's, or client's wish. A wish is something desired and is the same thing as a goal *only if it is attainable or potentially attainable.* It takes the application of *resources* and *social skills* plus real, favorable opportunities and some luck to convert wishes to goal achievement. Furthermore, to be realizable a goal must be real, tangible, and concrete. A therapeutic goal that visualizes the achievement of a set of behaviors, for example, fewer family fights, can easily be made concrete by making a baseline measurement of the current undesirable number of fights and formulating what lesser number will do. Simply to assert a goal of "improvement in communication," or "more positive relationships," however, is rhetoric and not readily visualized or capable of specific definition. For example, what I consider improved or positive in my life, you may consider highly unsatisfactory.

Rhetoric, however, serves a purpose. It encourages communication about a subject, and useful ideas arise from communication. Rhetoric can be a shorthand way to clarify—or obscure—a subject. Notions such as "improvement in communication," "positive relationships," or "personal maturity" are short-hand for expressing a wide variety of attitudes about what is desirable. To be loved, employed, or promoted; to graduate, have a good income, live in a nice place, have healthy children—all these are understandable goals because they refer to conditions in the commonsense real world; they are not abstractions. On the other hand, unlimited or nonspecific rhetoric can blur understanding and lead nowhere.

Therapeutic goals can include changes in feeling, thinking, beliefs, and attitudes that are not visible to the degree that "fewer fights" or a "a better job" are. But cognitive goals are tangible if they deal with real internal events such as fears and anxieties, lack of appropriate self-esteem, painful, depressed moods, excessive suspiciousness, unfocused anger, misperceptions of one's own or other's attitudes and behaviors, misperceptions of the reality of events, and so forth.

The notion that social services have goals is old and commonplace, but in contemporary practice the professional perception of goals in practice has undergone a change. Since the mid-1960s a climate of thought has developed that has put high value on programs and techniques that could demonstrate "payoff." Results are desirable if they are in accord with defined objectives and produced by efficient, economical, and accountable methods. Hence there has been an attempt to formulate goals in concrete, finite, and measurable terms.

The anticipated payoffs from using goal-directed interventions are that clients will benefit from direct, rapid action to cut down a problem; accumulated information about goal achievement (results) can be used to improve service by distinguishing among better or worse interventions; staff can be rewarded and their morale improved by seeing client change; and it is possible to shed light on the characteristics of problems and interventions, enabling better quality research to take place.

Goals Are Not a Panacea

Goal-directed interventions are not cure-alls for the ills of the social welfare system. Intervention methods to reach goals have to be constructed and learned, and that takes time, energy, and money. Issues of values emerge and create conflict among staff, agencies, and the public. Some goals may seem better or more important than others, depending on a person's viewpoint, habits, and beliefs. Techniques have to be constructed to monitor outcomes and effectiveness of interventions, that is, to measure the performance of clients, staff, and agencies. Studies of outcome, whether for a single case or a total agency clientele, have to be interpreted, and interpretations can be complex, inconsistent, contradictory. The complexity of economic and social problems often retards straight-line goal achievement. Incomplete and inadequate goal achievement raises questions about how much goal attainment is enough. Is the work a failure if some ultimate condition is not obtained? Is the work a success if a limited useful gain has occurred?

It has for decades been an ideal to *maximize* help to clients. To this end, the tendency developed to formulate goals that were broad, inclusive, and multiple (Siporin, 1975). Such an ample approach, however, cannot be put into practice readily, given the limitations of technology, staff, funds, and constraints in the general climate of public opinion and in norms of society. Maximization is an ideal that seems logical and desirable, but lack of resources and technology to achieve this ideal as well as lack of consensus about the definition of an ideal precludes achieving it. The present trend to simplify, reduce, make concrete, and put limits around intervention reflects the practical meaning of goals, an end set of client behaviors and attitudes, and conditions in the the environment. Goals should be achievable in a reasonably short period of time, and as economically as possible. They should result from relatively specific actions that the client and practitioner can and do take to alleviate a specified target problem.

Why Goal-Oriented Interventions?

Cost and efficiency considerations
As the social welfare system of the United States grew to billion dollar proportions financed largely through taxation and operated by large bureaucra-

cies, it became apparent that issues of cost and efficiency were priorities in administering service programs. The immense size of the system is indicated by some selected statistics. Total social welfare outlays (including state, local, and federal) were 52 billion in 1960 rising to 672 billion by 1984.

The size of public expenditures arouses intense scrutiny, debate, and considerable acrimony among influential sectors of the public. People want to know what is being accomplished by social welfare expenditures and whether the results are worthwhile. These questions disturb everyone. Today computers make it possible to collect detailed information and to conduct increasingly sophisticated data analyses that put out more and more information in an attempt to deal with the questions of what exactly is the welfare system doing, how is it doing it, and what are the results. There are no simple answers, of course, but the data does help human service professionals and administrators understand what the system is doing and how it is operating.

To control costs and enhance efficiency it is necessary to state the goals of intervention processes clearly and to specify what is to be done and what results are to be accomplished. Formulating goals is one of the accepted ingredients in setting up interventions that can be monitored to find out with some exactness what was done and what resulted. Such straightforward planning and implementation, in and of itself, is considered to improve efficiency. In addition, the gradual accumulation of information about the relative merits of different interventions may, in time, provide usable information about what kind of interventions should be emphasized and what kind de-emphasized, and what kind dropped from the repertoire. This kind of specificity and measurement in human services is only just beginning, but there is every reason to believe the trend will persist and produce, within a few years, interesting and potentially useful data.

Administrative and policy considerations
A decade ago concern developed about administrative practices in social welfare, which were thought to be partly responsible for poor results (Comptroller General, 1973). Since then, great strides have been taken in upgrading the training of adminstrators and in developing business practices for the purpose of increasing efficiency, controlling costs, and enhancing effectiveness of the services.

Formerly policy was often based on assumptions that the social services should make major alterations in family life styles and individual behaviors to enable disadvantaged and deviant people to achieve economic independence, and reorganize and "normalize" their personalities and family relations. From a contemporary viewpoint these aspirations not only sound naive, but also fail to give enough consideration to structural problems in society that engender and maintain these problems, no matter how much effort is expended for individual "rehabilitation." Revisions in practice and innovative practices directed at goal-oriented results are today seen as potentially capable of reducing limited, specific problem conditions and behaviors of substantial importance without necessitating dilute attempts at major overhauls of personality and relationships.

The issue of congruence: What about differences between client and agency over goals?

Differences of opinion between clients and helping practitioners and their agencies have long presented difficulties in the helping process. A good deal of theorizing has gone into explaining why clients will circumvent, oppose, ignore, and obstruct supposedly beneficial efforts. The most prominent explanation for the unwillingness of clients to accept a practitioner's appraisal is the theory of resistance. That hypothesis assumes a mostly unconscious tendency to cling to habitual perceptions, ideas,and behaviors and thus to resist change.

Professional practice that relies on the resistance explanation has a tendency to extrude an impasse that slows down problem solving. There may be a concentration on dissolving the resistance rather than getting rid of the the problem. The problem may become a struggle between client and practitioner over problem definition. The working through or working out of this impasse extends treatment time, and may develop client dissatisfaction, drop-out, or other unwanted events.

Resistance is thought to be activated and maintained primarily by the presence of feelings, attitudes, and habits of mind that go back to earliest childhood, and by transference and repression. The process of "working though resistance," derived from psychoanalysis, is used to resolve transference and repression.

Transference is the tendency to project feelings, thoughts, and wishes onto the psychoanalyst, who becomes in the patient's mind a representation of persons from the past, primarily parents. *Repression* is the process of keeping unacceptable ideas or impulses out of consciousness. Working through in psychoanalysis is thought to enable the patient gradually to relinquish accustomed but dysfunctional ways of thinking, feeling, and acting, and also the assumed satisfaction possibly attached to the "illness." It is thought that slowly pushing away at the impasse develops insight and enables the patient to experience new perceptions and appropriate conflict-free affects. (Hinsie & Campbell, 1970, p. 662 and p. 814).

The theory of resistance and guidelines for working through are influential in treatment practice and have been popularized in novels and movies, on TV and on the stage. Many practitioners think in these terms about the reluctance and unwillingness of clients to accept and consent to the focus determined by the practitioner. However, there are other, probably more practical, approaches with a problem-solving purpose.

It stands to reason that if practitioner and client were working on the same problem and headed in the same direction such cooperation would increase pressure to achieve good task performance. In fact research evidence supports this commonsense idea. Reid and Hanrahan (1982) reviewed controlled experimental studies of direct social work interventions published from 1973 to 1979. The most clearly successful interventions were those in which *the clients' motivations were directed toward what the social workers were attempting to provide*. Research in the University of Chicago Task-Centered Project indicated that target problems worked on at the initiative of the client or as a result of close client-practitioner agreement were those that showed the most successful results (Reid, 1978). This kind of "motivational congruence" between practitioners and clients was missing from most of the intervention programs with poor outcomes. Videka-Sherman (1986) offers additional substantiation in her larger meta-analysis of 38 studies and suggests that clients' commitment to working on the problem defined may be a critical component of effective practice.

There are differing perspectives about dealing with conflicts between clients and practitioners on problem definition and focus of problem solving. There is steadfast adherence in American society, shared by many human service practitioners, to psychic determinism, the belief that early and unconcious psychological patterning causes present unhappiness, misbehavior, deviance, and inadequate self-fulfillment. It is assumed that it is best to tackle "underlying" problems to achieve desired results and long-standing views contend that intervention dealing primarily with presenting problems is inferior and insufficient. The aspiration to resolve deep psychological problems at the foundation of personal character and life style conflicts with the pervasive observation that people do not change readily, if at all, that social structures change very slowly, and the causes of problems are as much in the realm of society and culture as they are in the realm of psychology.

It is obvious problems underlie all areas of life—history, economics, and politics as well as in psychology. The question for problem-solving therapists is not whether or not there are underlying problems that should be eradicated, but rather what problems are accessible to change and what immediate, contemporary problems ought to be addressed to make a difference in the life of the client. Changes of importance are never trivial and are often hard to effect. However, when the client's interests can be meshed with the practitioner's expertise, so-called resistance can often be reduced to manageable dimensions, and there can be a significant release of client effort.

We may be uneasy when clients concentrate on defining problems that put the blame or responsibility on some other person or on some large environmental, political, or economic structure. Ordinarily, in a direct service agency, neither the client nor the agency has an immediate ability to change anything in the macro-economic-political system, or in the behaviors of persons they do not know and who are not present in the problem solving effort at hand. An agency may have an advocacy function or a social action function, but normally proceeding in those ways is too slow to have an immediate impact on a particular client's troubles.

Clients focus on matters of great interest to themselves, regardless of how they formulate the problem statements. Their formulations are legitimate and deserve respect. They probably indicate the surest direction for problem-solving work that will be taken seriously and has a good chance of success.

Sometimes, the dissonance between practitioner and client is exacerbated by public pressure, particularly from the various media, demanding results beyond the present capacity of the helping professions. The practitioner may feel squeezed between the resistant client on one hand and the critical, demanding public on the other. This tension is natural in present day political democracy where human service issues are among the most important concerns of the society, but systematic public education could help alleviate this stress.

Types of goals

Agency goals   Agency goals are established formally by the service organization. They chart a direction for the administration to accomplish a whole program. Agency goals cannot be directly applied to individual cases because they are too abstract. Their accomplishment does not depend on single individual cases but on the collective results of all the cases considered together.

Agency goals determine case goals only indirectly. There is usually no straight-line connection between broad, abstract agency goals and individual case practice, and there is no technology for applying broad agency goals to individual clients. Only intervention techniques apply to individual cases. The programmatic interventions of an agency with large aggregations of individuals require macro-systems interventions, such as community organization, social planning, and social action.

The character of agency goals is normative; that is, agency goals express conviction about ideal abstract intentions, and intentions implicit in law and custom. They also reflect political aims. For example, an agency is operating to carry out a law to protect victims of child abuse. The agency goal may be stated as protection of children, rehabilitation of disorganized families, or prevention of multiple problems. No individual case goal can be visualized to carry out such lofty aims, although many a case plan, to its folly, does frame its individual goals in such rhetoric. An individual case goal would more likely be, "to eliminate physical abuse of Bill; to place Bill in a foster home; to teach the parents to control their rage; to get the father a job," and so forth. Accomplishing individual case goals can be measured: Bill's mother either does or does not stop beating him with an electric cord; she does or does not stop taking out here rage on her son; her husband does or does not get a job; Bill does or does not go to a foster home; he either does or does not thrive in the foster home.

Professional goals   Professional goals are *opinions* of what is good, effective, and valuable in furthering the well-being of people and society. Professional goals may be abstract or specific. If espoused by powerful leaders, teachers, and supervisors, they may exert substantial power over the opinions and actions of practitioners. Professional goals, like expert opinion, vary over time, vary from one locality to another, and rarely offer a firm consensus to guide individual case action. Professional techniques can guide action directly. Professional goals are indirect influences on actions and tend to be long range, philosophical, and political.

Personal practitioner goals   These goals reflect the private opinions of individual workers, their own view of life and their own biases. These may be highly individualistic and unexpressed; they may also reflect the cultural, religious, and socioeconomic background of the practitioner. Strongly held personal goals of which the practitioner is not sufficiently aware can exert the strongest influence on how the practitioner leads the client and sets up or imposes unrealistic and irrelevant goals. Such procedures are obviously detrimental to the client's well-being, and sophisticated professionals attempt to control excessive personal influence to avoid distorting the goal-setting process.

Client goals   Client goals are the most practical way to carry out a goal-oriented strategy for individual case action. A forthright expression from the client of what he wants to achieve provides a relatively clear idea of what the focal problem is and to what the client is ready and able to give the most attention and effort. When the professional doubts the relevance or feasibility of the client's expressed goal, discussion can explore, evaluate, and possibly alter the client's goal, with the client's participation and genuine agreement. (See Chapter 5.) When an agency or the courts authoritatively prescribe goals, these may need to be negotiated. The likelihood is that clients will not be motivated to work for goals of which they disapprove or that are counter to their strongest beliefs and wishes. The direct way to minimize dissonance between practitioner and client on goals is to accord the client's goals a prominent place in the intervention strategy. This is also the activity most likely to result in a satisfactory outcome.

FROM GOALS TO RESULTS
——————————— Developing a Plan ———————————

Elements of a Plan

Most contemporary approaches to treatment advocate planned, systematic procedures because they are generally the most efficient and effective (Epstein, 1985; Rosen, Proctor, & Livne, 1985; Siporin, 1975). Planning consists of designing or outlining the intervention components by

1. Defining the problem(s): "What is to be tackled or changed?"
2. Identifying goal(s): "What outcome will be looked for?"
3. Choosing intervention activities: "What will be done?"
4. Formulating a sequence: "In what order will the intervention activities take place; where, with whom, and for how long will the work take place?"
5. Making the contract: "What are the client and practitioner committed to do?"

Exercising Choice

At each step in planning, choices have to be made that involve judgment (Meyer, 1983; Mullen, 1983; Thomas, 1984). Deciding on the components of the plan involves subjective factors, including the practitioner's value orientations, his preferred habits and ways of working, and his attained level of skills. Other more objective factors, in the sense that they are easier to observe and confirm, include the client's problem and condition, the style and aims of the practice setting, and the guidelines for practice incorporated into various practice models.

Interventions are categories of action expected to ameliorate a problem. Purposefully selecting intervention activities (rather than relying on trial and error or happenstance) is essential. As much as possible, intervention activities should be selected from among those that have been tested in research or in codified practice, published in reputable sources, and which have achieved verifiably good records of success. Experimental and innovative interventions should be encouraged with the informed consent of clients.

General Types of Interventions

The general categories of interventions can be outlined briefly. Each general category, however, includes a very large number of separate and specific intervention items too numerous to list here. The intervention types listed here are not mutually exclusive and tend to overlap considerably.

1. *Practical help:* Straightforward informing, advising, arranging, and expediting in such matters as financial assistance, housing, clothing, referrals and applications, employment-seeking, day care centers, clubs, outings (Goldberg & Warburton, 1979).
2. *Referral and linkage:* Connecting clients with other agencies, such as physical and mental health facilities, educational and vocational services, financial assistance agencies, and the like.
3. *Negotiating, advocacy, and bargaining:* Dealing with other agencies through conference, discussion, and compromise on behalf of the client to settle conflicts between the client and other agencies, especially regarding such matters as eligiblity for benefits and terms and conditions of the client's relationships and behavior with other agencies.

4. *Task formulation and guided performance:* Moving along in a relatively orderly manner to pinpoint tasks, identify obstacles to task performance, overcome obstacles, acquire skills for task performance, all focused on actions to reduce the target problem.
5. *Emotional support:* Providing an empathic helping relationship in which adequate and relevant compassion, responsiveness, encouragement, and reinforcement are displayed and conveyed.
6. *Teaching and enhancing social skills:* Conveying needed information, directing, guiding, enabling, modeling, rehearsing, providing feedback, encouraging, and supporting in order to make possible the acquisition of behavioral skills needed to have impact on the target problem.
7. *Psychotherapy (including counseling):* Helping individuals develop themselves and their personal resources in terms of interpersonal relationships, self-regard, problem solving skills, moods and tensions, handling of stress, mental and emotional conflicts, and the like, using professional relationship and interviewing skills and other selected and combined processes described above.

Sequencing

The sequence is the order of the activities in the plan and includes such related matters as where the work will take place, with whom, in what order, and for what duration (time limit). In some settings administrative regulations limit the length of contact and may also influence or prescribe location and participants.

Contracting

The idea of a practitioner-client contract has wide currency in the human services field even though there is much variety in actual practice. Contracts vary from complex to simple, from general to detailed, and from written to verbal. As explained by Rothery (1980, pp. 179–180):

> Increased interest in contracts reflects the influence of a number of beliefs about practice, including: (1) that people can and should make informed choices about the nature and goals of the services they receive; (2) that this carries with it a concomitant share in the responsibility for their treatment and its consequences; (3) that this responsibility includes full participation in the process of making decisions and choices and acting on them; and (4) that there is value in maximizing a client's cognitive involvement in his or her own problem-solving from the outset of the helping process.

THE ISSUE OF EFFECTIVENESS

The effectiveness of social intervention has become a priority as the sums invested in it have risen to unprecedented levels and as there have developed widespread expectations that psychotherapy and counseling should improve well-being. Questions about the worth of programs and practices, about their ability to deliver what they promise, about whether or not they "work," and about their cost effectiveness demand credible answers.

In the last twenty years, there has been an explosion of systems, models, approaches, and techniques ranging from traditional approaches (usually meaning based on psychodynamic/psychoanalytical techniques) to cognitive and behavioral approaches, to problem-solving approaches, to other approaches not so easily classifiable (Germain & Gitterman, 1980; Norcross, 1986; Patterson, 1986; Pincus & Minahan, 1973; Reid & Epstein, 1972; Roberts & Nee, 1970; Roberts & Northern, 1976). A diverse cadre of professionals—psychiatrists, psychologists, social workers, nurses, and pastors—are practicing in the field. Strupp (1986) asserts:

> "Therapy" is now being applied to a virtually limitless number of problems of human adaptation beyond the "classical" neurotic conditions. "Therapy" has become a household word, and its consumers are legion. Psychotherapy has become a billion-dollar industry, lacking clear boundaries, with hazy quality control and relatively vague ethical standards. Within this maelstrom, the core mental health professions . . . have struggled to promote stability, respectability, and professional standards of training and practice.

The development of third party payers, that is, insurance companies, employer and union operated health plans, group health plans, health maintenance organizations (HMOs), government funded health insurance, and means-tested benefits, has increased the demand for accountability. The growth of a large group of researchers able to engage in evaluative outcome and process research has enhanced the capacity of the helping disciplines to undertake increasingly sophisticated research. Divisive issues about methodology and the philosophy of research in these fields exist (Mullen, 1985). Nevertheless, there appears to be no slackening of effort in the research enterprise devoted to identifying activities and results of the far-flung treatment enterprises.

Both outcome and process research about what actually is done in intervention practice is difficult for technical and conceptual reasons. It is complicated to pinpoint, operationalize, observe, confirm, and measure the events of treatment as they occur within the major unit of activity, the interview. Compounding the complexity is that therapeutic events have connections to the situations of family, peers, work and school, culture and community, socioeconomic status, gender, the avowed norms of society, the influence of economic recessions, unemployment, war, and politics. In fact, the contextual complexities are so unwieldly as to induce scholars and practitioners to avoid them. The tendency, especially in the United States, is to regard intervention as presumably capable of being analyzed as a technical operation. On the other hand, it is possible to view the treatment enterprise as primarily a matter of h social relationships, that is, compassionate, realistic, caring interacti client's behalf, bringing to bear such influence as is reasonable, and providing necessary resources and skills to enable people to negotiate the risks and dangers, the demands and requirements of contemporary life.

Given the complexity of this subject, it is necessary to be cautious about summarizing what is known about the active ingredients of the intervention process and about the question of what works, in what circumstances, for whom, as implemented by what type of personnel in what settings, and under what conditions. The state of knowledge about the efficacy of treatment is in flux and can be expected to be changeable for the foreseeable future. Briefly stated, the basic points about effectiveness appear to be these.*

1. Psychotherapy, counseling, and social interventions are beneficial and better than no treatment or intervention.

2. There is not at present, nor can there be expected in the near future, agreement on any one single model or set of techniques as the most superior. It is argued that the inability to identify a superior model or models is due to the inaccuracy and insensitivity of research procedures. It is also argued that the practices studied in research do not properly represent the best practice. To tackle this problem a number of new books and manuals are attempting to formulate how to undertake the various treatments. (This book, for example, is such a manual.) Training and texts can always be improved and might produce practice distinct enough to be observed and measured when outcomes are evaluated.

3. It seems possible that there may be common or similar activities across models, and that these activities may be the most powerful or among the most powerful. Certain practitioner attributes appear to be common across models: warm involvement with the client, for example, and communication of a new perspective on the client's situation; these are known as "core conditions"— warmth, empathy, and genuineness. Contemporary research has not contradicted the strong contribution of these relationship attributes to achieving good outcomes. However, some researchers have found it difficult to specify and measure these attributes and trace their role during the treatment process. Different theoretical viewpoints tend to shape the relationship factors according their individual explanations of interpersonal behavior and their value positions on human relatedness.

Therapists trained according to treatment manuals have shown that they practice in line with the manuals' specifications. Even therapists who merely assert their allegiance to a school of therapy have shown appropriate, systematic differences. These technical differences among practitioners, however, have not

---

*Bednar & Kaul, 1978; Bergin & Lambert, 1978; Koss, Butcher, & Strupp, 1986; Garvin, 1981; Johnson, 1986; Lambert, Shapiro, & Bergin, 1986; Newman & Howard, 1986; Reid, 1985; Reid & Hanrahan, 1982; Rubin, 1985; Strupp & Binder, 1984; Videka-Sherman, 1985,1986; Wood, 1978; Wells, 1982

been shown to be directly associated with differential effectiveness. Comparative outcome studies are generally deficient in describing comprehensively what practices were carried out, making evaluation difficult. Also, practitioner behavior is so individualized that it is rarely clear that the procedures were carried out in accordance with the rules of the approach or its best practice recommendations (Stiles, Shapiro, and Elliot, 1986).

   4. Certain attributes of practice tend to be associated with the likelihood of good outcomes. These attributes include:

☐ *Structured approaches addressed to specific problems, behaviors, or social skills. Structure* means planned content, order, and arrangement of the design and conduct of the intervention program. *High structure* means the quality of strong, tight specificity and uniformity of the treatment plan. *Low structure* means a diminished degree of specificity and uniformity, together with a high degree of practitioner independence in selecting and arranging the treatment components, their timing, and their type. The extremes of structure—high to low—are sometimes referred to as being tightly focused or diffuse.

☐ *Task-centered problem solving and behavioral contracting.* Behavioral contracting and the task-centered model call for securing from clients commitments to undertake specific problem-solving actions. What is to be done and what is to be gained from doing it are laid out clearly, and the client is engaged as a voluntary participant. According to Reid and Hanrahan (1982), "Within this arrangement are apparently potent ingredients for bringing about change in human problems" (p. 338). Rubin's review of research (1985, p. 474) confirms that

> Most of the studies with unequivocally positive outcomes tested forms of practice that relied heavily on problem-solving and task-centered methods, usually in conjunction with behavioral methods, such as social skills and training. These forms of practice were found to be successful with such diverse groups as mildly to moderately retarded adults; chronic schizophrenics in aftercare; young, nonchronic psychiatric inpatients; women on public assistance; and low-income children experiencing school problems.

Videka-Sherman (1985, 1986) found that conveying the structure to the client and preparing her for intervention and for her role in the change process (all part of contracting) were effective interventions associated with good outcomes.

☐ *Motivational congruence.* Particularly in dealing with involuntary clients, achieving a focus in keeping with the client's own interests has the effect of improving the probability of a good outcome.

☐ *Sharp focus.* Sharpness of focus is characterized by pinpointing the area to be worked on and putting related or distant issues in the periphery or background.

☐ *Case management techniques.* Brokering, linking, advocating, referring are activities designed to select, obtain, and monitor community services. Such techniques have been judged successful with both physically and chronically mentally disabled clients. With chronically mentally ill patients the most effective treatments appear to be structured, brief treatments. These programs focus on problems of role performance and basic living skills, provide material resources and social support, and reach out into the community to arrange the best possible environmental and social network conditions. Long-term "talking" programs do not appear to succeed with these clients.

☐ *Comprehensive treatment packages in aftercare of chronic schizophrenics.* Treatment packages include restoration of major role performance, instruction in basic living and social skills, drug therapy, support system development, family education, and provision of material resources. Distinctive in these successful approaches was a practice orientation emphasizing support, linkage, education, and rehabilitation and avoiding psychodynamic and cognitively arousing approaches. Succesful approaches sought to facilitate role performance and living conditions.

☐ *Socialization of the client for intervention.* Informing the client thoroughly and understandably about what will occur and what she should be doing has been shown to be strongly associated with good outcomes.

☐ *Short-term treatments.* Treatment programs that have a set, relatively brief, time limit are associated with effective interventions. It is not known what duration of treatment is best in particular circumstances. It is possible that the successful outcomes of brief treatments are the result of the structured effort induced by time limits or deadlines. In order to comply with deadlines, it is advisable to rely heavily on task-centered, problem-solving, behavioral, and cognitive approaches. Surveys of length, or duration, of treatment consistently show that most outpatient therapies last no longer than 20 sessions, and the average ranges from 5 to 7 sessions.

A growing body of research supports the effectiveness of brief treatments in work with families, in mental health outpatient treatments, in cases of marital conflict, problems involving children, and adolescents, in crises, and in social and interpersonal relationship difficulties. Brief psychotherapy is today considered to be an effective and efficient treatment option when treatment goals are appropriate to the time apportioned.

☐ *Behaviorally and/or educationally oriented family interventions.* Despite continuing and growing interest among practitioners in family oriented interventions, few studies meet criteria of adequacy in research. A newly formulated family problem solving approach based on the task-centered model is promising, depending on a variety of empirical findings from a number of research sources (Reid, 1985).

☐ *Group treatment of various types.* There is no clear evidence as to the superiority of group or individual modalities. Clear goals and use of contracts appear valuable aids in achieving satisfactory results.

☐ *Practitioner activity, including advice and direction.* Practitioner activity refers to verbal behaviors such as directing, guiding, advising, instructing, and modeling and to actions (such as obtaining resources, advocating, linking, referring, negotiating, and the like) taken on behalf of the client.

5. A proportion of cases shows little or no improvement and a degree of negative outcome or decline in functioning. This fact has caused considerable debate in all the helping disciplines. The extent of this problem and why it occurs are issues that are far from settled. The tendency has been to attribute the problem to practitioner errors such as insufficient personal behaviors (for example, a lack of warmth, empathy, and genuineness), insensitivity of various sorts (such as lack of time, adequate supportive relationships, hostile behaviors and aggressive actions), or lack of training and relevant knowledge (Mays and Franks, 1985). However, current analysis indicates additional factors are probably at work, suggesting that the practitioner's characteristics may not be the only or primary factor involved in negative outcomes. Thoits (1985) states that substantial research supports the commonsense idea that undesirable life events and chronic strains have deleterious psychological effects upon individuals. Recent work confirms that these negative effects may be reduced when individuals possess adequate social support or utilize coping strategies to buffer the impacts of events and strains (Camasso & Camasso, 1986). The likelihood is that negative outcomes result from a combination of factors including those already mentioned as well as constraints imposed on the helping situation by the structure of agencies, value and ideological positions, and features of practice methods.

The Effectiveness of the Task-Centered Model

The task-centered approach recommends many practices similar to those recommended by the whole group of short-term or brief treatment approaches: time limits, limited goals, focused interviewing and present centeredness, activity and directiveness, rapid early assessment, and therapeutic flexibility (Budman, 1981). Brief treatment approaches of various types have been attempted with almost every kind of psychosocial problem (Mandel, 1981).

There have been numerous studies of the task-centered model in the United States and England. Some are concerned with research and development of the model and some with evaluation of outcomes. A wide variety of settings, clients, and problems is represented, for example, medical and psychiatric clinics, public schools, corrections, services for the aged including residential care, child guidance clinics, public welfare, family service, child welfare, and employee assistance programs.†

These reports recount venturesome efforts at developing a general practice model. Developers used as much empirically tested information as could be assembled at the time to design and formulate descriptions of techniques or guidelines for practice.

The basic outcome research showed that the task-centered model was effective with a wide array of problems. In most instances the model was able to reduce a set of related problems that clustered around the target problem. The model was less effective if the problem was broad in scope, global, or loose in focus. Some "ripple effect" was observed; that is, good results sometimes fanned out to other problems. Although the quality and rigor of the studies varied, and despite the absence of desired results in some instances, the model was useful as a basic set of interventions for many, if not most, problems in living as they appear in ordinary practice. Taken altogether, the research reports on task-centered work indicate it produces satisfactory results over a wide area of problems. It does this efficiently, in a cost effective manner satisfactory to clients.

FROM GOALS TO RESULTS
_____ **Problem-Solving Methods** _____

Problem solving is essential to the practice of science, including scientific approaches to dealing with social and psychological subjects. People and their predicaments can be approached by reasoned methods of thought and behavior in systematic ways. These reasoned methods are *cognitive processes* thought to be "the distinctively human forms of gaining, storing, transforming and using knowledge of all sorts" (Bruner, 1984). Despite the prevalence of problem-solving ideas in human service practices, these views have critics. Applying technology to the human sciences meets with resistance because some fear that important moral, ethical, and value considerations will be put aside (Whan, 1986). Some fear that applying technological ideas to human services may lead to manipulation and covert social control (Castel, Castel, & Lovell, 1982).

In 1933, John Dewey's work, *How We Think*, was published; it was in that book that he worked out an analysis of problem solving that underpins contemporary approaches used in the helping disciplines. Dewey stated that

†Bass, 1977; Blizinsky & Reid, 1980; Brown, 1977, 1980; Butler, Bow, & Gibbons, 1978; Diekring, Brown, & Fortune, 1980; Epstein, 1977; Ewalt, 1977; Fortune, 1977; Garrien, Reid, & Epstein, 1976; Gibbons, Butler, & Bow, 1979; Gibbons, Butler, Urwin, & Gibbons, 1978; Goldberg & Stanley, 1978; Hanrahan, 1986; Hari, 1977; Hofstad, 1977; Jackson, 1983; Larsen & Mitchell, 1980; Macy-Lewis, 1985; Newcomb, 1985; O'Connor, 1983; Reid, 1975, 1978, 1981, 1985; Reid & Epstein, 1972; Reid, Epstein, Brown, Tolson, & Rooney, 1980; Rooney, 1977, 1978, 1981; Rzepnicki, 1981, 1985; Salmon, 1977; Tolson, 1977; Toseland & Coppola, 1985; Weissman, 1977; Wexler, 1977; Wise, 1977; Wodarski, Marcy, & Malcolm, 1982.

The two limits of every unit of thinking are a perplexed, troubled, or confused situation at the beginning and a cleared-up, unified, resolved situation at the close. The first of these situations may be called pre-reflective. It sets the problem to be solved; out of it grows the questions that reflection has to answer. In the final situation the doubt has been dispelled; the situation is post-reflective; there results a direct experience of mastery, satisfaction, enjoyment (pp. 106–107).

In the mid-1950s a steady development of emphasis on problem solving and problem solving methods occurred. In 1956, Dartmouth College was host to a conference on the problem-solving potentials of computers, which ushered in studies on problem-solving methods uncovered in the development of artificial intelligence (Gardner, 1985). In 1957 the publication of *Social Casework: A Problem-Solving Process* established the idea of problem solving firmly in the professional consciouness of social work (Perlman, 1957). In 1971, D'Zurilla & Goldfried published an outline for problem-solving steps in behavior modificaton (D'Zurilla & Goldfried, 1971), followed by the development of task-centered casework in 1972 (Reid & Epstein, 1972).

What becomes apparent is that there was growing belief in the merits of problem solving as a key concept for the helping disciplines. A similar development was occurring in the administration of social institutions, government and business; there it took the form of "management by objectives" that had a central theme of solving management problems and arriving at desired goals by structured, planned means.

There are many ways to classify problem-solving methods. The present discussion will group the common methods into "families" that have some essential features in common. Actually, each author explains methods differently; however, lack of uniformity among the adherents of a particular school or family of treatment reflects the flux characteristic of the field, the constant search and experimentation, the responsiveness to new ideas, and the influence of social pressures and fads.

The Task-Centered Approach

The task-centered model emphasizes the construction of interventions to reduce the impact of specified problems that are its focus. Specifically, it aims to decrease the frequency of the problem occurrences, the intensity of the problem, and the problem's undesired effects on behavior, relationships, rewards, and lifestyle. The reduction in impact is expected to decrease the impediments to the individual's or family's adequate social functioning and also to increase desired behaviors, relationships, rewards, and quality of life.

The major means of problem solving in the task-centered model are: (1) the provision or acquisition of resources with which to do effective problem solving, (2) the teaching and learning of social skills and problem solving skills, and (3) the actual performance of tasks that do in fact produce demonstrable improvement in the direction sought. It is assumed that in most environments n with the necessary resources and the necessary skills will be in the best position to manage. Resources and skills may be acquired by direct receipt of material funds and goods, and by combining various types and amounts of advice, guidance, instruction, therapy, and counseling.

The problems that the task-centered approach attempts to reduce are those often characterized as "problems in living," by which is meant conflict between persons (interpersonal conflict), dissatisfaction in social relations, difficulties with formal organizations, difficulties in role performance, reactive emotional distress, or inadequate resources (Reid, 1978).

Psychodynamic Approaches

Psychodynamic approaches have undergone considerable revision in recent years as theorists responded to criticism and questioning from such varied sources as, for example, the women's movement, sociologists, historians of science, and the helping professions themselves (Castel, Castel, & Lovell, 1982; Sulloway, 1979). Psychodynamic approaches, which are adaptations of classical psychoanalytic treatment theories, reflect powerful intellectual trends in the modern world and have many strong adherents, especially in the United States. Furthermore, some of these ideas have saturated modern international culture, literature, drama, art, and everyday habits of thought, as well as human service programs.

Psychodynamic approaches emphasize interventions to enhance and restore personal well-being, to help people meet their needs for self-actualization and self-fulfillment more fully, and to promote more adequate functioning in social relationships. The improvements intended are envisaged in broader terms than the target problem defined in the task-centered model. In the psychodynamic approach the changes hoped for are personality growth and development (to overcome childhood conflicts and needs preserved into the present and creating inappropriate reactions), reduction in current life pressures, and correction of poorly functioning ego and superego (resulting in distorted perception of the outside world or the self, poor judgment, excessive anxiety, insufficient ability to control impulses or to direct behavior, poor reality testing, and inappropriate uses of defenses) (Hollis, 1979).

The major means of problem solving in psychodynamic therapies is the therapeutic relationship in which the helping practitioner guides the client through processes of acquiring insight, that is, understanding herself, significant others, and the social environment; acquiring resources and skills along the way; achieving diminution or resolution of intrapsychic conflicts as a means to self-fulfillment and improved relations with others. Benefit from these processes is expected to decrease the impediments to adequate social functioning.

The problems that psychodynamic approaches attempt to affect are the same ones that the task-centered model formulates; but the ideal or preferred form of the psychodynamic approaches considers that the internal (that is, the private mental or intrapsychic) reflection of the problem takes priority in the treatment. However, if the client and/or her circumstances bar effective attention to underlying problems, psychodynamic practitioners are realists and settle for limited goals.

Cognitive Behavioral Approaches

Cognitive behavioral approaches are relatively new on the scene and were first formulated and published in the 1970s. As is the case with other treatment models, various writers, based on their different experiences and interests, have made unique contributions to the ideas that are now called cognitive-behavioral approaches. These writers emphasize interventions to help clients cope with immediate, pressing problems and acquire knowledge and understanding useful in managing future life problems (Berlin, 1983). Some evidence suggests, for example, that clients who learn problem-solving skills achieve more gains in treatment than clients who receive only treatment (Brown, 1980).

Cognitive-behavioral approaches relate to cognitive theory, a developing body of knowledge that is enlightening while still tentative and speculative (Gardner, 1985). These approaches offer new possibilities for the clinical practitioner. They suggest that the client come to understand and appraise the essential nature of her situation and options and then take steps to improve those options and reduce those problem states. Berlin (1983) suggests a wide range of activities that may facilitate change. How a client feels and thinks about problems may be changed by constructing more adaptive meanings and expectations and providing experiences that support changed views. New behaviors may be developed through modeling, rehearsing, and repeated enactments. Relevant social-environmental strategies may achieve new social supports for clients, enhancing their abilities to solve problems.

> The strategy is to get a little change going—to give the client the skills, supportive conditions, and incentives to assist him in attributing mastery to his own abilities and efforts—and then to build from there by guiding the client's performance through increasingly difficult and independent tasks (Berlin, 1983, p. 1106).

The problems that cognitive-behavioral treatments attempt to affect are those of central concern to all the intervention models, problems in living. Congitive behavioral approaches, like others, are addressed to how people think, feel, and believe, in other words, to psychological or mental aspects of their situations, but also to interpersonal transactions and transactions with the environment, in much the same way as the task-centered model.

Planned Brief Treatment and Crisis Intervention

Intervention sequences of relatively brief duration have always been used in practice, and are probably the dominant form of treatment. They were not taken seriously as a major modality until research findings began to reveal their effectiveness. Of great importance has been the demands of insurance companies and cost-conscious health service planners for specific cost effective treatments. The therapy establishment has also begun to insist on economical interventions. Today, brief treatment is a rapidly developing field of interest to practitioners of all persuasions and considered applicable to a wide range of problems. Treatment of choice in this area as elsewhere is unsettled, however.

Various types of quick, immediate responses to emergencies and to acute, sudden onset of problems, often resulting from some outside agent (for example a sudden beating or rape), are included within a broad, general category of crisis intervention. Sometimes included are acute emotional crises, such as grief. Crisis intervention approaches are responsive to public events, such as natural disasters and wrecks, and to traumas induced in special populations by newly emerging or newly recognized social problems such as child abuse and wife battering. There is no single unified crisis theory or intervention method. Crisis intervention is in fact a variant of planned brief treatment adapted to the circumstances of particular intervention programs (Lemon, 1983).

Family Approaches

Family treatment represents another collection of related but dissimilar approaches. Problems in living are explained as an expression of the way the family system functions. There are numerous views about the processes involved in the family system. Walsh (1982) has summarized the activities of various family intervention approaches as follows:

- [ ] reorganizing the family structure (structural approach)
- [ ] resolving the presenting problem (strategic approach)
- [ ] improving concrete, observable behavior (behavioral-social exchange approach)
- [ ] developing insight into and resolving family conflict and losses, reconstructing relationships, and stimulating individual and family growth (psychodynamic approach)
- [ ] modifying relationships in the family system (family systems therapy)
- [ ] enhancing clear, direct comunication and individual and family growth through immediate shared experience (experiential family therapy)

These various approaches overlap of course. Available research does not indicate the superiority of any one approach over any other, and it is not established in what circumstances family treatment is the treatment of choice. Many practitioners, however, prefer treatment to include all or part of the family when several members are involved in the problem. The problems that are the focus of family treatment are the same array of problems that are the focus of other treatment models. The psychodynamic approaches concentrate upon theoretically identified internal conflict areas in the family treatment mode as they do in the individual treatment mode.

From its inception the task-centered model has included family treatment within its scope (Reid & Epstein, 1972; Epstein, 1985; Reid, 1985) both with respect to focal problems and methods of intervention adjusted to take account of multiple participants. Adaptations of the task-centered approach have been worked out to enhance permanency planning for children in foster care (Rooney, 1981; Rzepnicki, 1985).

Group Approaches

A group is a collection of unrelated persons who have some explicit connection to one another that makes them interdependent. Groups consisting of individual adults, parents, children, or couples are formed in human service organizations. People facing similar illnesses, social problems, or seeking increased competence in social skills are typical examples of those who might consititute problem-solving groups.

Groups may be effective in ameliorating problems in living. Their problem-solving processes are augmented by group processes such as convening the group, integration and disintegration, the development of intragroup conflicts, and subsequent reorganization of the group (Epstein, 1985; Garvin, 1981; Yalom, 1985). Groups are complex phenomena and difficult to research. Available information comparing group and individual treatment does not indicate that either is more effective than the other. Like individual treatment, group treatment may result in casualties (Bednar & Kaul, 1978; Lieberman, Yalom, & Miles, 1973; Parloff & Dies, 1977).

The task-centered model has been applied to work with groups since its inception, adapting the steps and processes to take account of multiple participants and group processes (Coppola,1985; Fortune, 1985; Macy-Lewis, 1985; Newcome, 1985; Rooney, 1977). Some of these adaptations include:

- ☐ Selecting group members whose target problems and anticipated tasks are similar;
- ☐ Using group tasks as well as individual tasks;
- ☐ Using visual aids to clarify actions and keep attention on goals; and
- ☐ Using formats for achieving task performance, such as consulting pairs and buddy systems.

Blending Approaches: Eclecticism

Intervention practice cannot get along without developing and using technology. Real practice, however, must be eclectic. But this does not mean a hodgepodge; it *does* mean a reasoned selection from a number of sources of what seems or is judged best at a particular time under specific circumstances. What is best depends on one's viewpoint and philosophy of practice. Many today are persuaded that the best techniques are those most closely connected to the target problem, having a published record of effectiveness, developed from empirical testing and research, and making sense.

Eclecticism is the selection of elements from different systems of thought, without regard to contradictions between the systems. It differs from syncretism, which tries to combine various systems while resolving conflicts. Eclectics are frequently charged with being inconsistent. The fact is that practitioners are habitual borrowers and continual developers of their own practice procedures, based on experience, personal preference, loyalty to influential agencies, teachers, and supervisors, their own therapists, and attention to keeping up-to-date.

After a decade of muddle during the seventies, when followers of various schools of therapy engaged in combat with followers of other schools of therapy, there has now emerged a wiser atmosphere. Many contemporary practitioners do not "belong" to any particular system of psychotherapy, although they seem to have preferences or habits. They sometimes elevate their preferences by calling them "principles" or even "theory"— rhetoric that is not always deserved. However, many of today's practical and result-minded practitioners attempt to put some organization into collections of what they believe to be significant phenomena, based on their experience and the experience of trusted colleagues and relying on research data whenever possible (Garfield, 1980; Norcross, 1986; Tolson, in press).

Present-day eclecticism is based on an awareness that no one model or approach can be universally applied, cover any and all circumstances, or produce an effective outcome across the board. Although little is known with any certainty about what procedures work best in the multitude of practical circumstances, there is nonetheless an awareness that useful strategies and ideas may be found in many various sources.

The lens of problem solving was used as the centerpiece in organizing the characteristics of the main classifications of intervention approaches. The problem-solving lens reveals what is common among the approaches, namely, that they all deal with the same or similar problems in living and that they all use verbal discourse in which one person (the practitioner) helps the other person (the client) overcome difficulties. The differences among the basic categories of models are in the different emphases put on defining or focusing the problem; formatting an intervention into individual, group, or family mode; determining the comprehensiveness or specificity of goals; or deciding on the nature of the structure of the intervention sequence (for example, from the manifest steps of the task-centered model to the intricate constructions of the psychodynamic approaches).

Observation and available research findings suggest that practice in the real world is eclectic. Kolevson and Maykranz (1982) obtained information from 670 responding clinical educators (mostly field instructors) in ten graduate schools of

_____ *Appologetic?* _____

social work. The results indicate that their ideas about intervention action were only slightly influenced by their model preferences. Garfield and Kurtz (1976) surveyed 855 clinical psychologists and found that over half indicated they were eclectics. An additional study of a sample of these eclectic psychologists showed they thought that relying on only one pschyotherapeutic approach was inadequate for working with the wide variety of problems they encountered (Garfield & Kurtz, 1977). Jayaratne obtained information from 515 respondents to a questionnaire sent to a random sample of clinical social workers. Of the total respondents, 267 (or 54.6 percent) identified themselves as eclectic practitioners (Jayaratne, 1978, 1982).

What seems important at the present time is a commitment to what is most effective to the extent that can be ascertained from research and analysis of various theories of practice and practice reports from reliable sources. It is possible and practical to blend the task-centered approach with a wide variety of other approaches. In fact, the increasing literature about the task-centered model suggests that this kind of adaptation is constantly occurring. It would be desirable if these developments were to take place in a more systematic manner; Chapter 9 deals with this subject in more detail.

Professional Relationships

The consensus among the helping professions is that the relationship between client and practitioner is a prominent part of the treatment. This therapeutic alliance is believed to be crucial to the interaction between practitioner and client and to a good outcome for the intervention. Both client and practitioner experience this relationship in the same way they experience other human relationships, through their feelings, thoughts, and their perceptions of themselves. Both client and practitioner contribute to this relationship in terms of the work each does to assess and identify problems, collaborate on plans, and implement problem-solving tasks. This professional relationship is an important, some would say the most important, facilitator of getting problem-solving work done.

The professional relationship is composed of the thoughts, feelings, attitudes, perceptions, and interactional stimuli and responses occurring between the practitioner and the client. A relationship always exists when two or more people are together in any social endeavor and takes on a charged quality when people are communicating about intimate and significant matters as is the case in human service work. The emotional charge in interactions is heavy when clients want something that they hope practitioners can provide such as surcease of stress, food, money, a job, a skill for acquiring a promotion, a husband, a wife, a divorce, a child placement, an education, better health, or parole from jail.

Establishing and maintaining a positive practitioner-client relationship depends on the quality of communication (including the attitudes communicated by appearance, manner, and body motions), and expressions of concern and support, both verbal and nonverbal. Much research has attempted to analyzethe operational attributes of the practitioner-client relationship (Pope, 1979; Frieswyk, Allen, Colson, Coyne, Gabbard, Horwitz, & Newson, 1986; Luborsky, Crits-Christoph, & Mellon, 1986). Attitudes and personal characteristics that facilitate the client's communication, that is, that put the client in a frame of mind to talk to the practitioner, seem to contribute to a good relationship. One of these characteristics is the practitioner's close attention to and grasp of the client's problems in the way they are formulated and understood by the client in her particular environment, setting, and cultural, economic, and social context. Another facilitating attribute is the collection of attitudes subsumed under the term "empathy" (that is, the imaginative participation in the client's feelings and ideas) and the related ability to project warmth, positive regard, and genuineness.

PROBLEM SOLVING IN COMPLEX, _____ NATURAL CIRCUMSTANCES _____

Many human problems evade reduction. We do not know the answer to many problems. We ought to put forth our best efforts on those likely to be improved by presently known methods and invest as much as possible in research on the more obdurate problems.

It seems to be the nature of the helping disciplines to expect more and better solutions through technology. However, we ought not be naive about the capability of social science to produce all-purpose technologies to solve problems. While some problems lend themselves to clear-cut asssessment and relatively neat and straightforward solutions, others are difficult or intractable. In live, natural circumstances, personal and social problems are often obscure in their origins, confounded by multiple circumstances, and resistant to quick fixes. Knowledge may be fragmented or lacking. Practice has to take place without the certainty of thorough, complete, valid, and reliable knowledge. This is the essence of problem solving in complex, natural circumstances.

The daily encounter with clients involves methods (or technology), theories, and values. In our scientifically minded society, practice—doing, acting, intervening—is underpinned by technology. That underpinning is the problem-solving process. Of equal importance is *prudence*, that is, practical wisdom or practical commonsense, with which one mediates between the universal and the particular, between the theories and their application, between the practice guidelines (as in this book) and the live case. Practice decisions get made by applying theory or principles with judgment, choice, and reflection on what constitutes the good for which one acts (Whan, 1986). In spite of many different motives that may coexist when defining problems or deciding on intervention strategies, the final, legitimating value is the concerned judgment about what is best for the client.

The Influence of Helping Organizations

Except in the case of individual private practice, intervention is conducted in bureaucratic organizations, such as welfare agencies of various types, clinics, hospitals, schools, housing authorities, employment and training facilities, or correctional facilities. The organization influences the way practice is conducted. It usually affects the selection of practice models. Policy decisions may direct the specific ways models are used. The types and training of personnel hired will strongly influence the way practice is conducted. The organization emphasizes work in a particular service domain and makes decisions about what interventions are appropriate for the problems or sets of problems over which it assumes responsibility. The organization establishes the terms and conditions for the availability of resources needed in the helping process.

The Role of Organized Professional Judgment

Clients of human service professionals are vulnerable because they must reveal personal, intimate information in order to be helped. Consequently they have no choice but to depend on and trust the practitioner. They must have greater confidence than if they were using a service with more technical control over its processes, for example, engineering. However, not everybody can be comfortable with that amount of dependence and many lack confidence.

To protect the client and to maintain their authenticity before the public, the human service professions support a wide variety of mechanisms that organize professional opinion. The organized professional associations collaborate with universities in sanctioning professional education. Through publications and conferences, the professions formulate preferred views and practices; that is, they set standards. Professions are not immune to being influenced by prevailing winds on the political scene and in the funding organizations. They are not immune to the dominant directions of their culture and body of opinion about what norms to uphold, what priorities to set, or what goals and results to shoot for.

Organized professional judgment makes itself felt at the level of the client's personal problem solving through the practitioner and what he has learned or selected from the whole body of shifting professional judgment. The power of that judgment is strong because professionals acquire much of their status, security, power, authority, and prestige from the identification with their own profession. Because the helping professions are divided into numerous parallel and subsidiary strata, they diverge in general outlook and specific practice rules and recommendations. This creates some confusion, but professionals in these fields learn to live with that confusion as a regular part of their professional work.

Effects of Environment

It is all too obvious that the characteristics of the environment are a major determinant of problems in living. The physical environment comprises the natural world and the man-made world. The social environment encompasses the system of socioeconomic stratification, the distribution of equality and opportunity, the repressive mechanisms of discrimination, the advantages enjoyed, and the micro-environment—the network of family, friends, community and neighborhood, resources, work and school. Enfolding all environments are culture, values, knowledge, and beliefs that guide our choices and form our consciousness.

The immensity of the environment, the multiple sources of information and knowledge about it, and the complexity of intervening to change the environment have all combined to turn the attention of helping professionals to more manageable sectors of problems in living, namely the individual and her most immediate environment, the family. Furthermore, the environment is enmeshed in politics, in conflicts between management and labor, and in crucial conflicts over domestic and foreign social policy. It is difficult for any profession sanctioned by law, society, and custom to put itself in a position where it is actively participating in working out large scale social conflicts, played out mostly in the political arena. Most persons in the helping professions do not have the taste for such conflicts, rather seeing themselves as mediators at most. A stream of social activists surfaces at various historical times, the latest being during the civil rights struggles of the 1960s–1970s. But for the most part, helping professionals attend to the individual and the close family-neighborood environment.

Within that small arena, the profession of social work has historically possessed a special expertise in connecting people to resources through referral, linkage, and advocacy. This is service much valued by clients and of growing interest to other helping professions such as nursing.

In the live case, the environment saturates the problem circumstances. For purposes of practice (that is for practical judgments about problem identification, focus, and intervention design) assessments ought to be attempted that judge the degree to which environmental factors are dominating the problem. Understanding those factors or intervening in some of the environmental circumstances may ameliorate the situation. Should that be the case, even partly, the intervention may be efficient and successful.

Effects of the Personal Characteristics of the Client and Practitioner

The client's response to the helping process is only partly a product of the techniques of problem solving used. Clients' responses are conditioned by who they are and where they come from and are shaped by their expectations and their views of themselves, other people, and social institutions arising from their ethnic background, culture, social class, personal traits, values, and circumstances.

Mental or physical illness, handicaps, and background affect the manner in which a client presents herself and perceives the practitioner's intentions and actions. The client's characteristic mood, anxiety level, education, cultural background, talkativeness, interests and expectations all combine to produce the individuality that each person contributes to the treatment situation.

The individual characteristics of the practitioner also influence the process. The practitioner acquires a professional posture or professional "self" that is the result of knowledge, experience, discipline, and socialization. At the same time the practitioner is an individual with his own characteristics. Personal and professional selves coexist, however; we do not do away with our personal self and substitute a cardboard character, scripted and made up to look "professional." Like the client, the practitioner has ideas about what to expect, what is preferred, and how to appear. These ideas are personal, derived from the practitioner's background, culture, values, and circumstances. The importance of self-awareness lies in appreciating that practitioner characteristics are present and affect the process of interacting with the client.

SUMMARY

This chapter examines the characteristics of intervention in the helping services. It analyzes the frameworks for intervention and gives an overview of its technologies.

Intervention in human service work means acting upon the client's problems in such a way as to improve or alter them for the better. The main purpose of intervention is to cause desired actions to occur. Intervention takes place within the context of social control and/or therapy.

There are numerous types of intervention models and approaches: cognitive-behavioral types, psychodynamic approaches, group treatment, task-centered, brief treatment and crisis intervention, and so forth.

Goals are powerful in determining intervention content and substance. Goals include changes in feelings, thinking, and beliefs and attitudes, and in environment, social relations, and behaviors. Goals are important in controlling work to produce results that are as economical as possible and efficient. The contemporary view of goals is to visualize them as reductions in limited, specific problem conditions and behaviors of substantial importance without necessitating major overhauls of personality and relationships.

Differences between clients and helping practitioners and their agencies present difficulties in the helping process. It is advisable to minimize these differences as quickly as possible. The most direct and feasible way is to accept the client's statement of target problems as a straightforward focus for the work, modified, to the extent necessary and possible, on the basis of professional judgment and with client understanding and agreement.

There are several types of goals, all of which may be present: agency, professional, personal practitioner goals, client goals. Goals need to be explicit and lead into the development of a plan. Planning involves making choices about interventions and selecting types of interventions expected to be effective in the particular case circumstances, choosing from types of practical help: referral and linkage; negotiating, advocacy, and bargaining; task formulation and guided performance; emotional support; teaching and enhancing social skills; and psychotherapy. The intervention plan includes a plan for the sequence or order of the activities, and for contracting which is primarily a way to assure that the client is well informed about the nature of the intervention and her part in the process and is willing and agreeable to proceeding.

Although the helping professions have only recently developed research means for evaluating the effectiveness of interventions and there are no absolutes that will guarantee results, some major findings suggest the kinds of interventions most likely to succeed. The techniques employed in the task-centered model closely fit the protocols of effective treatment.

Problem-solving methods provide the means to get from goals to results in intervention practice. The task-centered approach is a way to conceptualize problem solving to make it applicable to human service practice. Other approaches (such as selected psychodynamic, cognitive-behavioral, planned brief treatment and crisis intervention, family, and group techniques) may be used to add to the repertoire of techniques. The task-centered model can be used to organize eclectic approaches that augment the model, according to the judgment and expertise of the practitioner and also taking into account the preferences of the client and practitioner.

Most practitioners and theorists agree that certain aspects of intervention are important to effective interventions: for example, a satisfactory professional relationship or therapeutic alliance and the presence of facilitating conditions (and absence of strongly limiting conditions) in the environment and in the helping organization or agency. The intervention program may be affected by prevailing professional opinion and by unique effects of the client's and practitioner's personal characteristics.

———————————————————————— **REFERENCES** ————————————————————————

Bass, M. (1977). Toward a model of treatment for runaway girls in detention. In W. J. Reid & L. Epstein (Eds.), *Task-centered practice* (pp. 183–194). New York: Columbia University Press.

Bednar, R. L., & Kaul, T. J. (1978). Experiential group research: Current perspectives. In S. L. Garfield & A. E. Bergin (Eds.), *Handbook of psychotherapy and behavior change: An empirical analysis* (pp. 769–816). New York: John Wiley & Sons.

Bergin, A. E., & Lambert, M. (1978). The evaluation of therapeutic outcomes. In S. L. Garfield & A. E. Bergin (Eds.), *Handbook of psychotherapy and behavior change: An empirical analysis* (pp. 139–190). New York: John Wiley & Sons.

Berlin, S. (1983). Cognitive-behavioral approaches. In A. Rosenblatt & D. Waldfogel (Eds.), *Handbook of clinical social work* (pp. 1095–1119). San Francisco: Jossey-Bass.

Blizinsky, M., & Reid, W. J. (1980). Problem focus and outcome in brief treatment. *Social Work, 25*(March), 89–98.

Brown, L. B. (1977). Treating problems of psychiatric outpatients. In W.J. Reid & L. Epstein (Eds.), *Task-centered practice.* New York: Columbia University Press.

Brown, L. B. (1980). *Client problem solving learning in task-centered social treatment* (Doctoral dissertation, University of Chicago).

Bruner, J. (1984). *In search of mind.* New York: Harper and Row.

Budman, S. H. (1981). *Forms of brief therapy.* New York: The Guilford Press.

Butler, J., Bow, I., & Gibbons, J. (1978). Task-centered casework with marital problems. *British Journal of Social Work,* (Summer), 393–409.

Camasso, M. J., & Camasso, A. E. (1986). Social supports, undesirable life events, and psychological distress in a disadvantaged population. *Social Service Review, 60*(3), 378–394.

Castel, R., Castel F., & Lovell, N. A. (1982). *The psychiatric society.* New York: Columbia University Press.

Dewey, J. (1933). *How we think.* Lexington, MA: D. C. Heath.

Diekring, B., Brown, M., & Fortune, A. E. (1980). Task-centered treatment in a residential facility for the elderly: A clinical trial. *Journal of Gerontological Social Work, 2*(3), 225–240.

D'Zurilla, T. J., & Goldfried, M. R. (1971). Problem solving and behavior modification. *Journal of Abnormal Psychology, 78*(August), 107–126.

Epstein, L. (1977). A project in school social work. In W. J. Reid & L. Epstein (Eds.), *Task-centered practice* (pp. 130–135). New York: Columbia University Press.

Epstein, L. (1985). *Talking and listening: A guide to the helping interview.* Columbus, OH: Merrill.

Ewalt, P. (1977). A psychoanalytically oriented child guidance setting. In W. J. Reid & L. Epstein (Eds.), *Task-centered practice* (pp. 27–49). New York: Columbia University Press.

Fortune, A. E. (1977). Practitioner communication in task-centered treatment. (Doctoral dissertation, University of Chicago).

Fortune, A. E. (1981). Communication processes in social work practice. *Social Service Review, 55*(March), 93–128.

Fortune, A. E. (1985). Treatment groups. In A. E. Fortune, *Task-centered practice with families and groups* (pp. 33–44). New York: Springer.

Frieswyk, S. H., Allen, J. B., Colson, D. P., Coyne, L., Gabbard, G. O., Horwitz, L., & Newson, G. (1986). Therapeutic alliance: Its place as a process and outcome variable in dynamic psychotherapy research. *Journal of Consulting and Clinical Psychology, 54*(1), 32–38.

Gardner, H. (1985). *The mind's new science: A history of the cognitive revolution.* New York: Basic Books.

Garfield, S. L. (1980). *Psychotherapy: An eclectic approach.* New York: John Wiley & Sons.

Garfield, S. L., & Kurtz, R. (1976). Clinical psychologists in the 1970s. *American Psychologist, 31*(1), 1–9.

Garfield, S. L., & Kurtz, R. (1977). A study of eclectic views. *Journal of Consulting and Clinical Psychology, 45*(1), 78–83.

Garvin, C. D. (1981). *Contemporary group work.* Englewood Cliffs, NJ: Prentice-Hall.

Garvin, C. D., Reid W. J., & Epstein, L. (1976). Task centered group work. In R. W. Roberts & H. Northern (Eds.), *Theoretical approaches to social work with small groups* (pp. 238–267). New York: Columbia University Press.

Germain, C. B., & Gitterman, A. (1980). *The life models of social work practice.* New York: Columbia University Press.

Gibbons, J., Butler, J., & Bow, I. (1979). Task-centered casework with marital problems. *British Journal of Social Work, 9*(no. 2), 393–409.

Gibbons, J. S., Butler, J., Urwin, P., & Gibbons, J. L. (1978). Evaluation of a social work service for self-poisoning parents. *British Journal of Psychiatry, 133,* 111–118.

Goldberg, E. M., Gibbons, J., & Sinclair, I. (1984). *Problems, tasks, and outcomes.* Winchester, MA: Allen and Unwin.

Goldberg, E. M., & Stanley, J.S. (1978). A task-centered approach to probation. In J. King (Ed.), *Pressures and changes in the probation service.* Cambridge, England: Institute of Criminology.

Goldberg, E. M., & Warburton, R. W. (1979). *Ends and means in social work.* London: Allen and Unwin.

Hanrahan, P. (1986). Task-centered system: Review of the research. Unpublished manuscript.

Hari, V. (1977). Instituting short-term casework in a long-term agency. In W. J. Reid & L. Epstein (Eds.), *Task-centered practice.* New York: Columbia University Press.

Hinsie, L. E., & Campbell, R. J. (1970). *Psychiatric dictionary.* New York: Oxford University Press.

Hofstad, M. O. (1977). Treatment in a juvenile court setting. In W. J. Reid & L. Epstein (Eds.), *Task-centered practice* (pp. 195–202). New York: Columbia University Press.

Hollis, F., & Woods, M. E. (1981). *Casework: A psychosocial therapy* (3rd ed.). New York: Random House.

Jackson, A. A. (1983). *Task-centered marital therapy: A single case investigation* (Doctoral dissertation, University of Alabama).

Jayaratne, S. (1978). A study of clinical eclecticism. *Social Service Review, 52*(4), 621–631.

Jayaratne, S. (1982). Characteristics and theoretical orientations of clinical social workers: A survey. *Journal of Social Service Research,* (4), 17–30.

Johnson, H. C. (1986). Emerging concerns in family therapy. *Social Work, 31*(4), 299–307.

Kolevson, M. S., & Maykranz, J. (1982). Theoretical orientation and clinical practice: Uniformity versus eclecticism? *Social Service Review, 56*(1), 120–129.

Koss, M. P., Butcher, J. N., & Strupp, H. H. (1986). Brief psychotherapy methods in clinical research. *Journal of Consulting and Clinical Psychology, 1*(54), 60–67.

Lambert, M. J., Shapiro, D. A., & Bergin, A. E. (1986). The effectiveness of psychotherapy. In S. L. Garfield & A. E. Bergin (Eds.), *Handbook of psychotherapy and behavior change* (3rd ed.). New York: Wiley.

Larsen, J. A., & Mitchell, C. (1980). Task-centered, strength-oriented group work with delinquents. *Social Casework, 61*(March), 154–163.

Lemon, E. C. (1983). Planned brief treatment. In A. Rosenblatt, & D. Waldfogel (Eds.), *Handbook of clinical social work* (pp. 401–419). San Francisco: Jossey-Bass.

Lieberman, M. A., Yalom, I. D., & Miles, M. B. (1973). *Encounter groups: First facts.* New York: Basic Books.

Luborsky, L., Crits-Cristoph, P., & Mellon, J., (1986). Advent of objective measures of the transference concept. *Journal of Consulting and Clinical Psychology 53*(1), 39–48.

Macy-Lewis, J. A. (1985). Single-parent groups. In A. E. Fortune (Ed.), *Task-centered practice with families and groups.* New York: Springer.

Mandel, H. P. (1981). *Short-term psychotherapy and brief treatment techniques: An annotated bibliography, 1920–1980.* New York: Plenum.

Mays, D. T., & Franks, C. M. (1985). Negative outcome: What to do about it. In D. T. Mays & C. M. Franks (Eds.), *Negative outcome in psychotherapy and what to do about it.* New York: Springer.

Meyer, C. H. (1983). Selecting appropriate practice models. In A. Rosenblatt & D. Waldfogel (Eds.), *Handbook of clinical social work.* San Francisco: Jossey-Bass.

Mills, P. R., Jr. (1985). Conjoint treatment within the task centered model. In A. E. Fortune (Ed.), *Task-centered practice with families and groups.* New York: Springer

Mullen, E. J. (1983). Personal practice models. In A. Rosenblatt & D. Waldfogel (Eds.), *Handbook of clinical social work.* San Francisco:Jossey-Bass.

Mullen, E. J. (1985). Methodological dilemmas in social work research. *Social Work Research and Abstracts, 21*(4), 12–20.

Newcome, K. (1985). Task-centered group work with the chronically mentally ill in day treatment. In A. E. Fortune (Ed.), *Task-centered practice with families and groups* (pp. 78–91). New York: Springer.

Newman, F. L., & Howard, K. T. (1986). Therapeutic effort, treatment outcome, and national health policy. *American Psychologist, 41*(2), 181–187.

Norcross, J. C. (Ed.). (1986). Handbook of eclectic psychotherapy. New York: Bruner/ Mazel.

O'Connor, R. (1983). A study of client reactions to brief treatment (Doctoral dissertation, University of Chicago).

Parloff, M. B., & Dies, R. T. (1977). Group psychotherapy outcome research, 1966–1975. *International Journal of Group Psychotherapy, 27*(July), 281–319.

Patterson, C. H. (1986). *Theories of counseling and psychotherapy.* New York: Harper and Row.

Perlman, H. H. (1957). *Social casework: A problem-solving process.* Chicago: University of Chicago Press.

Pincus, A., & Minahan, A. (1973). *Social work practice: Model and method.* Itasca, IL: F. E. Peacock.

Pope, B. (1979). *The mental health interview: Research and application.* New York: Pergamon.

Reid, W. J. (1975). A test of the task-centered approach. *Social Work, 20*(1), 3–9.

Reid, W. J. (1978). *The task-centered system.* New York: Columbia University Press.

Reid, W. J. (1981). Family treatment within a task-centered framework. In E. R. Tolson & W. J. Reid (Eds.), *Models of family treatment* (pp. 306–331). New York: Columbia University Press.

Reid, W. J. (1985). *Family problem solving.* New York: Columbia University Press.

Reid, W. J., & Epstein, L. (1972). *Task-centered casework.* New York: Columbia University Press.

Reid, W. J., Epstein, L., Brown, L. B., Tolson, E., & Rooney, R. H. (1980). Task-centered school social work. *Social Work in Education 2*(1), 7–24.

Reid, W. J., & Hanrahan, P. (1982). Recent evaluations of social work: Grounds for optimism. *Social Work, 27*(no. 4), 328–340.

Roberts, R., & Nee, R. (Eds.). (1970). *Theories of social casework.* Chicago: University of Chicago Press.

Roberts, R. W., & Northern, H. (1976). *Theories of social work with groups.* New York: Columbia University Press.

Rooney, R. H. (1977). Adolescent groups in public schools. In W. J. Reid & L. Epstein (Eds.), *Task-centered practice* (pp. 168–182). New York: Columbia University Press.

Rooney, R. H. (1978). Separation through foster care: Toward a problem-oriented practice model based on task-centered casework (Doctoral dissertation, University of Chicago).

Rooney, R. H. (1981). A task-centered reunification model for foster care. In A. N. Maluccio & P. A. Sinanoglu (Eds.), *The challenge of partnership: Working with parents of children in foster care* (pp. 135–150). New York: Child Welfare League of America.

Rosen, A., Proctor, E. K., & Livne, S. (1985). Planning and direct practice. *Social Service Review 59*(2), 161–177.

Rothery, M. A. (1980). Contracts and contracting. *Clinical Social Work Journal, 8*(no. 3), 179–187.

Rubin, A. (1985). Practice effectiveness: More grounds for optimism. *Social Work, 30*(November), 469–476.

Rzepnicki, T. L. (1981). Task-centered intervention in foster care services (Doctoral dissertation, University of Chicago).

Rzepnicki, T. L. (1985). Task-centered intervention in foster care services: Working with families who have children in placement. In A. E. Fortune (Ed.), *Task-centered practice with families and groups* (pp. 172–184). New York: Springer.

Salmon, W. (1977). A service program in a state public welfare agency. In W. J. Reid, & L. Epstein (Eds.), *Task-centered practice* (pp. 113–122). New York: Columbia University Press.

Siporin, M. (1975). *Introduction to social work practice.* New York: Macmillan.

Smith, M. L., Glass, G. N., & Miller, T. T. (1980). *The benefits of psychotherapy.* Baltimore: Johns Hopkins University Press.

Stiles, W. B., Shapiro, D. A., & Elliot, R. (1986). Are all psychotherapies equivalent? *American Psychologist, 41*(2), 165–180.

Strupp, H. H. (1986). Psychotherapy: Research, practice, and public policy (How to avoid dead ends). *American Psychologist, 41*(2), 120–130.

Strupp, H. H., & Binder, J. L. (1984). *Psychotherapy in a new key.* New York: Basic Books.

Sulloway, F. J. (1979). *Freud: Biologist of the mind.* New York: Basic Books.

Taylor, C. (1977). Counseling in a service industry. In W. Reid & L. Epstein (Eds.), *Task-centered practice* (pp. 228–234). New York: Columbia University Press.

Thoits, P. (1985). Negative outcome: The influence of factors outside therapy. In D. T. Mays & C. M. Franks (Eds.), *Negative outcome in psychotherapy and what to do about it* (pp. 267–273). New York: Springer.

Thomas, E. J. (1984). *Designing interventions for the helping professions.* Beverly Hills: Sage.

Tolson, E. R. (1977). Alleviating marital communication problems. In W. Reid, & L. Epstein (Eds.), *Task-centered practice* (pp. 100–112). New York: Columbia University Press.

Tolson, E. R. (in press). *A meta-model for clinical practice.* New York: Columbia University Press.

Toseland, R. W., Coppola, M. (1985). A task-centered approach to group work with older persons. In A. E. Fortune (Ed.), *Task-centered practice with families and groups* (pp. 101–114). New York: Springer.

U.S. Bureau of the Census. (1987). Statistical Abstract of the United States, 1987. (107th edition). Washington, DC: United States Government Printing Office, 1986.

United States General Accounting Office. (1973). Report to the Congress. *Social services: Do they help welfare recipients achieve self-support or reduce dependency?* Washington, DC: The Office.

Videka-Sherman, L. (1985). *Harriet M. Bartlett practice effectiveness project, report to NASW Board of Directors, July 10, 1985.* Unpublished report.

Videka-Sherman, L. (1986). A meta-analysis of research on social work practice in mental health, I: Outpatient mental health settings. Personal communication to author.

Walsh, F. (1982). Conceptualizations of normal family functioning. In F. Walsh (Ed.), *Normal family processes* (pp. 3–42). New York: The Guilford Press.

Weissman, A. (1977). In the steel industry. In W. J. Reid & L. Epstein (Eds.), *Task-centered practice* (pp. 235–241). New York: Columbia University Press.

Wexler, P. (1977). A case from a medical setting. In W. J. Reid, & L. Epstein (Eds.), *Task-centered practice* (pp. 50–57). New York: Columbia University Press.

Whan, M. W. (1986). On the nature of practice. *British Journal of Social Work, 16*(2), 243–250.

Wise, F. (1977). Conjoint marital treatment. In W. J. Reid, & L. Epstein (Eds.), *Task-centered practice* (pp. 78–88). New York: Columbia University Press.

Wodarski, J. S., Marcy, S., & Malcolm, F. (1982). Using research to evaluate the effectiveness of task-centered casework. *Journal of Applied Social Sciences, 7*(Spring), 70–82.

Wood, K. M. (1978). Casework effectiveness: A new look at the research evidence. *Social Work, 23*(6), 437–458.

Yalom, I. D. (1985). *The theory and practice of group psychotherapy* (2nd ed.). New York: Basic Books.

CHAPTER
4

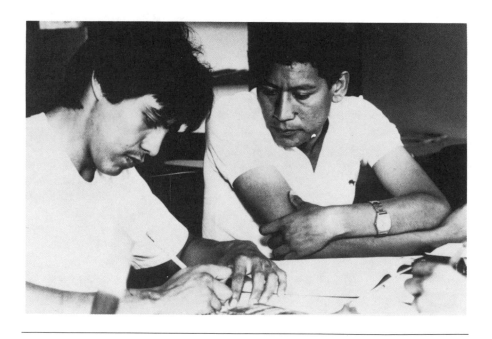

STARTING UP

Receiving Referrals and Applications

Start-up	Client referred by an agency source	Client applies, independently and voluntarily
Chapter 4	**Find out** • Source's goals **Negotiate** • Source's specific goals • Source's resources to achieve goals	Not needed

FIGURE 4–1 Map detail

_____ WHAT IS A REFERRAL? _____

A referral is the sending or dispatching a client from one agency to another in search of or to obtain resources, concrete resources, counseling, therapy, or any other type of welfare or social service. In complex, multidepartmental and multidiscipline staffs, one department may make referrals to another department within the same agency. Issues arising in interdepartmental referrals and in interagency referrals are similar. In the following discussion, the parties to a referral will be called "agencies," but it should be understood that the parties may in fact be departments within agencies.

Arranging to transfer a case from one agency to another or to collaborate on a case with another agency may be done by letter, phone call, or conference. In other words, practitioners may link clients to the other agency by making an appointment for him, identifying the person the client needs to see, discovering any special requirements of the receiving agency, and doing whatever else is indicated to make the referral "stick." If possible, the referral should make a bond between the person and the resource (Pincus & Minahan, 1973). The practitioner can enhance the effectiveness of the referral by following up with the agency and the client to check on progress and problems and intervening when necessary to make the linkage work.

The client can sometimes be _steered_, or sent to another agency without prior arrangement. This usually, but not necessarily, has less certain results. Steering may be appropriate if an agency has rules against accepting cases without the clients' having shown an initiative in seeking the referral and the ability to act on his own. Steering may be used to save time or to pass the buck.

A referral is also an exchange. One agency exchanges the client with another. Though clients may obtain resources through referrals, they may also receive the runaround. When agencies accept, reject, or lose referrals, their supply of resources is affected. Their funds, staff, time, and position in the social welfare system are diminished or augmented, depending on whether resources are used, used well, used up, or wasted (Kirk and Greenley, 1974).

The fates of clients referred to an agency varies. Weissman estimated (1979) that about one third of those referred will not follow through and contact the agency. They will give up, change their minds, forget the matter, or get help from informal channels or alternative services that do not report into official statistical data banks. Two-thirds of those referred will make contact with the agency, but about a third of those will subsequently drop out.

In any year it is likely that hundreds of thousands of persons pass in and out of the referral mechanisms. No one knows exactly the frequency and scope of referrals or why about half fail to receive service. Attrition has been attributed to various causes including the practitioner's lack of skill and lack of total resources in a community.

Organizational processes, however, affect the rate of acceptance of clients. A client can be an asset or a liability to an agency. Clients are assets if they commit their time and effort and pay a fee or if the agency is reimbursed by the referring agency or receives grants from funding agencies to support the services. Clients are a liability if they consume staff time, occupy room in a scarce facility, fail to change in the desired ways, expand the caseload to an extent that lowers staff morale, or affect the agency's public reputation in a negative manner.

An agency's organizational objective to accept clients who for the most part are assets cannot usually be fully attained. Human service agencies may be obliged by law or custom to accept referrals from authoritative agencies such as the courts or police. Thus, clients and agencies may be involuntary participants in intervention programs imposed on them by third parties.

Agencies develop traffic patterns to stabilize and regularize the flow of clients within certain networks of the welfare system. These networks evolve over time as a result of habit, preferences, legal mandates, and reimbursement or purchase of care arrangements (for example, contracts may provide that one agency pays another to perform certain services for a client who is shared between them).

Barriers to the flow of referrals are created by budget allocations among agencies. For instance, problems defined as "mental health" tend to be referred to a department of mental health; those defined as "child abuse" tend to go to a department of child welfare; "financial support" problems go to a department of public aid, and so forth. Referrals may be blocked if agencies differ about how to define the case: Is it a child abuse case for child welfare service, or a mental health case for the department of mental health? Such disputes are not only time consuming but are also the reason why some cases fall through the cracks.

_____ **WHY REFERRALS ARE MADE** _____

Referrals, or exchanges, are made for many practical reasons.

☐ An agency may be short of staff and may attempt to refer a client elsewhere to cut down on internal pressure and still get the client to some needed service.
☐ An agency's staff may lack necessary skills and believe the client will be more appropriately served elsewhere.
☐ Clients or their problems may be outside the normal and usual mission or function of the agency.
☐ Another agency is presumed to have some quality or quantity of service that would make a better fit with the client's application.
☐ Another agency is believed to be vested with responsibility for certain classes of clients and problems.

For example, when Lester (see Chapter 1) was referred for vocational training, his practitioner attempted to exchange his case. The practitioner lacked time and expertise in vocational assessment and knowledge of the labor market. The initiating agency had no job training program, but another agency was funded to develop and provide those resources. The first referral did not stick; the other agency did not seem to be able to get the client to commit himself to following its procedures and fitting into its pattern of service. The referring practitioner had to stretch himself to do the work.

Divisions of Labor

In every community a formal division of labor and responsibility among agencies exists. Figure 4–2 demonstrates this formal division of labor in a general way. Fields of service are often highly stable. A particular agency or a sector of a field may have a tradition of providing certain services. It may be sanctioned by law and custom to monopolize a particular service, or it may be funded to provide a particular service. Supplementing or substituting for earned income, for example, is exclusively the domain of public welfare agencies. Other agencies give very little cash to clients except small amounts, amounting to petty cash, for the most extreme emergencies.

However, some subdivisions of fields of service are less stable or highly unstable. Ever-changing funding patterns, trends of public attention, and innovations in practice create flux. It is difficult to keep up with new and defunct agencies and new programs. In this fluctuating domain, traditional agency boundaries meet, cross over, solidify, and liquify again.

Agencies initiating a referral are often uncertain how that referral will be received. For this reason agencies that make many referrals often work out interagency agreements to guide the staff decisions made case by case. Agencies receiving referrals are ordinarily not prepared to give a quick response, especially

Private sector ◄──► Public sector

Interconnection

Grants
Subsidies
Purchase of care contracts
Argreements and understandings

Fields of service
Child Welfare
Corrections
Physical health
Mental health
Community development
Family services
Income supplements
Institutions
Job training and placement
Schools
Others

FIGURE 4–2 Fields of service

if there is no definite detailed agreement about what they will accept and under what conditions. The referral has to be evaluated by the receiving agency, that is, judged in terms of the current position of the agency. The way the problem is defined often influences how a referral will be made or received.

Problem Definition and Referrals

Behind a referral lies an implicit or explicit problem definition and specification. As discussed in Chapter 2, the problem definition explains the problematic issues at hand by describing the problem briefly and succinctly, formulating its scope and limits, specifying it by sharply pinpointing the focus, and naming the problem to improve communication about it. The problem specification is the concrete individualized problem definition that individually characterizes the problem, such as "The couple fights six hours in the evening almost every night about what bills to pay, what purchases to make, and who will control the money."

Problem definition and specification practices vary according to the prevailing style of an agency. Practices also vary according to the particular practitioner's or agency's style and beliefs. Whether the process of defining is explicit or implicit, soundly based or vague, a referral agency will have made its problem definition. Its referral assumes that the receiving agency can or should alleviate the problem it has identified.

NEGOTIATING REFERRALS

Negotiations are carefully planned and conducted discussions that aim at determining who will do or give what to whom and in return for what. If a referring agency is going to purchase the service for a client, there is little difference between negotiating to use the service and negotiating to purchase an airline ticket. Ordinarily, however, agencies conducting negotiations must also deal with issues of function, prestige, and rank; in other words, human service agencies, being customarily nonprofit, find many intangible rewards by being recognized for doing good jobs in worthwhile work, being well-regarded in the professional community, and commanding a high position as a result of public approval.

Negotiating Inter- and Intra-agency Understanding

When negotiations are being conducted with a referral source or an agency is being requested to accept a client, a plain, straightforward approach controls the potential for producing anxiety. Straightforward negotiations increase the confidence of the referral source and the receiving agency in each other because expectations are practical and realistic.

Practitioners need to follow up on a good initial negotiation, however, with reports to the referral source and collaborate with that source as new conditions emerge. The expected payoff from ongoing contact between agency representatives is worth the time even when it means letting some other things go (Rooney, 1978).

Problems in negotiating inevitably arise, and some are not easily solvable. Many times the agency making the referral, seems to require the receiving agency to make massive changes in the client's life-style, culture, basic personality, or intellect. A reasonable explanation of practical limitations often reduces this kind of demand, but it is not unknown for a referring agency to set up unreasonable or impossible goals. A practitioner may need to bear this conflict stoically, but it is better to have upper-level agency administrators work out a compromise with which all parties can live.

In follow-up conferences (by phone or letter, or perhaps in person), the practitioner may need to negotiate one additional area: the client's own target problem, the center of intervention. A referral source may have a long list of problems, and the client a short list. The referral source may emphasize a focus for intervention that contradicts the client's focus. The receiving agency has to deal with this disagreement by negotiating a compromise. The referring agency will very likely respond to the practical value of such a compromise, especially in order to create the conditions for the best outcome.

Negotiating Conflicts with Other Agencies and Departments

It would be ideal if the social agencies in a community all had reliable knowledge about what is best and what works best, but as discussed in chapter 3, they do not. Furthermore, the individual histories of agencies, along with their aspirations, community relationships, and the caliber of their staffs, make for different viewpoints and interagency conflict. Nevertheless, since service components are distributed unevenly among agencies, coordination is necessary in order for clients to receive needed packages of service.

The typical interagency discord that requires negotiating occurs when

☐ A case is referred with a specific service request (often really a recommendation),
☐ The client's target problem is not consistent with what the referring agency wants, and
☐ The receiving agency disagrees with the referral source, or at least is not ready to agree or disagree definitely.

For example, a teacher refers a child who is underachieving, fearful, passive, and has a good deal of conflict with parents and siblings. The child's target problem is singular: only poor grades in math and social studies. The parents' target problem is singular: poor grades in math and social studies. If the grades do not improve, they want to transfer the child to another school. The negotiating strategy called for here is to persuade the referral source that the child's and family's position is reasonable and that the clients are probably capable of good achievement on problems of high importance to them (learning math and social studies, in this case). Reasonably regular reports to the referral source normally alleviate this kind of dissonance. If this process is repeated several times with the same referral source, and if they see some satisfactory results, conflict tends to disappear or be cut to a low level.

Negotiating Strategies

In general a negotiating strategy can be conducted along a continuum from:

1. Explanation to referral source;
2. Explanation, plus mutually agreed participation of referral source on its services and actions;
3. Explanation, plus solid position statement; and
4. Explanation and solid position, plus plan for available backup and alternatives.

Specific strategies recommended here have been adapted from Fisher and Ury's study of negotiation processes (1981).

☐ *Don't bargain over position.* Instead, discuss problem-solving alternatives on a principled basis. For example, the *wrong* thing to say is "I'm calling to get temporary shelter for a couple of weeks." The *right* thing to say is "I'm calling about a child who needs shelter. I'd like to discuss how your agency might help."

☐ *Confront the problem, not the person.* For example, a good response to a refusal might be: "Your program is full? Hm . . . I really think your service would be best for this particular child. I wonder what might be worked out?" Put yourself in the other practitioner's shoes; don't blame her for your problem.

Discuss each other's perceptions, and have the other practitioner participate in the process. Help the other practitioner save face. Allow her to let off steam and don't react to emotional outbursts. Listen actively and acknowledge what is being said. Speak clearly and to the point.

☐ *Keep the focus on the interests of both agencies and talk about those interests.* Do not stray from the particular purpose of the discussion, except for personal pleasantries.

☐ *Introduce options for mutual gain.* Present many tentative ideas; one may catch on.

☐ *Frame each issue as a joint search for objective criteria.* Always converse from an assumption that the other practitioner is a collaborator of good will, not an adversary.

☐ *If the other practitioner has more muscle than you do, stand on principle.* Bring all your knowledge to bear on the subject. Take your time; don't be rushed. Use your wits.

☐ *If the other person turns you down cold, avoid a confrontation.* Start reconsidering terms.

☐ *If you feel you have been deceived and pressured, don't be a victim.* Be polite and make your principles clear.

Task-Centered Approach to Negotiating

In the task-centered model it is necessary for the receiving agency to pin down the problem defined and identified by the referral agency and the goals it seeks in order to collaborate with a client on the client's target problem. The client, the referring agency, and the receiving agency have to negotiate any incongruence among their target problem identifications and goals. They must also negotiate—and, if possible, contract—the resources possessed by the referral source that can or should be supplied to the client. These resources can be tangible (goods and services) or intangible (attitudes and skills).

Some problem identifications passed on to a receiving agency from a referral source are nonnegotiable. These are mandated problems. The receiving agency dealing with involuntary clients (that is, clients required to apply or appear) secures these referrals usually by a letter or a written order from a court. Sometimes such referrals are made on the phone or result from a case conference.

The crucial first step is finding out the referring agency's reason for the referral, that is, its particular reason, not only its general reason.

Negotiating Goals in Referrals

Implicit assumptions about the goals are attached to every referral. But if the goals are only implicit and are not concrete and particular, they are often excessively ambiguous. Ambiguous goals hinder systematic intervention procedures and create dissonance between the agencies and the client that can impede the making or receiving of referrals. In the task-centered model, goals should be negotiated at the referral point so they can be stated as explicitly as possible.

CASE 4–1

Ron

A public child guidance clinic received a referral from a teacher and the school social worker in a conference. The teacher said that Ron, 11 years old and overweight, was well behaved and compliant. His problem was wanting other children to praise him for being good and making himself obnoxious by soiling his pants in school. The social worker said that Ron was clinging and "bizarre." She believed the mother was the chief problem and thought the mother should be helped to focus on her own problems and learn how to allow Ron to be independent.

Analyzing this referral, one can make a chart as follows:

TABLE 4–1 Ron: problems identified by source and goals

Source	Identified Problem	Goal
Teacher	Ron wants praise for good behavior.	Not stated
	Ron soils himself.	Not stated
Social worker	Ron is clinging.	Not stated
	Ron is bizarre.	Not stated
	His mother has personal problems.	Not stated
	His mother keeps Ron dependent.	Not stated

In this case, the absence of specific goals stated by the referral sources, necessitates an analysis of the possible implicit goals. Without pinning down, or specifying, the concrete goals of the referral source, a practitioner could get the idea that the goals were to deliver Ron in two to three months as an independent, nice 11-year-old who would be self-confident, modest, neat, and clean and whose placid, comfortable mother would take joy from having an independent son. Undoubtedly the referral sources are not so foolish, but without specific understanding of the objectives and an evaluation of their feasibility, who is to know?

Once goals have been put in feasible terms, a referral source should be able to provide the results of their observations and other information to describe Ron's praise seeking, soiling, clinging, bizarreness; his mother's problems and what she does to keep him dependent; any medical cause of his soiling problem; medical care; and assessment of Ron's capabilities.

The troublesome gaps between assumed goals and actual feasible goals are depicted in the following table. It states what may have been the assumed goals in Ron's case and what kinds of questions still have to be answered before the goals can become explicit.

Ron's case illustrates the unnecessary technical complexity caused by failure to clarify the referral source's goals. Ambiguous assumptions about what was wanted opened the door to unrealistic and fictive goals.

TABLE 4–2 Ron: analysis of assumptions about goals

Assumed goal	Analysis and questions
Reduce Ron's praise seeking.	How much reduction does the teacher want? In what explicit praise-seeking actions? What exactly are the praise-seeking actions that are considered obnoxious? Since most of us enjoy and seek praise, why should such an ordinary characteristic be eliminated? What would be the result? Might the teacher be misstating what is obnoxious? Does she mean that Ron lacks appropriate self-esteem? What specific behaviors does the teacher want changed?
Stop his soiling.	First, are there any medical problems? Exactly what are his toilet habits? Is there a history of previously competent toilet behavior? Any evidence of upset or trauma that interfered with competent behavior?

Reduce his clinging.	We all cling. What is special about Ron's clinging? What would be the desirable change?
Stop Ron's bizarre behavior.	In what way is Ron "bizarre," meaning odd, extravagant, eccentric? When and how often? What would absence of this quality look like?
Reduce his mother's problems.	All mothers have problems. What particular problems does the social worker think Ron's mother has? What does mother's problems have to do with Ron?
Stop his mother from keeping Ron dependent.	What does she do and how does she do it? What would the desired independence look like?

CASE 4–2

Myra

Some interagency discord is very complex. More actors or highly charged ambitions are involved.

A prestigious, private psychiatric institution for residential treatment of children referred Myra, a teenaged girl, for placement. It named a long-term residential treatment institution as its preferred placement. The referring institution's policy was to provide care for no longer than three months, a period of time needed, in their opinion, to do a diagnostic work-up and also in keeping with the time-limit in many hospitalization insurance policies.

The following analysis shows the situation of each of the actors.

Myra's Target Problems

1. Mother antagonistic to her
2. Cannot live with mother
3. Will not agree to further institutional placement

Her Mother's Target Problems

1. Afraid of her daughter
2. Distress about her own personal circumstances (nature of distress obscure)
3. Heavy indebtedness (reason obscure, since income from employment average for working-class woman)

The Referral Agency's Objective

It wants to place this girl in a long-term institution of its choice on the grounds that psychotherapy is needed for a borderline psychotic condition

Response of the Receiving Agency

1. Would consider Myra if referred by public agency on purchase of care contract, but had no immediate vacancy
2. Not sure if it had the resources to provide treatment

Public Child Welfare Agency (the agency with central responsibility—Myra's legal guardian)

1. The policy is to place in institutions as a last resort
2. The agency is not convinced that the girl is psychotic
3. This diagnosis was not confirmed by a public mental health consultant
4. The agency knows that a maternal aunt is interested in the girl's living in her home with the aim of eventual return to the mother
5. The agency is willing to consider foster home placement

Negotiating Strategy

The public agency has a firm opinion. Therefore, it must be prepared to take a solid position against institutionalization and for placement with the aunt or foster home care. It must offer counseling services to the girl to help her learn to cope with her distress about being rejected by her mother. It must be prepared with a backup plan for institutional psychotherapy in case the diagnosis of the referral agency proves accurate.

Myra's case illustrates the extreme complexity of deciding on goals when there are many actors in the referral. The greater the number of actors, the greater the likelihood for conflict among agencies in setting agreed-on goals. In Ron's case there were only two referral sources, working in tandem: the teacher and the school social worker. In Myra's case there were three powerful agencies, one of which was the child's legal guardian; each of the other agencies had at least a service worker, a supervisor, and a consultant. All together at least nine actors in the referral process. The large number of participants and their power created a pronounced conflict over the objectives for the case and the intervention strategy. The presence of that many actors tends to overpower the client's own personal focus unless care is taken to preserve the client's rights.

CASE 4–3

Sally Roscoe

The case of Sally Roscoe illustrates another type of referral issue, the difference in focus between agencies about who is the identified client.

Eight-year-old Sally was referred to a multiservice community agency by a school teacher who thought Sally was underachieving in her school work. Sally seemed agitated and was not clean. Following normal procedure, a practitioner interviewed Sally briefly. She explained the reason for the referral. The child acknowledged doing poorly in school and was willing to work on improving her grades. She did not speak of any other problems. She gave permission for the practitioner to talk with her mother, a necessary step required by the school.

The practitioner made an appointment to visit the mother at home. On the first home visit the practitioner found a timid young mother. Mrs. Roscoe was tense and worried, troubled about her child's school problem. She knew no details of the school problem and had not conferred with the school. She thought it likely that Sally was not doing her homework but had done nothing to schedule homework time for Sally. The mother showed concern but no interest in taking any action. If the practitioner wanted to get Sally some extra help at school, that was all right.

Because of the mother's weak response to her daughter's school problem, the practitioner asked Mrs. Roscoe if there was something she wanted help with. That question caused a flood of problems to emerge. The father, Mr. Roscoe, had failed to pay the rent for three months. After several weeks of threats, the landlord had now obtained a court order permitting the authorities to evict the family. There was no money to rent another apartment. Mr. Roscoe was not looking for another apartment. He became enraged when Mrs. Roscoe said she would look. In addition to Sally, Mrs. Roscoe had a 3-month-old infant to care for. Mr. Roscoe was bringing in food, but no rent money and no moving money. Desperately and strongly, Mrs. Roscoe asked for help with her target problem—eviction.

Exploration of how this problem came about brought out the story. Mr. Roscoe was a painter whose work was seasonal and erratic. Sometimes he made good money and sometimes he made nothing. Before the infant was born, Mrs. Roscoe worked on an electrical parts assembly job. Her steady income took up the slack when her husband was not employed. She was no longer able to work because of the young child's care. She could not afford a baby-sitter. Her relatives were in another state; her husband's relatives were not friendly. There was just no one to care for the child. Mr. Roscoe did not want her to work anyhow.

Mr. Roscoe was at home while this discussion was taking place. Asked to join, he refused although he was obviously listening at the doorway. Lowering her voice to keep him from hearing, his wife explained that he was sick and so was she. He had no company group medical insurance. Her insurance lapsed when she quit her job. They could not afford medical care.

To Mrs. Roscoe's relief, the practitioner contracted with her on the target problem of eviction. The goal was to prevent the eviction, if possible, or to help her find, rent, and move into another apartment. The other target problems—the parents' ill health and Sally's school situation—were put into a pending status, to be activated or not, depending on the outcome of the eviction problem.

Discussion

Sally Roscoe did indeed have a serious school problem and had shown a low but definite interest in working on that problem. The referral source expected action to reverse Sally's underachievement. Tutoring her had a reasonable chance to improve Sally's grades.

However, here was a mother who could not participate in the reduction of Sally's problem because of a real and imminent threat to her and her family's survival. Mrs. Roscoe could work on solving her problem and would have to let Sally's problem go.

It has been said, "When the house is burning down, do not stop to wash the curtains." Figuratively the Roscoes' house was burning down. The referral source, the school, had no difficulty in agreeing to a delay in taking up Sally's problems so that time could be spent with the mother on safeguarding the home.

Frequently a referral deals with a peripheral problem. Interviewing the identified client and the other significant persons, the practitioner often comes upon a problem condition that is closer to the client's interests than the problem identified and defined by the referral source.

In the Roscoe case, Sally's school problem was attended to in a second contract, much later, after the housing crisis was solved; after public assistance was obtained, including medical care for the parents; after Mr. Roscoe joined in the effort; and after the family settled in a new apartment. There were fourteen interviews in all over four months. To have worked with Sally on her schoolwork while her family life was a shambles would have been ineffective. To have ignored Mrs. Roscoe's plight would have been cruel.

APPLICATIONS

Applications are distinguished from referrals because in applications there is no obvious intermediary. The applicant comes to an agency on his own. In a referral, his coming has been prearranged, recommended, strongly recommended, or imposed by an authority with warnings or penalties in case of noncompliance. Most practitioners and many agencies prefer the voluntary client to the involuntary one because there is an inherent dissonance in conducting treatment under duress. (This is why the attempt is so often made to transform the involuntary client into a voluntary client). However, even when there has not been any official or authoritative intermediary, applicants learn about various treatments through relatives and friends, the media, courses they take, suggestions made by employers, teachers, ministers, physicians, and other respected sources. Often, what people know about treatment is inaccurate, and their expectations may be unrealistic. The publicity given to treatment can be misleading and create false expectations. For all these reasons, the voluntary client is also likely to have reservations, reluctance, and resistance more commonly associated with involuntary clients but present also in varying degrees with the voluntary applicant.

Task-Centered Approach to Applications

The task-centered approach to applications emphasizes finding out what the problems are as defined by the client, what the client's priorities are, and making a rapid, early assessment. This process logically determines whether or not the client fits the eligibility rules of the agency, whether the receiving agency is the one that can serve him, or whether another agency should be suggested instead.

Normally, the answer to whether or not the agency can bring effective resources to bear on a problem is a straightforward "yes" or "no." Sometimes, however, the answer is not obvious and the decision is "maybe." In such instances the practitioner should clearly explain to the client what is uncertain and make a contract to explore possibilities. These processes are the subject of Chapter 5.

———————————— SUMMARY ————————————

A referral is sending or dispatching a client from one agency to another or from one department to another in search of and to obtain resources: concrete resources, counseling, therapy, or any other type of welfare or social service. Referrals may be made because of staff shortages, or lack of skill in an agency for dealing with a particular problem or type of client. The request may be outside the agency's function; another agency may have some quality or quantity of service that would better fit the client's situation; or another agency may have undertaken responsibility for the class of clients and problems involved in the case. Behind a referral there is an implicit or explicit problem definition and specification.

There is considerable chance that disagreements and ambiguities will arise when making and receiving referrals. To work efficiently and to preserve the client's active participation, it is advisable to conduct planned negotiations with referral sources. These negotiating discussions should mediate conflict and promote understanding about what the client is seeking and can do, what resources can be provided, and what goals are feasible and realistic.

The essential actions in responding to a referral are to find out as neatly, specifically, and concretely as possible what the source's goals are; to negotiate with the source directly to reach an agreement on feasible goals and on what resources, if any, the source will provide to get these goals in place; to make explicit to the source what resources the receiving agency can apply; and to negotiate the strongest possible support for reducing the client's target problem.

When a referral is received, the receiving agency or staff member may feel obliged to do that which the referrer is asking. What the referring agency or staff wants represents its best judgment at the moment. Referring agencies are obviously within their rights to ask for service in whatever way they deem best, particularly if they have an appropriate rationale. Given that differences of opinion are likely to exist about how a referral should be handled, the receiving agency can surreptitiously pursue its own opinion and wait for a conflict of interests to emerge. Or the receiving agency can impose the referral agency's opinion and wait for an impasse to take place with the client. The best action is to explain, interpret, and reach agreement with the referring agency.

The position of the task-centered approach is that being able to work unimpeded on the client's target problem is the necessary condition to using the guidelines properly, and to conducting the case in the best possible way to obtain good results. The first aim, therefore, is to negotiate with the referral source to achieve understanding and agreement on the target problem. The second aim is to conduct planned negotiations with referral sources to obtain the resources that are expected to support problem solving, also in the interests of obtaining good results.

============================ **REFERENCES** ============================

Fisher, R. & Ury, W. (1981). *Getting to yes: Negotiating agreement without giving in.* Boston: Houghton Mifflin.

Kirk S. A., & Greenley, J. R. (1974). Denying or delivering services? *Social Work, 19*(4), 439–447.

Pincus, A., & Minahan, A. (1973). *Social work practice—Model and method.* Itasca, IL: F. E. Peacock.

Weissman, A. (1979). Linkages and referrals (Doctoral dissertation, University of Maryland at Baltimore).

CHAPTER
5

FIRST STEP

Target Problem Identification

Deciding on Problem Focus
Problems defined by clients
Dealing with our own assumptions
General Orientation to the Elements of a Problem
The needs orientation
The personal deficiencies orientation
The lack of social skills orientation
Classification of Problems
Task-centered problem typology
Mandated Problems and Services with Involuntary Clients
Facilitating Client Target Problem Identification
The problems arrayed
Target problem preeminence
Clients who cannot state their target problems
Suggesting and recommending target problems
The problem search process
Dilemmas of the problem search
Crisis problems
The Role and Responsibility of the Practitioner in Deciding on Target Problems
The Essence of Targeting Problems
Principles
Basic actions
Determining priorities
Rapid Early Assessment
Assessment defined
Focus and assessment
Rapid early assessment described
Relationship Management
Suggested practitioner behavior for creating good relationship conditions
Summary
How to specify target problems: summarized

This chapter will describe how to identify a target problem, how to define the problem through the processes of describing, specifying, and naming it, and finally, how to decide on a problem focus. Frequent practice issues of targeting a problem will be discussed and guidelines for dealing with them will be suggested. Among the practice issues of most concern are deciding on problem focus; handling mandated problems; facilitating client's participation in target problem identification; both expanding and also drawing boundaries around problems; preventing trivializing problems; handling long-standing and deep problems, problems that appear to be constantly changing, and crises; establishing priorities; conducting a rapid early assessment; and managing the relationship.

_____ **DECIDING ON PROBLEM FOCUS** _____

Problems Defined by Clients

Analyzing a problem situation in order to pick out a focus is a crucial step in task-centered work. Given the amount of uncertainty and inexactness in the social sciences about defining *problems* as a concept, it is little wonder that there is confusion about how to pin down or operationalize this concept in professional practice (see Chapter 2).

Dealing with Our Own Assumptions

In approaching the process of determining the problem as defined by clients, we tend to start with traditional assumptions.

The assumption of universal criteria. It is often assumed that there are universally known and accepted criteria for defining problems. In fact, as we have seen, a problem to one person may be no problem to another. The

Step 1	Client target problems identified
Chapter 5	**Find out** • Problems defined by client • Client priorities (hold to three) • Referral source priorities (mandated problems) • Preliminary rapid early assessment

FIGURE 5–1 Map detail

definition depends upon what each is interested in, and upon how aware the person is of her own interests. How problems are stated and what priority is given to them rests upon changeable methods, theories, values, and societal norms and expectations.

To guard against undue influence on the client, the practitioner should always keep in mind what tendencies and inclinations dispose us to adopt a particular mode of problem definition and simultaneously attend to the exact and precise form the client gives to the problem definition. In that way a problem definition may be worked out mutually and openly with the client to legitimate the client's perception and to give the practitioner an appropriate opportunity to influence how the client makes this choice.

The assumption of total coverage.   Another assumption is that a problem defined should turn into a problem solved. Human services, almost universally recognized as problem-solving enterprises, often behave as if they are obliged to act upon whatever appears dysfunctional. That thrust often fails to consider the likelihood that some things may be better left alone, that no intervention or minimal intervention, in some instances, may be better than maximal interventions. More is not necessarily better. Another way of putting this is that a problem identified is not necessarily a problem to be worked on now.

It is not feasible to provide total coverage of the whole array of problems in someone's life. The techniques of professional helping are indeed of modest power and availability. To deal with this assumption that total coverage is the way to go, it is necessary to discriminate among problems on the basis of what problems need priority attention to make an important difference in the present situation.

Assumptions about self-actualization.   Some practitioners believe that helping clients to become self-actualized, to grow, to potentiate themselves, to be involved "in new and possibly more productive ways of reasoning about his or her problem" . . . [is] "the most vital aspect of the helping experience" (Goldstein, 1986, p. 355). These expressions refer to influencing personal beliefs, attitudes, feelings, and capabilities and creating in the client good feeling, personal satisfaction, and control over her circumstances.

Self-actualization is an attractive viewpoint. Many people are making reasonable or better salaries. They have leisure to contemplate art, architecture, and decoration of themselves and their homes. They have time and money to have fun, travel, and study. Self-actualization seems a reasonable preoccupation in the context of today's highly ambitious consumer society and contrasts with the frustrations of real limits on achievement, high prices, strangling red tape, and the dangers of fire, theft, mugging, catastrophic illness, old age, desertion, terror, nuclear accidents, and waste of people.

It is commonly acknowledged that frightening social forces in modern society are turning people's attention inward. But believers in self-actualization are also problem solvers. They may prefer the language of feelings (that is emotions, sentiment, attitudes, and other subjective states), but they help their clients alleviate crises, overcome depressions, get public aid, medical care, better housing, jobs, child care. They help clients repair the thousand mean, destructive slings and arrows of outrageous fortune that real people face, the so-called "problems in living."

In dealing with our own preferences for self-actualization goals, it is advisable to refrain from imposing on clients problem definitions restricted only to the emotional and cognitive realm. Clients, as do all of us, usually prefer to deal in the realm of tangible practicalities as well as in the realm of feelings. Reducing tangible problems or increasing tangible resources goes far in improving a problem situation.

Assumptions about client reluctance-resistance as pathology. An inherent tension exists between problems as defined by clients and as defined by helping practitioners. Professional definitions are the product of specialized training and occupational socialization. Client definitions are the product of ordinary living and commonsense experience. Experts tend to define the client's problems in terms that fit their expert's views. Clients tend to define problems in terms that make sense to them, preserve their competence and dignity, and are consistent with their knowledge of the world.

These two viewpoints—the practitioner's and the client's—come out of different worlds of personal experience, culture, and class. They are the same to the extent that the life experiences of client and practitioner have been similar. Differences *may* be caused by resistance; pathological processes of thought and personality *may* be at work to maintain the status quo and avoid the change needed for progress. On the other hand, the differences may be mostly due to the client's strong interests in her own aspirations, reluctance to undertake what the practitioner wants, lack of understanding and know-how, fear, or differences in cultural, moral, ethical, or normative views.

A practitioner using the task-centered model should be in touch with the problem as it is perceived and defined by the client, understanding it as much as possible in the client's terms, and sensing how it is relevant for the client. The client is thus responsible for describing and explaining the situation, for participating in how the problems are defined, and for being a real partner in what the solution is to be.

Assumptions about history as destiny. All accounts of one's own life (autobiography) or of another's life (biography) are arranged selections chosen at the time of telling, in the present. These narratives explain and make sense of what happened. When clients tell us of their lives, and when we practitioners inquire about their history, we are following deeply embedded and old traditions that a story or narrative has to have a beginning, middle, and end (Whan, 1979).

Erikson

Many theories explain present problems in terms of the past. On the whole, these theories, or the uses to which they are put, are reductionist in their effect. Too often simplistic and linear reasoning results in conclusions about the causal effects of previous experience, particularly of hypothesized phases, stages, or patterns that supposedly predetermine a person's life.

Systematic studies have questioned the extent to which the course of life can be understood as an ordered and predictable developmental sequence. A person may make sense of her life by continually reconstructing her view of it, that is by telling her story in changing ways while we hear and interpret it according to our own views at a given time. Cohler (1982) suggests that life seems to be characterized by often abrupt transformations determined both by expected and eruptive life events and by intrinsic, but not necessarily continuous, developmental factors. Shifts from early to middle childhood, the transformation to middle age and then old age are particularly conducive to disruption and subsequent revision of the personal narrative. Lives are much less ordered and predictable than some deterministic hypotheses suggest, and changing social context has much influence on what happens to us and how we interpret ourselves.

To avoid undue attribution of the causes of present problems to hypothesized past events or an interpretation of those events, the task-centered approach recommends that practitioners accumulate and use past history cautiously. The history of a problem can be explored for practical clues as to what the problem means currently, but the practitioner's primary effort should be in understanding the problem in its contemporary setting and form.

GENERAL ORIENTATION TO
THE ELEMENTS OF A PROBLEM

To get a problem into focus we need a general orientation. We need to perceive the problem in relation to the persons involved, the environment in which the problem is occurring, and the knowledge available to describe and explain the problem. Four perspectives (needs, personal deficiencies, lack of social skills, and classification or boundaries) used by practitioners and clients alike represent ways to become acquainted with and arrange the terrain of the problem.

These perspectives are not mutually exclusive, but adopting one or another as a major approach to a problem tends to shape what problem will be emphasized and what will be the content of the intervention.

The Needs Orientation

The needs viewpoint makes the basic assumption that a person's needs are the results of deficits in social and personal resources. The client is perceived to need certain material goods, skills, personal attitudes, relationships, or services. For example, consider these statements:

☐ *"Mrs. A needs daycare."* This means Mrs. A does not have the resources to care for and teach her children during the day, does not know where to get daycare, and probably does not have funds to purchase daycare.

☐ *"Mr. B needs a psychiatric evaluation."* This means Mr. B is thought to lack normative interpersonal skills and the knowledge, will, and funds to procure an expert opinion from a mental health professional.

☐ *"John needs treatment."* This means John is thought to lack normative interpersonal skills and lacks the knowledge, will, and funds to procure advice and guidance from a mental health professional. This statement assumes that treatment can improve his interpersonal skills and well-being.

A needs viewpoint may be the result of reliable information about a client's concrete deficits. Examples of presumably reliable information that show the existence of needs deficits are intelligence test results; measurement of degree and type of malnutrition; economic status above or below a poverty line; number and quality of rooms in an apartment; sufficiency of a welfare grant; stability of the home environment; health; and so forth. Perceived needs may also be consensually held beliefs about what it is good for people to have, for example, loving and caring parents and spouses, personal self-sufficiency, fulfilling work, the ability to give love and to care, flexible attitudes and responses to other people, and so forth.

Needs can be converted to social welfare service categories such as daycare, protection, health service, family planning, foster care, and so forth. Needs are an indirect way of stating a problem. Although subject to inaccuracy, they also have a commonsense basis.

A needs viewpoint is both a moral and rational accompaniment to understanding the social context of a client's target problem. Identifying perceived needs helps a practitioner be specific about the particular resources and social skills in which the client and her situation are deficient and about the presence of disordered emotional states, mental illness, ill health, employment and vocational problems, and other complex personal troubles. However, the needs viewpoint must be tailored to match a client's particular target problem; otherwise, it may do harm to aggressively fulfill some "need" that is not real to that client. For example, a practitioner or agency may impose professional or personal standards about what the client should have or should do and disregard the client's individual appraisal of what she should have or do. Imposing actions on a client can cause harm by introducing pressures that cannot be handled under all the circumstances. The case of Mr. and Mrs. Chris illustrates how a needs viewpoint shapes the problem definition.

CASE 5–1

The Case of Mr. and Mrs. Chris

Mr. and Mrs. Chris, both in their eighties, were brought by the police to the emergency room of a local hospital. They were weak and incoherent, and their bodies and clothes covered with coal dust.

Their weakness was diagnosed as malnutrition. The coal dust was accounted for by their living in a basement amidst the furnace and coal bins. A social worker attached to psychiatry was called in, but Mr. and Mrs. Chris were so incoherent that he could not find out what the situation was and what had happened to them. The couple were hospitalized, bathed, and fed.

The next day Mr. and Mrs. Chris were coherent. It was learned that the malnutrition was the result of their trying to live on the husband's meager social security. They did not know they were eligible for a supplementary public assistance grant. A neighbor who used to give them food had recently moved away, and so they were more hungry than they used to be. They had lived in the basement for fifteen years, rent free, because they watched the coal. The landlord was—he thought and they thought—befriending them. The couple had no children. They were very attached to one another. They were old and their lives were restricted.

The social worker perceived their problem as "needs protective housing because of age." He offered to locate and help them be admitted to a nursing home. The couple blew up. They eagerly accepted intervention to get them a supplement to their social security and help them apply for public aid. But they would only return to their accustomed living quarters—the coal bin! No place else.

The question of whether this couple did or did not need housing has no single or simple answer. More than an obvious need for better housing was involved and had to be taken into account.

The Personal Deficiencies Orientation

Deviant behavior is objective in the sense that it can be observed and verified if adequate criteria for identification exist. It is subjective in the sense that judgments about what constitutes deviance are often based on unverifiable inferences and a variety of moral judgments. Deviant behavior has conflicting definitions in the sociological literature as well as in the popular literature and the media.

It is conventional to think that a client's or a family's specific problem consists of the deviant behavior of individuals, and that the deviance is revealed by the part of their conduct that departs from consensual norms (Chapter 2;

Thio, 1978). It is more difficult to understand how particular social and economic conditions interact with specific personal situations to extrude problems.

The personal deficiency framework is useful in the task-centered approach but should be combined with an assessment of the social context. The practitioner needs to evaluate personal deficiencies to see if and how altering the environment, providing resources, making some changes in how significant people relate to one another, or increasing the client's store of social skills through education, advice, and guidance can ameliorate the focal problem.

If the practitioner manages only to isolate certain personal deficiencies and place them in the central focus, he may ignore real difficulties in the physical and social environment. He may overlook the extreme difficulty of altering some personal deficiencies without also—or instead—altering crucial environmental conditions. He may overlook the opportunity of making relatively simple and direct change in the socio-physical environment which might improve the situation promptly and efficiently. (For a related view, expressed differently, see Greif and Lynch, 1983.)

The Lack of Social Skills Orientation

Ordinarily the social skills needed for carrying out a reasonable life-style include

- ☐ Providing child care (minimum basic parenting skills)
- ☐ Maintaining reasonable personal hygiene
- ☐ Maintaining a home
- ☐ Learning subject matter from school or special training courses
- ☐ Perceiving relatively accurately the intentions and expectations of other people, especially parents, close friends, siblings, spouses, authorities, and peers
- ☐ Communicating understandably to other people, especially parents, close friends, siblings, spouses, authorities, and peers
- ☐ Earning a living, especially finding and doing a job, getting along with fellow workers and employers, and getting the rewards of work
- ☐ Planning problem-solving steps
- ☐ Taking problem-solving actions

Identifying deficits in social skills is another way of organizing thought about needs and personal deficiencies. There are, however, potentially important differences among these three ways of formulating a viewpoint about problem definition. The *logic of the needs* is to provide what is missing as directly as possible, for example, a clean home, a father figure, a mutually satisfying marital relationship, psychotherapy, medical treatment, and so forth. The *logic of the personal deficiency approach* is to provide therapy that is intended to develop a mature (or more mature) person. The *logic of the lack of social skills approach* is to educate, teach, and train a person how to do necessary things.

Because of the different tilt of each of these viewpoints, it is possible that each one could lead to a unique way of identifying the problem and designing the treatment. In actual practice, however, all these viewpoints tend to merge; in fact, it is possible to argue convincingly that all of these orientations to problems are different facets of the same thing or that the nature of problems is so complex and changeable that they (problems) appear in different guises at different times.

——————— THE CLASSIFICATION OF PROBLEMS ———————

A broad classification of problems affixes a name or label to social problems that are collective, aggregated troubles judged to be afflictions of sizable groups of individuals. Examples are delinquency, crime, illegitimacy, academic under-achievement, unemployment, female-headed families, child abuse, child neglect. Of course, labeling has a role in organizing information about different conditions in social life, but broad labels are useless as guides to understanding individuals or particular social situations. They give no information usable in planning interventions on a case basis. A more useful problem typology is one that can capture features of problem conditions and behaviors illuminating the individual problem of concern at the moment. The task-centered model has this kind of a problem typology.

Task-Centered Problem Typology

The task-centered model suggests a rough typology useful for putting systematic boundaries around target problems (Reid, 1978). It helps to visualize the classification as a fence that contains the content of the assessment, the interviews, the treatment plan, and the implementation. The task-centered approach classifies problems in

1. *Interpersonal conflict.* Overt conflict (such as marital conflict, parent-child conflict) between two or more persons who agree that the problem exists.
2. *Dissatisfaction in social relations.* Deficiencies or excesses that the client perceives as problems in interactions with others, such as dissatisfaction in a marriage, with a child or parent, or with peers.
3. *Problems with formal organizations.* Problems occurring between the client and an organization, such as a school, a court, or a welfare department.
4. *Difficulties in role performance.* Problems in carrying out a particular social role such as that of spouse, parent, student, employee, or patient.
5. *Decision problems.* Problems of uncertainty, such as what to do in a particular situation.
6. *Reactive emotional distress.* Conditions in which the client's major concern is with feelings, such as anxiety and depression, rather than with the situation that may have given rise to them.

7. *Inadequate resources.* Lack of tangible resources such as money, housing, food, transportation, child care, or job.
8. *Other.* Any problem not classifiable.

MANDATED PROBLEMS AND SERVICES _____ WITH INVOLUNTARY CLIENTS _____

In innumerable instances a problem is mandated by an authority. The consequences of ignoring that mandate may result in severe losses to the clients' interests and well-being. Agencies cannot ignore mandated problems, for instance, those ordered by courts or required by law, without jeopardizing their public sanctions and funding. Therefore, the agency is obliged to insist that certain mandated problems be part of the work. Normally, mandated problems are agreed to by clients on the basis that the client's own target problems are accepted by the practitioner. Few clients are so foolish as to completely flout authority by refusing any kind of participation. Clients may not state a mandated problem in the same way as an agency, or they may take a different or opposite view from the agency, but they will nevertheless be expected to select the same area for attention.

FACILITATING CLIENT TARGET _____ PROBLEM IDENTIFICATION _____

The Problems Arrayed

The practitioner's first activity in the first step of the task-centered model is eliciting the client's views on the problems in the present situation as she sees them now. This array of problems will undergo change and be organized and reorganized as the first step proceeds. But the problem array is the building block of all that comes later to shape the problem definition and problem-solving work. It is common to put this list of problems in writing and to use the written document, which may be pencilled notes, as a guide to grouping problems. Once grouped, these problems become a basis for discussion that ends up with a description and eventually a name that symbolizes the centerpiece of the work.

Target Problem Preeminence

The task-centered approach puts the client's expression of the target problem in the central position. This position is practical because it mobilizes as much power as possible from the client's own individual particular motivation. Concentrating on the client's target problems is the most direct route to taping the reservoir of problem-solving effort in the client. It eliminates endless struggles to influence the client to want and do things she does not care about. At the same time, it concentrates the client's effort to tackle important problems she wants to work on.

This single-minded concentration on the client's target problems is consistent with the observation that intervention is usually more effective when client and practitioner agree on problem focus. To minimize drop-out and increase the probability of good results, the practitioner needs to put and keep the focus of intervention on a problem that both he and the client define in the same or a similar way.

The task-centered approach concentrates primarily on those problems explicitly acknowledged and stated by the client, spontaneously or as a result of client-practitioner discussion. The target problem emphasis is a way to get a general orientation to a problem that may include needs, deficiencies, or lack of social skill.

Clients Who Cannot State Their Target Problems

Sometimes clients are unable or seem unable to come forth with target problems. Such clients tend to be extremely fearful or confused. Extreme fears are the result of experience. A client may have learned that it is too risky to reveal herself to a representative of an agency. Her relatives or friends may have told her of negative consequences brought about by too frank statements to persons in authority, or the client may have experienced negative consequences first hand. Some clients have learned to transfer fears of teachers, police, physicians, or other officials to all or most helping persons. Clients may have suffered punishments or reprisals from unsympathetic relatives and peers. It is difficult, perhaps impossible, to risk exposure with a strange practitioner when a client's experience suggests caution.

Internal fears are probably also learned from experience, but they seem to have become a permanent part of an individual's character. Some people are afraid and suspicious even when the evidence is that no harm will come to them in reality. They have become so habituated to being suspicious that almost no amount of checking out will convince them to come out of their protective shells.

Some fearful people can take the risk of stating a target problem with a reasonable amount of encouragement, but they require a steadfast and trustworthy practitioner with patience and persistence. It ought to be expected that these clients will remain tentative in their trust which is as it should be in view of the known realities that caused their distrust in the first place.

Confused persons

Some people may also evince an inability to clearly identify their target problems; they may blur their thoughts, mix their ideas in illogical ways, and make important mistakes in the way they think. They may lack experience in sizing up situations. Young children may misperceive an offer of help because of limited experience in deciphering the intentions behind the offer. Some people, adults and children, may be handicapped because of low intelligence or disordered thought processes.

Experience with the task-centered model used with elementary school children reveals that, with rare exceptions, children of school age can develop clear and cogent target problems (Epstein, 1977). Many mentally handicapped and ill persons make relevant statements of their problems (Brown, 1977; Newcome, 1985). Although it is not to be expected that all confused people can be straightened out, it is important not to assume serious pathology in situations that may be only passing, superficial, or temporary.

Suggesting and Recommending Target Problems

The practitioner working with fearful or confused persons can make suggestions, recommendations, and/or institute a problem search and work toward alleviating fear and confusion to the extent the circumstances permit. These remedies go together and will often be carried out together or inter-woven.

The practitioner will normally form an assessment impression and as a result may have some tentative ideas about possible and relevant focuses. These can be put before the client for consideration as suggestions, or more strongly, as recommendations. In either case, the practitioner should state and explain the suggested or recommended target problem as fully as necessary in order to be clear and provide ample opportunity for the client to question, react, and consider.

The Problem Search Process

The problem search is a one- or two-interview special phase designed specifically to assist the practitioner in helping a client establish a target problem in circumstances where there is little if any spontaneity. Problem search can be initiated in the start-up phase or in Step 2 and is used with clients of two types: those who are referred by an authoritative agency but acknowledge no problem; and those who apply to an agency for a specific service but who seem to need broader or different service. The agency, or the practitioner, would like the client to expand the request. The agency possesses other services, believes them to be more appropriate, and the practitioner wants to interest (engage) the client. The problem search, or an adaptation, may be useful in other circumstances also. A practitioner may use this process at any time when there is an impasse about establishing practical and relevant problems for work.

The essential ingredient of the problem search is that the client is informed exactly what the subject of the interview is: namely to come up with a notion of her problem from her viewpoint. The practitioner then leads a discussion to explain what the contact is for, what it is about, how it will be done, what the client can expect from participation, why he stands to benefit, and what the alternatives are. To the extent the client will cooperate, she should be afforded ample opportunity to examine all these questions and give whatever responses she will.

A client who gets involved in this process can be expected to develop for herself and for the practitioner background and contextual information that helps get hold of an understanding of her predicament. If this effort is not successful or sufficiently successful to start intervention, the case can be terminated. On the other hand, it is often neither wise nor practical to terminate. It may be necessary to monitor the situation, to confer with the referral sources and the client's close relatives to help them affect the problem. It may also be possible, and often is, for the practitioner to reach agreement with the client upon some problem of seemingly secondary or peripheral importance that may or may not lead to more significant contact. When there is a mandate, however, that is, when a client is obliged to participate, it is necessary to invoke the practitioner's authority and make insistent demands.

Rationale for the problem search

The rationale for the problem search is that it provides a structured, purposeful opportunity for the practitioner to concentrate on assisting a client with the process of developing her own ideas about what problems should be attended to and what she is willing and motivated to attend to. Many clients find this a novel opportunity. It can have much importance because it clearly is respectful. It provides a chance for the client to dig into issues and decide matters that are often decided for her.

Problem search in mandated cases

Practitioners are faced with an obligation and a responsibility when problems are mandated, despite a client's lack of acknowledgment of problems. Typical circumstances that suggest a problem search when the client has no self-formulated problem include a child referred for misconduct or underachievement in school, a mother referred for correction of child management practices as a condition of having her children returned from foster care, and parents referred for correction of child abuse.

A practitioner has two options under these and similar circumstances. First, the practitioner can insist on attending to the mandated problem. The legitimacy of such insistence is the authority vested in the practitioner. Second, the client can be offered an extra two-session problem search. If the client does not come up with a personally perceived target problem in two interviews, further attempts will probably not be useful. The first option then becomes the operating procedure, that is, the practitioner will have to set the agenda authoritatively.

Under normal conditions clients authoritatively referred because of serious, incapacitating, threatening problems do state problems of their own accord, related logically to the mandate. If nothing else, the pressure placed on them by authorities is aversive. They want to be rid of an implied or overt threat, such as not graduating, going to jail, or having children placed in foster care.

Sometimes the problem comes down to "getting that agency, teacher, judge, doctor off my back." It is often sufficient to deal with a mandated problem in terms of what the client has to do to reduce the pressure of authorities.

Dilemmas of the Problem Search

The problem search is a way to try to draw out specific client target problems under an adverse condition, one in which the client is either a nonparticipant or a reluctant participant. The client has not revealed what she is concerned about or will not share her concerns with the agency. It can be argued with conviction that a practitioner ought to refrain from intruding into aspects of the client's life that the client has closed off. In fact, the value position of the task-centered model supports a nonintrusive posture. However, when an agency has the legal responsibility for investigating wrongdoing, as in the case of child abuse, it is obligated to intrude into family matters to the limit permitted and required by law and administrative regulations.

Problem search procedures have been devised from practical experience. They are plausible procedures if an agency has the responsibility to try to influence and convince a client to use services maximally or in the way the agency thinks best and if the agency has the resources for providing more services.

The problem search is a way to deal with clients who appear to need time to accustom themselves to the idea that intervention may take time and may require their commitment in a way they had not previously contemplated. The problem search is an adaptation of outreach, common in many sections of practice, which is based on assuming responsibility to extend maximum services, with the hope that those services can support problem solving and contribute to a client's well-being. However, there has never been any firm evaluation that supports the success of outreach (Mullen et al., 1972; Fischer, 1976).

Many clients will view the problem search and its implication of outreach as intrusion and be reluctant to participate. Although its effectiveness is unproven, outreach will be done because in many instances it is a moral and ethical practice to extend services, even in the face of client reluctance that may be self-defeating. It is advisable that the intrusiveness be limited, constrained to problems clearly and explicitly stated by practitioners, and offered in a climate respecting the client's right to refuse.

Dealing with fear and confusion

If it appears that the client is not able to focus because of fears, the practitioner should try to learn just what she is afraid of. Common fears have to do with the client's believing she will not be believed or respected, believing the meaning of the situation will be distorted, or thinking she will be jeopardized in some way. Provided that the situation is not really unfair, exploitative, or manipulative, the client has little to fear in actuality; it is often possible to convince her by means of careful and painstaking discussion. Above all, a fearful client can learn the truth about these fears by observing the actual behavior of the practitioner and the agency.

The client whose fears have become internalized may not be accessible to a logical discussion although the practitioner should attempt to discuss unfounded fears. It may not be possible to accomplish much by way of fear reduction, in such instances; but it may be possible for the practitioner to avoid behavior that will trigger a client's deep fears.

The confused state of some clients may be temporary and due to crisis emotions, stress, illness, or shock. In such instances just waiting a bit probably will abate the confusion. On the other hand, the confusion may be the result of some permanent or almost permanent state of mind and health. If the client is severely handicapped, the problem-solving work has to be limited to those areas where the client is functioning, and the work must be supplemented by involving family and the available social network. In other words, the task-centered approach and all other treatment approaches require, as a basic condition, a functioning social person with verbal capacity. If the major client lacks those abilities, the practitioner must work with the persons responsible for the client.

Dealing with laconic, taciturn clients
From time to time practitioners encounter laconic clients who use a minimum of words and are concise to the point of seeming rude or mysterious. Persons who present themselves in this way are often taciturn, that is temperamentally disinclined to talk. On the whole, this is an inconsequential personality trait. Nontalkative people do what they think is important with an economy of expression that contrasts with the conventional emphasis in our society on communication and talking things out. Sometimes, however, the laconic client is deeply afraid and protects herself by underinvolvement. There is no unique technique known to dissolve either the character trait or the fear.

If it is fear that is stopping the client from communicating, it will take some convincing experience to convey to her that it is safe and possibly helpful to communicate. If the client is unskilled in communication, it may be desirable to confirm this lack of skill and, with the client's agreement, provide her with relevant skill training.

Resolving an impasse in stating a target problem
What we call an impasse is the deadlock that occurs when there is strong, important disagreement between practitioner and client on what the target problem is and should be. Unresolved, this situation produces the prototypical incongruence between client and practitioner associated with poor outcomes.

The client's persistent and enduring disinterest and refusal to accede to professional opinion calls up the explanation of client resistance, a condition often not subject to much, if any, change. The client may not be able to deal with the recognition of the problem. The practitioner may be overly invested in certain stereotyped explanations of problems because of preference and adherence to a given occupational viewpoint.

When such a deadlock arises, it is advisable to be flexible and to accept the client's way of thinking about the problems, at least tentatively, in order to see where that leads. In other words, this deadlock situation is the acid test of the practice of the task-centered approach. It should not be assumed that confused or unskillful people do not know their trouble and cannot state it. Most clients know, or can develop in a discussion, what their problem is.

Skillful, flexible practice with the task-centered approach often results in a serious effort to accomplish what it is the client wants and what it is she will give a lot of effort to. Often this effort pays off with good results. The attempt to pursue the client's aims may produce failure as predicted by the practitioner, but if it does, the client has the actual experience of finding out what the difficulty is for herself. Now the client is in a better position to deal with the practitioner's suggestions and recommendations, either at this time, or in the future.

Voluntary clients nearly always produce reasonable, relevant target problem statements. An impasse often arises when a practitioner is reluctant to deal in the client's terms. The most common difference is that the client believes the problem lies in the environment or the attitudes and behaviors of other persons and that she is only tangentially responsible. The client often tends to target the problem in a narrow area and in a relatively specific manner.

On the other hand, the practitioner may be inclined, by preference, experience, and training, to assume that the problem is broad, that the client is the important actor causing and maintaining the problem, and that the client is the one who must do the changing. Furthermore, unless the case is being handled as a family matter, with important others participating, the practitioner usually has no leverage with which to affect the behavior of someone who is not part of the treatment transaction.

Practitioners worry about what to do if a client should propose a target problem that is unrealistic, trivial, or involves illegal or immoral activities. It is obvious that the practitioner should not participate in anything that is trivial, unethical, immoral, or illegal. However, it is exceedingly rare for such situations to occur. What may happen is that the client proposes work on problems that in the practitioner's judgment are wrong or bad target problems. It is usually possible to discuss changes and influence the client's view so she can accept a formulation considered reasonable by the practitioner.

Expanding the scope of the target problem
A practitioner may believe that the mandated problem or the problem selected by the client is embedded in a host of other problems. Many human behavior theories assert the existence of underlying problems that require attention in order to make effective changes. A practitioner has a right and an obligation to explain this or any other professional reasoning to a client. The obligation is

especially pertinent if resources exist and are accessible for reducing other suspected problems. To persuade the client to open up other problem areas, the practitioner can propose the problem search.

In the absence of a mandated problem, the practitioner's professional judgment may still suggest that the client ought to consider other problems and that resources exist for their solution. The practitioner may believe there should be an attempt to broaden the problem scope from a specific concrete problem identified by the client to other areas. For example,

☐ A discharged mental patient, receiving posthospitalization follow-up, finds that the boarding house landlord is failing to provide services for which payment has been made.
☐ A mother, trying to live up to child and home management standards required by the court, is in jeopardy because the public aid department has inexplicably cut off her grant for homemaker service.
☐ A married couple, both employed, are threatened with loss of income due to garnishment of wages, or wage assignments, from bill collectors.

Most human service practitioners would feel obligated to suggest exploration beyond the concrete remedies implied in the target problems. For the examples just discussed, the practitioner might attempt to have some authority put pressure on the landlord to provide the service, put pressure on the public aid department to resume homemaker service, and get legal counsel to stop the bill collectors from harassing the couple. It is often correctly assumed that problems such as these are embedded in a web of circumstances that ought to be dealt with and probably can be dealt with successfully.

To proceed with a problem search to broaden the client's target problem, the following steps could be taken:

1. *Provide an explanation of the rationale for a broader examination of the problem.*
   For example, "I suggest that you and I discuss whether this boardinghouse is the right place for you to be living. I can probably help you find and move into a better place to live and also help you deal with your landlord so you won't have to worry about him all the time. It seems to me that the whole atmosphere of this house is upsetting and that you ought to have a more pleasing home base from which to rebuild your life out of the hospital."
2. *Inquire about how the client perceives the relevance of an extension of exploration to these other areas.*
   For example, "What would you think about discussing your housing and its effect on you? It seems to me that there are quite a lot of problems you might be having there. No? Why would you prefer not to discuss this with me?"
3. *Recommend a problem search and plan on two interviews for that purpose.*
   For example, "Since you think that maybe you could benefit from more discussions, let's set up one or two interviews to see if we can hit on the

problems it would pay you to work on." Or, "I strongly urge that you come to see me once or twice more before you decide against doing nothing about the hospital's child abuse report. The police and the department of child welfare may find that your child is in danger and may place your child in foster care. I could help you."

4. *Suggest no more than three problems. The client should be fully informed why these three are chosen.*
   For example, "I suggest we review your medication to see if it is giving you trouble. You might be lethargic due to your medication and that could give your landlord ideas about taking advantage of you."

5. *Follow the regular procedures for exploring and specifying the target problem with a problem search.*

The difference between this approach to problem targeting and the normal task-centered approach is that the focus is initiated and largely determined by the practitioner who must be highly active and talkative, ask questions, reflect verbally on responses, and make explorations and suggestions. The research on task-centered intervention suggests that the results of practitioner-initiated target problems are not likely to be as satisfactory as those defined by the client. To promote the likelihood of a good outcome, the practitioner should provide the client with ample opportunity to consider the relevance of his suggestions, to become interested in them, and to formulate a rationale for not acting on them. The client can be expected to spin off on her own into a problem formulation more befitting her situation. If this does not happen, then the practitioner's obligation is fulfilled and the problem search is ended.

Drawing boundaries around problems

In the task-centered model problems must be limited by boundaries to minimize loose, diffuse, and rambling work. Boundaries permit specifying the locus of the problem, its substance or content, and its scope and range. In other words, boundaries help set the focus so that the client and practitioner can concentrate effort on specified sectors of a problem situation. Depicting a clearly bounded problem area starts the process of structuring, or systematic planning, essential to efficiency and good outcomes (see Chapter 3).

Boundaries are readily devised if the target problems are assigned to the best fit within the task-centered target problem typology discussed earlier in this chapter. Using a specific classification focuses only on those problems that can logically be subsumed under the classification. Classifying the target problems according to the typology provides a relatively simple way to separate those problems to be addressed from those to be put aside. However, many practitioners find that referring to the typology is not a comfortable process for them. Since the problem types are not discrete and tend to overlap, it requires a decision to classify the problem. Many practitioners lack confidence in drawing boundaries in a live case and would prefer to depend on practice wisdom to judge what is in and out of the boundary. This is a weakness of the typology, but it is still a useful tool in putting necessary constraints on a process that easily gets overly expanded. Problem boundaries can be set by a practical commonsense process of grouping together those immediately related to the target problem.

Excessive number of problems

The task-centered model is capable of embracing two or three problems within its normal eight session sequence. (Time limits and duration techniques will be discussed in Chapter 6.)

The need to limit the numbers of problems comes up if the client perceives complex and interwoven problems covering a wide scope and lists a long array of problems of various types. Sometimes referring agencies may also infer or observe a long array of problems. It is the practitioner's immediate task to help the client select the two or three significant problems on which to concentrate her energies.

Cases where the sheer number of perceived and defined problems are large have been labeled in various ways over the past two decades: problem families, multiproblem families, hard-to-reach, crisis-ridden, difficult, urban girls, single mothers, child abusers, chronically mentally ill, substance abusers, and, lately, underclass. These labels are not well-defined and researched entities. Rather, they are temporary and convenient code words that generally have a short life in both the professional literature and the media. Problem definitions that encompass the breadth of deficits and disadvantages suggested by these terms are not useful.

. The guide to constructing target problems in overloaded circumstances is to adhere to the preeminence of the target problem as perceived and selected by the client, modified to the minimum judged necessary by the practitioner, and in mandated, involuntary cases, adhering to the essentials of the mandated problem in the form in which it is negotiated so as to be feasible.

Other problems, beyond the two or three that can be accommodated in the six- to eight-session time frame, need to be put aside. They may be taken up at a later time if doing so proves necessary or possible. It is naive to imagine that we could take up and resolve every stated problem, or that clients, supervisors, and the public actually expect us to do that. In real life, problem solving seems to be accomplished through the creation of improved conditions that have some spillover effect. Reducing some problems puts others in a new light, making it possible to reduce those with less effort, or making it possible to live with them.

Trivializing problems

In the interests of formulating problem definitions in a specific and bounded way, it is possible to become mechanical. This process is observed when problems are broken down into minuscule pieces, each piece being dignified as a central focus. This results in problems being taken up that are of little worth or importance, trifling, too simple, and in the end meaningless.

Changing target problems constantly
It is common in practicing with the task-centered model to see some clients, from interview to interview, for the whole sequence, changing the form of the target problem, adding on, subtracting, and expressing uncertainty about whether the focus is right. In fact, this phenomenon is so common that it should be expected. It does not necessarily mean that the practitioner has erred in conducting the process of problem definition, although that possibility exists and should be checked; it does not necessarily mean that the client is fickle, impulsive, or erratic although that may be and should also be considered.

Usually what these constant changes mean is that problems in general are not finite entities but are perceptions, viewpoints, and tentative explanations (see Chapter 2). Normally, the "new" problem is the problem already targeted but seen in a new light because the client and the practitioner are undergoing new experiences and consequently revising their perceptions.

When such constant changes seems to be a problem the practitioner's judgment on boundaries to be observed in the treatment becomes useful. As long as the new facet or new problem can be logically included within the boundary, relatively small alterations in the problem mean a change in the rhetoric. If the problem really does take large swings, it will be necessary to reformulate the problem to get at a more stable formulation. Unless changes are real and substantial, they should be incorporated in a somewhat altered phrasing of the originally defined problem.

Long-standing and deep problems
Old problems that hang on and appear to take on new life and new forms as time goes on are what is usually meant by "deep." "Deep" may also refer to problems that are recondite, obscure, grave in nature or effect, and pervasive.

Many old problems are relieved by correcting present conditions. To the greatest extent possible, the most feasible way to deal with old problems is to rearrange the present to minimize their impact on the present. The problem of old wounds and hurts, and entrenched, habitual ways of responding may be intractable; people often learn to manage without necessarily obtaining basic change in long-standing patterns and problems.

Should wounds from the past defeat efforts to ameliorate the present, the practitioner can ascertain whether other treatments are available and if the client can use them. These treatments may be those customarily planned to take long periods of time, or they may be family-oriented or group treatments that aim for a broader scope than the task-centered model.

Crisis Problems

The term *crisis problem* is used so indiscriminately and is so dramatic that it has come to be practically indistinguishable from the term *problem*. The term *crisis* is often reserved for *a stressful problem due to an emotional upset touched off by a disruption* such as:

☐ A substantial *change in the environment* (moving, disaster, flood, fire, war)
☐ temporary or permanent *loss of physical function* (accident, sudden onset of severe illness)
☐ *maturational development points* (starting school, leaving school, starting new job, getting fired, being forcibly retired)
☐ *loss of important interpersonal supports and personal identity* (rape, battering, abuse, death, separation, abandonment)

When applying the task-centered model to crisis problems, the practitioner should confine the problem definition to the boundaries of the crisis.

In the past some theories suggested that intervening in a crisis was a good way to enter into a client's deeper problems, which are aroused by the emotions surrounding the crisis. Indeed, one often observes people who are very upset (say after a fire has destroyed their home) easily talking about old and painful problems. However, it has not been established that treatment occurring in a crisis is a real route to uncovering and pursuing deep problems. It may also be asked whether or not it is ethical to take advantage of the emotions of a very upset person to dig around in the past. An extensive literature about crisis intervention in specialized problem areas, such as rape, battering, and other forms of interpersonal violence has developed, but it is too specialized to include in this discussion and the interested reader will need to seek it out when needed (Dixon, 1987; Golan, 1978).

THE ROLE AND RESPONSIBILITY OF THE PRACTITIONER ———— IN DECIDING ON TARGET PROBLEMS ————

The role of the practitioner in arriving at the target problem as perceived by the client is to elicit fully and in detail what the client sees as the problem; to aid the client in trying to understand what that problem means to her; to form an independent professional judgment (assessment) on what an appropriate and feasible problem definition should be; and to arrive at a mutual formulation with a minimum of resistance and a maximum of cooperation.

———— THE ESSENCE OF TARGETING PROBLEMS ————

Principles

1. A practitioner is obliged to define and identify problems. The whole sense of the human service enterprise is to solve or abate problems.

2. The way to reach a practical focus is to start with and stay with the particular client's definition.
3. It is practical to state a problem definition that is congruent with the client's sense of the situation.
4. Staying with the client's definition clarifies the issue of motivation. Task-centered practice gives priority to the areas in which the client is motivated.
5. It is unlikely that a client's motivation can be readily enhanced, or that she can be maneuvered into a genuine commitment for a personal change not wanted, not sought, and not accepted.
6. Clients seek and value help that makes sense to them, is useful in their daily lives, gets or keeps them out of trouble. The whole purpose of the task-centered model's emphasis on target problems identified by clients is to take maximum advantage of the existing client motivation.
7. The client's statement of the target problem puts necessary boundaries around the exploration and intervention.
8. Assessment begins as the target problem becomes relatively definite, and is carried out more fully in Step 2 (contracting and planning), proceeding to be more developed in Step 3 (problem solving).
9. The client's target problem determines the focus.

Basic Actions

1. Specify the problem

Normally, with a little encouragement, the client states and at least partially describes the nature and location of the problems as she defines them. The client establishes the actual presence of a problem. The practitioner helps the client name and state what the problem is explicitly and in detail. The practitioner must phrase the problem in a definite and specific way so that it can be developed into a statement of what is to be changed. The phrasing of the problem is important in the same way that a label is important. It formulates the problem in a distinctive way and is an aid to focus.

There are right and wrong ways to phrase target problems. The right way gives information that leads to plans for change, that is, to specific tasks. The wrong way contains insufficient information to lead to ideas about what can be changed. A wrong formulation may not do any harm; it just blurs the process, impairing the direction and efficiency of the work. A few examples of target problem specifications clarify the differences between correct and incorrect phrasings.

> *Right:* Arthur fights too much with his foster father.
> *Wrong: Conflict in the foster home.*
>
> *Right:* Ben hits his mother every day. He broke windows in the apartment three times in a fit of rage. Mrs. C believes her son is too interested in sex.
> *Wrong: Mrs. C cannot control Ben.*

Right: Mr. and Mrs. D quarrel too much.
Wrong: Marital conflict.

Right: They leave the children alone.
Wrong: Inadequate parenting.

The "wrong" statements may be accurate, and they may be useful shorthand statements, but they are wrong as target problem statements because they convey both too much and too little information. They are abstractions. A target problem statement must be a concrete, individualized description of the condition to be changed. "Arthur fights too much with his foster father" means that a goal will probably be reduction in the frequency of these particular fights. "Conflict in the foster home" has no boundaries and no specificity. This wording can refer to matters all the way from leaving the cap off the toothpaste to a vague, general climate of unease and resentment among the family members.

2. Specify the conditions or behaviors to be changed

What is to change is implicit in the target problem. "Arthur fights too much with his foster father" implies that the change desired is reducing the frequency of those fights. To be particular and explicit about the conditions to be changed is to be sure that the problem is consistent with the goal. If practitioner and client do not specify conditions to be changed, it is easy to disconnect the problem from the goal. This disconnection can be illustrated with the case of Ben. Take the target problem "Ben hits his mother every day." This problem implies that the goal will probably be to eliminate Ben's hitting his mother. Supposing, however, we did not specify that the condition to be changed is Ben's physical aggression. We could easily transform our goal from stopping Ben's aggression to improving the mother-son interactions. Making that transformation could lose the mother's attention, open up an area too broad for Ben to handle, stretch the boundaries of the target problem too much, and possibly overtax our ability to intervene with good results. If broadening the problem is indicated and acceptable, the broader problem should be specified *in detail.*

3. Make tentative goal statements

Tentative goal statements are preliminary, *working goals,* that are needed to help make problem definitions that are practical and worthwhile (because they will lead to something attainable, desired, and significant). These tentative goals may very well be honed later. They are needed from the start, however, to frame the problem definition. The obvious reason for having a tentative and realistic goal in mind as background for developing the target problem is to prevent wishful thinking from driving the decision on the target problem.

Goal statements confirm what the end product of the sequence is supposed to be. If a goal statement is not concrete, there is no way to find out if it was attained or how much was attained. A diffuse goal statement prevents achievement or lack of achievement from being recognized.

Goals are not limited, nor are they ultimate or stretchable. Mr. and Mrs. D, who "quarrel too much" and "leave the children alone," acknowledge those problems and want to do something about them. The only logical goal for the first target problem is to cut down on the quarreling. There are two alternatives for the second problem: making safe child care arrangements when they are gone or staying home. (See Chapter 6 for more discussion of goals when pulling together the contract.)

4. Explore the target problems

Defining target problems involves discussion. Sometimes the problem seems to change as the interview or series of interviews proceeds. Although the practitioner should try to get hold of firm statements, he should explore the issue further if the target problem is uncertain or is starting to appear uncertain after being stated.

Exploration means a systematic search and examination. In the task-centered model, the exploration concentrates on scrutinizing the target problems and their social context and discerning the client characteristics that shed light on the problem. This information is of immediate use for getting a first assessment impression. The first impression pushes the process along. Later on this impression will also be honed. Increased accuracy and relevance of the assessment information may help select what interventions are going to be most effective with this client in this situation at this time. Exploration and assessment occur together. In Step 1, making the target problem identification, the purpose of exploration is to be clear and quick in settling on target problems so that intervention can start as soon as possible.

Exploring the social context   The social context consists of housing and neighborhood conditions, work and school conditions, socioeconomic status and financial constraints, health conditions and health-care provisions, family and peer relationships, and cultural and ethnic background. The social context is a primary source of information on which to base assessment of the meaning of the problem. Conditions in the social context and the client's transactions with elements in the social context will provide clues to stresses and dysfunctions that cause, contribute to, and maintain the problem. Environmental alterations may be feasible and may make a significant difference in the client's well-being.

Normally, a client provides a good deal of information about the social context spontaneously during the process of problem specification. Noting this information and expanding it with a few questions provides the practitioner with essential facts about who clients are in their particular circumstances. It is not necessary to go into obscure, hidden, and old information. The gross exploration outlines the circumstances in which the problem exists.

A gross exploration of this type is likely to identify important deficits or exploitive and oppressive conditions. The practitioner should secure enough information to show how much these conditions are responsible for the problem. His observations and inquiry should attempt to identify the source of the stresses that are precipitating and maintaining the client's problem. Attention should be held to present environmental stress. A long history of environmental stress has a cumulative effect and may give a strong coloration to the client's situation. However, some of the undesirable effects of long stress are reversible if the stress is lifted. There are various theories about the debilitating effect of stress (Golan, 1978). From the point of view of the practitioner handling a case, common sense and experience are good guides to pinpointing grave stress in the environment.

Among those conditions likely to produce excessive stress are separation from and loss of close relatives and friends, status changes, unemployment, tedious, demeaning, and poorly paid work, hostile authorities, unsanitary, ugly, and unsafe housing and working conditions, poor health, discrimination, and poverty. Some problems are closely associated with socioeconomic status, particularly the condition of the poor and those at the low end of the income scale. The social context of poverty gives a rough gauge of what opportunities exist for problem solving.

Exploring client characteristics and mode of functioning   A practitioner can acquire a great deal of the necessary information about a person by simply observing her during the interview. A practitioner can size up whether a client is timid or aggressive, suspicious or trusting, angry or calm, reasonable or unreasonable, logical or illogical, lethargic or active.

Sometimes, if a client is upset or confused, the practitioner must confer with other people who know the person. Information about intellectual and psychiatric status is sometimes important, particularly if the client is hard to understand. Information obtained from others, however, can be misleading. Judgment always has to be made about how much credence should be given to secondhand information. Having a firm grasp of a client's target problem will keep the practitioner from making unnecessary explorations and help him make a decision on the appropriateness of the views of other informants.

Exploring previous problem-solving efforts   Finding out about previous problem-solving efforts, particularly recent past efforts around the same target problem, can be enlightening. These past experiences offer analogies that can be drawn on for good ideas about actions to repeat, change, or avoid.

Determining Priorities

The types of problems handled in human service programs are characterized by lacks of resources and lacks of social skills. The resource deficit may be extreme or minor, obvious or inferred. People perceive resource deficits as serious restrictions on their freedom and well-being. Deficits in social skills may vary from being simply awkward to life threatening.

Resource deficits are both tangible and intangible. The basic tangible resources are those essential minimums that sustain and maintain body and subsistence: food, clothing, and shelter. Beyond the basic minimums are other tangible resources also considered in modern societies to be necessities: furniture, utilities, laundry equipment, pots and pans, heating and cooling equipment, telephones, medical care, and educational opportunities.

Social skills deficits are always intangible. Social skills are a developed and acquired power to perform physical and cognitive acts and to use knowledge effectively and proficiently in the performance of particular and necessary acts. Deficits in social skills vary from the inability to talk to abrasive garrulousness; from the inability to concentrate to a rigid obsessive fixation on a single idea; from the inability to learn to the inability to play; from the obsessive concentration on one's own internal state to total ignorance of one's own feelings, attitudes, and beliefs; from an absolute insensitivity to others to offensive attention to others; from the inability to be alone to complete withdrawal into one's private self.

Most social skills deficits include a lack of problem-solving skills. Persons referred to social agencies as well as those who seek help voluntarily often come with a long "laundry list" of problems. Being deluged with problems is one sure way for a person to become overwhelmed and immobilized or frantic. To restrain this tendency to immobilization ("I don't know what to do: I can't do anything.") or frenzy ("These things have to be all done at once or else!"), a person must establish realistic priorities.

The practitioner and client can establish these priorities according to several criteria, including the characteristics of the method being used to address the problem in question, mandates from authorities, and the client's viewpoints. All three of these criteria play a part in all decisions on priorities. However, which viewpoint is the most powerful determinant of priorities makes an important difference in how the priorities are structured within an intervention strategy.

Methods priorities

Methods priorities come from a style of thinking. Ideological preferences and beliefs, theoretical concepts, and values combine to explain a problem. The particular method may favor certain explanations of how problems are caused although, ordinarily, beliefs about causation are incomplete and variable. The method may favor certain interventions thought to be best.

Practitioners learn and agencies support actions called for or consistent with a method. The key action in carrying out a methods priority is that the practitioner's decision about priorities is thought to be an application of the method. There is a tendency to reify methods. Emphasizing their assumed priorities may result in distorted treatment strategies. For example, priority may be accorded a client's compliance with the method, attending sessions regularly, achieving insight, facing problems, forming a good relationship, and so on.

Mandated priorities

Mandated priorities can be set according to an authoritative directive from a powerful institution, usually the referral source. Mandated target problems, as discussed earlier, originate with a legal or social authority, whether or not the client is in agreement. Such target problems can be ranked according to the power of their source. Mandates to act in a certain manner imply that the client and agency are obliged to change a situation, sometimes in a predetermined way, by restraining, curbing, or requiring identified action: for example, being drug-free, or giving a child regular medical home care.

Sources of mandated problems can be classified into several broad categories that vary in power according to their degree of influence and jurisdiction.

Legislation   Some legislation requires that agencies or clients act according to the provisions of specific statutes. The client's problems are governed by rights and restraints set forth in the applicable statutes, for example, legal prohibitions of assault and theft.

Police and court orders   When problems of the client are public, the client may be ordered to act differently, for example, in the case of a police arrest and a court order.

Impending police and court order   When problems of the client are public or in danger of becoming public, there may be a threat of police or court order, for example, in case of a complaint of child abuse by a legally designated authority.

Professional opinion   If problems are identified because of professional opinion, for example, an opinion registered by a school official or mental health professional recommending foster care for a child, the client may feel pressure to conform but can avoid changing behavior fairly easily.

Public opinion   Problems of the client may be identified because of a complaint about the client's behavior from a person in the community: a relative, neighbor, acquaintance, newspaper reporter, or government official.

How powerful are mandates?

Only legislation and police and court orders have real power to create consequences of the highest seriousness for the client: deprivation of liberty, coercive removal of children, or coercive commitment to correctional institutions. *Threats* of police or court orders, if real, have almost the same power.

Professional and community opinion are ambiguous. Professional opinion is likely to be more powerful to other professionals than to clients who dislike or reject the opinion. Community opinion, since it may express the wishes of prestigious or significant persons on whose goodwill the agency depends, may, like professional opinion, exert much pressure on an agency. Staff may easily feel compelled to maneuver the client, if possible, into submitting to the wishes and expectations of other professionals and influential community people. Professional and public opinion is, at times, capable of acquiring such general acceptance or prestige that new laws evolve that become high-order mandates on agency clients.

Practitioners in agencies have authority, as legally sanctioned agents, to inform the client and explain exactly what consequences are to be expected if they ignore mandated problems. A list of specified actions the client will have to take to avoid negative consequences should be drawn up. The client should be helped to avoid those consequences by making the change specified.

When it comes to clients who ignore professional and public opinion, that is another matter. Clients have the right morally to make a voluntary choice about the propriety of opinions held about them by others. Professional helping people sometimes have an inclination to give out opinions with more authority than is warranted by the state of their knowledge. The ability of professional opinion to predict harmful acts is low. This is not meant to suggest that professional opinion should be ignored at will. But experts frequently disagree about psychosocial diagnosis, treatment of choice, and predicted consequences. There are degrees of expertness; in the helping disciplines it is sometimes hard to know who is and who is not really an expert. Public opinion about a client is capable of being genuinely altruistic but may also be spiteful, prejudiced, and exploitative.

It is difficult to motivate, influence, and induce unwilling clients to agree to recommendations and commands of referring professionals and community people. However, it is common that clients referred, if given the opportunity, will target a problem differently from the referral source. They may or may not include an item from the referral source's list of problems.

When the involuntarily referred client is under a low-power mandate, the practitioner should accept the client's target problem choice and begin work on it. However, if the mandated problem is identified by a source with real and legal power, capable of imposing important negative sanctions for disobedience, two parallel sets of target problems can be established: one mandated and the other identified by the client. It is likely that these two sets will be related and may merge.

Legislative mandates do not ordinarily identify, specify, or command the focus of cases directly. Legislative mandates are direct for persons charged with crimes: homicide, theft, sale of prohibited drugs, and so forth. Even for persons who are so charged, the court and welfare systems mediate and interpret the application of the law to individuals. Legislation establishes rules for conducting the affairs of society and enforces them by punishment or threat of punishment. Legislation reflects history, social conflict, and social change, but there are always ambiguities in what the law is and how it should be applied in individual instances.

Court orders are one of the ways laws are transformed from general rules to specific rules to govern the management of a particular case. Because violation of a court order can have disastrous consequences for a client, a problem identified in a court order is a high-power mandate commanding great attention and highest concentration. Police powers result in high-power mandates because they contain the possibility, sometimes the probability, that ignoring the police will result in the client's being arrested. When the police refer a case to a welfare agency, their problem identification cannot be ignored.

Administrative regulations are a source of many mandated problems. Agencies are established, sanctioned, and funded to effect types of outcome or results with certain classes of persons identified as deviants. Partly to carry out their mission as they perceive it and partly to continue to receive public sanction and funds, agencies develop complex regulations, some highly specific; for instance, a person is ineligible if her income exceeds a stated ceiling (a means test). A variant of the means test is fixing a sliding-fee scale for applicants above a stated income ceiling. Beyond the means test, agencies develop regulations about various circumstances in which they will or will not provide goods and services. Most of these regulations contain large amounts of discretionary power and are interpreted variously case by case. Usually supervisors and higher-echelon staff exercise the formal power. But in the daily routine of practice, the regular practitioner is powerful.

Mandated problems with involuntary clients or semi-voluntary clients are a major source of difficulty in practice. The prevailing intervention custom is that direct service provision (resources) and social treatment (skill training or therapy) are one inseparable package. On the one hand, the ethics of social treatment support client voluntarism. On the other hand, the expectation that agencies will exercise benign social control is always present. The dissonance between voluntarism and social control is immense. The reality of much practice makes the separation of voluntary engagement and social control often impossible: it is often *not* possible to fuse treatment and social control. Therefore, it is advisable to deal with them separately, even though both are present. This means confronting ourselves and our clients with the opportunities and requirements of both social treatment and social control and using the authority we have been given by legislation and collaboration (as with courts and police).

Since clients understand the source of authority very well, open admission of it is no surprise to them. Covert disguise of authority as treatment gets the distrust it deserves.

Problems mandated by professional opinion probably cause practitioners more distress than more powerful mandates. Professional opinion sets our internal standards for ethical and appropriate practice. However, we have no right to impose our views by using our authority over vulnerable clients who may see their world differently.

Client priorities

Client priorities can be selected from the client's statements of how the problem is perceived in particular circumstances. Client statements are prioritized by asking a leading question, namely, which three problems—if fixed—would make the most difference to you in solving your problem?

The most effective way to set priorities is to

☐ Establish the client's priorities among the target problems. The three problems most important to the client make up the priority list.

☐ Include the mandated priority (if any) as one of the three.

☐ Recommend to the client, if necessary, a preferable priority list. It is unlikely that the client will work on any but his own priorities. However, many clients are receptive to professional advice about a preferable priority list when it can be shown that another order will achieve more.

To establish client priorities, *start* with the client's list. This produces the array of problems. *Introduce* the practitioner's recommendations, if any; include any mandated problems, stating the degree of authority they carry. *Classify* the problems according to logical combinations. The task-centered problem classification assists in making such combinations. Alternative ways to classify problems are according to their similarity in behavioral or situational characteristics or according to their expected consequences. *Name, state, and review* each problem as specified. *Make an independent judgment* about which elements in a multiple-problem list are most important. Judging importance means considering which problems weigh most heavily on the client's situation, have the most negative consequences, would have the most positive consequences if corrected, interest the client most, and are most amenable to change. *Engage the client in making* a judgment about importance. *Put aside* prioritized problems that exceed the rule of three. They will be activated later if there is time and if it is necessary. The *rule of three* refers to constraining the sequence to three prioritized problems.

EXAMPLE 5–1

Specifying Client Target Problems

Ron (Chapter 4), in interviews 1 and 2 acknowledged two target problems, specified the behavior to be changed, and stated his target problem and goals as follows:

1. He is too fat. He has been fat for the past four years. His peers humiliate him because he is fat. They call him insulting names. His mother and sister are overweight. In addition to three full meals Ron eats snacks four times each day—leftovers, pie, potato chips. He would like to lose weight. He would like to be normal size. Ron's goal is to lose forty pounds.
2. He soils his pants. At home after he wakes up and before he leaves for school, Ron has one to three loose bowel movements. In the past seven days he had such bowel movements on six days, every day of the week except Sunday. After he gets to school, he has loose bowels again. He is embarrassed about leaving the room to go to the toilet so often and so he soils his pants. Ron thinks his eating so much food and so much junk causes the loose bowels and soiling. The teacher says he soils on four out of five school days. Ron says he has had this problem since he started school and that he used to soil at home before he started school. Ron's goal is to stop soiling.

Reviewing the Social Context and Past Problem-Solving Efforts
Information was obtained from the first two interviews with Ron; two separate interviews with the mother, and the teacher. Items are listed separately to emphasize their distinctions.

Social Context of the Problem
1. Ron is 12 years old.
2. He has an unkempt appearance.
3. He is worried about his problems.
4. Peers avoid him.
5. He is interested in a girl who is friendly to him but
6. He fears he will lose her.
7. He is inactive.
8. Mostly he watches TV
9. And eats.
10. He plays basketball occasionally.
11. He would like to bike,
12. But his bike is always broken.
13. He thinks of food all the time.
14. His three basic meals are heavy on fats and carbohydrates.
15. His demeanor is friendly.
16. He acts as if he would like to be close to people and less lonely.
17. His attention span is short.
18. He does not sit or stand still, jiggling around most of the time.
19. Ron lives with his mother and 9-year-old sister.
20. His parents were divorced seven years ago.
21. His father died less than a year ago.
22. Ron does not want to discuss his family.

23. He has to be pushed to give basic information.
24. He says that the family is supported by social security benefits.
25. The mother is generous with food and toys.
26. She prefers the children to stay in the house or close by.
27. The mother is overweight.
28. Ron's mother said that he was a colicky infant who did not sleep soundly.
29. He was given enemas.
30. He had surgery at 4 years for undescended testicles.
31. The surgery scared him.
32. That was when he started soiling.
33. He refused to use the potty.
34. The mother is intelligent and conscientious.
35. She pays lots of attention to Ron, but she is critical of him.
36. For the past year, the mother has been dating a man about whom she seems to be serious, and they are thinking about getting married.

Past Problem Solving

1. Medical information contains no known physical basis for Ron's incontinence. A report from the physician and a psychiatrist concluded that Ron has a moderately severe behavior problem.
2. As a result of getting medical and psychiatric reports, the mother enrolled Ron as a patient in a child guidance clinic.
3. He did not change, and so
4. He was sent to a residential treatment center.
5. After the insurance ran out, Ron was sent to a special education school, where he is at present.
6. He takes three prescribed medicines: one for diarrhea, one for hyperactivity, and one for depression.

Working Explanation

The several therapeutic agencies that Ron has attended have been in agreement about the presumed cause of his problems: a strong fear reaction to his surgery years ago, and an anxiety about his mother's serious consideration of remarriage. The present agency has a different view:

1. Whatever conditions led to Ron's undesired behavior in the past, at present Ron wants to lose weight and stop soiling.
2. These problems cause him to be seriously unhappy as he enters his teen years.
3. He knows how unattractive these problems are and he wants to become a more normally behaving teenager.
4. Overeating and soiling have become bad habits he has acquired to get some control over his inner feelings of emptiness and his desire for attention from his mother, teacher, therapists, and the like.

> **Mandates**
>
> The referral source, the teacher and the school social worker, thought Ron's problem was an obscure deep-seated conflict involving his mother in some way. The school personnel were determined that something substantial be done to relieve Ron of his problems and to relieve the school also. In the negotiating discussion with the referral sources, it was found that the teacher and social worker were willing to focus on Ron's selected target problems (being fat and soiling).
>
> The teacher was willing to schedule trips to the bathroom as an aid in forestalling soiling. There were no powerful mandates with drastic consequences. No destructive acts were being committed or needed to be controlled.

RAPID EARLY ASSESSMENT

Assessment Defined

The assessment is a professional formulation, a systematized statement. It is produced by combining the information acquired and developed from interviews, observation, supervision and consultation, thoughtful professional consideration, and other sources. It is a set of interpretations, judgments, and hypotheses that provide a working explanation of the person or persons, the problems of present concern, and the situation or social context in which the problems are found. In some practice theories, the assessment attempts to identify the etiology, origins, and development of the problem. Historicity of this type has limited use in the task-centered approach. There is, however, no bar to exploring history if there is some appropriate use for the information in the present problem-solving effort.

The assessment formulation outlines the nature and major characteristics of the problem, the persons most closely associated with it, the major circumstances, and an estimate of the problems' seriousness, that is, its intensity, frequency, and duration. It tells what is going on, where, with what consequences, with what frequency, over what period of time, and involving what people.

Practitioners form impressions and images of each client, define the client's problem, and make a judgment about its seriousness. From these impressions, images, and judgments, he makes a tentative explanation (hypothesis) regarding the nature of the problem, the people, and the situations involved. These impressions and his explanations constitute the assessment, leading to the intervention plan. He assumes the assessment will suggest what actions are needed and what actions can be expected to correct the problem.

The process of problem definition, as described in this chapter, is the basis of the assessment. As the problem definition is developed, it produces information about the problem, the client's characteristics, social context, and past problem-solving practices and suggests a working explanation of the problem. In the course of the interviews in which the problem defining process is conducted, the practitioner will have many opportunities to observe the client's behavior and personality, to receive reports about significant other people and personal relationships, and to learn about relevant socio-economic factors.

Thus the processes of problem definition in the first step of the task-centered model and the observations made in the course of the interviews together provide the information that makes up the rapid, early assessment. Defining the problem and attempting to understand the people and their social situations lead to an idea of what needs to be changed, restored, or enhanced. A practitioner can make a judgment about how much change is necessary, desirable, and feasible. Resources can be examined to judge their availability and usefulness.

Focus and Assessment

The assessment is the practitioner's way to define the problem in professional terms, in accordance with the set of theories to which he subscribes and any pertinent rules and regulations of the agency and profession. The assessment stabilizes the treatment processes to the extent that it provides a degree of certainty about what is wrong and what should be done. The assessment is a guide to the possibilities and constraints on treatment planning, which must take into consideration the limits and opportunities suggested by the assessment. Thus, the focus of the case activity comes about by extracting from the assessment what point or area is thought likely to be the most effective concentration.

Rapid Early Assessment Described

It is customary to think of assessment as a thorough and long process because of the importance attached to it as a determinant of treatment. However, in real practice conditions, assessment conclusions have to be reached rapidly. Treatment is brief by plan. Or the person is in crisis and the only humane and ethical approach is to take useful action right away or as soon as possible. Or, there is strong pressure from the community to do something at once. These conditions indicate the need for rapid assessment, at least of a tentative type. More complex and comprehensive assessments may have to be made in complex and obscure situations or when required by regulations. Comprehensive assessments take time and, if needed, may be conducted subsequently.

Keys to rapid, early assessment

1. *Provide an appropriate interviewing atmosphere.* Adopting a straight-forward, moderately assertive, friendly, cordial, and generous manner lowers the client's defensiveness and encourages confidence. This atmosphere, together with a commitment to legitimate the target problems as perceived by the client, provides the best opportunity to obtain needed information.

2. *Depend on the immediate interviewing situation for the data from which to generate significant assessment hypotheses.*

☐ Collect information constrained to the target problems and the present time.

☐ Explore selectively areas of strength and weakness in personal traits, immediate environment, culture and ethnicity, family and peer relationships, and work and school situation.

☐ Draw full value of immediately available interviewing data from observing interview behavior, relationship, and communication patterns with practitioner, and from information elicited regarding problems and social context.

3. *Exploration should be parsimonious.* Extensive explorations are conducted on the assumption that the fullest accumulation of information will be a hedge against error. The flip side of this belief is that we cannot profitably make use of excess information. Explorations should not exceed what is needed to form a commonsense understanding of the target problem and its most immediate area. Uncertainty can be checked against available professional literature, with supervisors, colleagues, and consultants.

What is the assessment data available in the immediate interviewing situation?

1. *Broad sensing of personality traits and typical behaviors under stress.* This means making gross observations, without special attention to detail. The purpose is to get hold of a working image of the other persons. These gross observations are interpreted according to personal and professional experience, practical common sense, augmented by behavior theories espoused by the practitioner.

Gross observations focus on physical appearance, bodily demeanor, facial expression, vocabulary, and manner of speaking and expressing oneself. These characteristics portray a person's self-image, something about his or her expectations, interpersonal demands, personality traits, manner of relating to others, and some idea of his or her income level. Ways of dealing with stress are shown in the way the person makes requests, whether fearful, anxious, unreasonable, overly reasonable, submissive, suspicious, manipulative, controlled, disciplined.

How the client deals with an interviewer, a person in authority, who is a man or a woman, can usually tell a good deal about the person's customary pattern of relating with men and women in authority. One can infer how it is likely the person is now dealing with similar figures in real life—such as spouse, children, employer, for instance.

2. *Observations should be put into a tentative pattern, configuration, or diagram based on behavior theory and practical experience that explains who the client is, what her background is, and what is the matter at present.* This pattern is constrained to explain only the problem situation related to the problem definition. Information the client supplies that is not related to the target problems can suggest areas about which the client is concerned and possibly confused or upset, but including of a wide range of problem areas defeats focused attention and decreases the probability of successfully intervening to accomplish some problem reduction.

3. *Impressions of a person form very quickly.* Considerable evidence from research studies suggests assessment is formulated impressionistically in the first few minutes of a contact and that the rest of the time allotted is used for checking and verifying. The final assessment is most likely to be the same or similar to that created in the very first impressions (Kendell, 1975; Sundberg, 1977).

Since this is so, the question arises: why do more? For one thing, in order to work effectively with a person in her situation, the practitioner needs to understand more than the name or label to give to the problem. He usually wants to have a feel for the human being with whom he will be working, for her qualities and characteristics, and for a sense of how she lives and what she suffers. That kind of feeling for the person and situation takes more than a few minutes of technical appraisal.

Some situations are harder than others to assess. The less difficult are situations that have been extensively studied and described and for which assessment and intervention have been somewhat standardized, for example, adjustment disorders with depressed mood, the straightforward depressive reaction consisting of depressed mood, tearfulness, and hopelessness, or the clear-cut, uncontradictable evidence of violent assault on a child.

However, few situations are truly clear-cut. Even those that seem clear-cut in a general way show much variation from individual to individual. Hence, it is important to try to avoid imposing mechanical stereotypes and allowing them to pass as assessments that may have an important effect on a person's life. It is a delicate matter to balance between the tendency toward extensive data accumulation to be on the safe side, while postponing interventions, and acting on a rapid assessment.

The balance is best achieved by starting intervention as soon as possible, based on the rapid early assessment. Meanwhile, one should be scrutinizing what happens in order to alter the assessment and alter the plan when the evidence turns up to indicate error. There is no such thing as an error-free assessment. But there are varying degrees of rigidity that become installed in a case process, making people continue on a less than useful path and feel abashed or embarrassed about changing course. Flexibility should be the byword. Flexibility does not mean whimsical changing, but rather, disciplined alterations based on new information and new insights.

_____ RELATIONSHIP MANAGEMENT _____   ___

Despite much research on the characteristics and dynamics of the therapeutic relationship, the subject remains elusive. The therapeutic relationship is some combination of communication and social interactions occurring between practitioners and clients as influenced and shaped by their backgrounds and the present environments including the helping organization involved.

Social interactions are among the most difficult phenomena to study because researchers and practitioners are totally immersed in the subject being studied. Scientific objectivity is hard to come by in these circumstances. Furthermore, the subject of client-practitioner relationships is encumbered by our feelings that something super-natural or supra-natural is involved, something that partakes of human essence or soul, that makes the subject mysterious.

As if this were not enough, relationships are powerful. We all need and want to possess, enjoy, manipulate, and exploit relationships because we all need and want the good things obtainable from intimate relationships, from good relationships with people in power, and from soothing, compassionate, and loving relationships with parents, mates, friends, and others.

The helping relationship has become idealized and virtually enthroned as a necessary and almost sufficient condition for successful treatment. The helping relationship is often conceived as something ephemeral, distinct from its empirical moorings that are influence, attraction, confidence, inspiration, communication of support, warmth, and respect. Something about the client-practitioner relationship is very powerful, if not magical; and a good relationship matters.

Suggested Practitioner Behaviors for Creating Good Relationship Conditions

In the task-centered model, and particularly in its beginning phase, a few suggestions are worthwhile following to create the right atmosphere for helping clients to participate fully in targeting problems and providing enough self-disclosure to enable the practitioner to form a reliable rapid, early assessment.

1. Use a manner that is plain, straightforward, and overtly friendly, but not effusive.
2. Verbalize understanding of major feelings and attitudes of the client: that is, say you understand and, especially, what you understand.
3. Verbalize awareness of overall stress and dominant mood or dilemma: that is, say you are aware and especially, of what you are aware.

4. Foster identification between yourself and the client.
5. Assume an assuring and supportive posture and demeanor.
6. Discuss and clarify what you and the client mean to one another, realistically.

SUMMARY

Identifying target problems is the first step in the task-centered model. It is a distinguishing mark of this model that the problems identified by the client are placed in the center of attention. It is the responsibility of the professional practitioner to discuss openly with the client what difficulties there may be in attempting to implement a program of intervention focused on problems as perceived by the client and to offer suggestions and recommendations to change the client's view if necessary. However, in case of impasse or strong reluctance on the part of the client, the client's view will prevail. In real practice, a respectful handling of these discussions is likely to produce a mutually satisfactory conclusion.

The basic actions for targeting a problem are establishing the actual presence of a problem, describing the problem, formulating the tentative assessment, determining the conditions or behaviors to be changed, stating the tentative goals, getting information about the social context, and getting relevant information about the social context of the problem. Clients who have difficulty in formulating target problems on their own can be assisted by a problem-search process. In cases of involuntary clients required by an authority to participate in making changes they do not seek themselves, practitioners must be sure that clients know the exact consequences of avoiding the mandated problem and also that clients are assured that problems of particular concern to them will be attended to.

Rapid early assessment develops from the process of targeting the problems and becomes the basis for treatment planning. A supportive, friendly, but not effusive, relationship posture on the part of the practitioner is most likely to encourage the desired self-disclosure and confidence needed to move rapidly into assessment and intervention.

How to Specify Target Problems: Summarized

Purpose

1. To name, state, and describe the target problem(s)—not to exceed three
2. To establish the center (*focus*) of intervention activity
3. To organize the treatment efforts so that they are efficiently directed to reducing the problem(s)

Basic actions (order is approximate)

1. Establishing the actual presence of a problem acknowledged by the client
2. Describing and naming each problem specifically
3. Formulating the tentative rapid early assessment
4. Determining the conditions or behaviors to be changed
5. Stating the tentative goals, that is, what the desired changes are to be
6. Getting information about the client's social and physical environments (social context) and the client's characteristics and mode of functioning
7. Getting information about the necessary history and development of problem to the degree the information is usable in conducting the present interventions

—————————————— **REFERENCES** ——————————————

Brown, L. B. (1977). Treating problems of psychiatric outpatients. In W. J. Reid & L. Epstein (Eds.), *Task-centered practice*. New York: Columbia University Press.

Cohler, B. J. (1982). Personal narrative and life course. In P. B. Baltes & O. G. Brim, Jr. (Eds.), *Life span development and behavior,* (Vol. 4, pp. 205–241). New York: Academic Press.

Dixon, S. L. (1987). *Working with people in crisis.* Columbus, OH: Merrill.

Epstein, L. (1977). A project in school social work. In W. J. Reid & L. Epstein (Eds.), *Task-centered practice* (pp. 130–146). New York: Columbia University Press.

Fischer, J. (1976). *The effectiveness of social casework.* Springfield, IL: Charles C. Thomas.

Golan, N. (1978). *Treatment in crisis situations.* New York: The Free Press.

Goldstein, H. (1986). Toward integration of theory and practice: A humanistic approach. *Social Work, 31*(5), 352–357.

Greif, G. L., & Lynch, A. A. (1983). The eco-systems perspective. In C. H. Meyer (Ed.), *Clinical social work in the eco-systems perspective.* New York: Columbia University Press.

Kendell, R. E. (1975). *The role of diagnosis in psychiatry.* London: Blackwell Scientific Publications.

Mullen, E. J., Dumpson, J. R., & Associates. (1972). *Evaluation of social intervention.* San Francisco: Jossey-Bass.

Newcome, K. (1985). Task-centered group work with the chronically mentally ill in day treatment. In A. E. Fortune (Ed.), *Task-centered practice with families and groups* (pp. 78–91). New York: Springer.

Reid, W. J. (1978). *The task-centered system.* New York: Columbia University Press.

Sundberg, N. D. (1977). *Assessment of persons.* Englewood Cliffs, NJ: Prentice-Hall.

Thio, A. (1978). *Deviant behavior.* Boston: Houghton Mifflin.

Whan, M. W. (1979). Accounts, narrative and case history. *British Journal of Social Work, 9*(4), 489–500.

CHAPTER
6

SECOND STEP: CONTRACTING

Plans, Goals, Tasks, Time Limits, and Other Agreements

_____ **CONTRACTS AS CASE PLANS** _____

A contract is a contemporary form of the conventional client-worker agreement, a basic ingredient of intervention. The assumption underlying an agreement is self-determination. The assumption underlying a contract (a formal agreement) is a commitment to work. A *contract* in direct service work is an agreement to work toward the reduction or alleviation of stated personal problems.

The contemporary professional climate values the client's right to exercise maximal choice in connection with decisions and acts that will seriously affect the quality of his life. The client's participation in such choices is thought to be right in and of itself. In addition, client participation is thought to have a strong payoff in terms of better outcomes. Practitioners can make bad decisions. The client's knowledge of what is to be done and why can help avert such mistakes. A client who understands the risks and benefits of intervention and the alternatives to treatment is likely to be more cooperative than one who is a passive recipient of authoritative actions from "on high." Information about purpose, forms, and structure helps demystify intervention and strengthens realistic client-practitioner relations and expectations of treatment (Lidz et al., 1984).

Planning treatment or intervention is necessary for the practitioner to handle cases purposefully and intentionally. Formalizing the plan in a written or oral contract makes the matter explicit. Rosen, Proctor, and Livne (1985), in developing the concept of planning in direct practice, describe the plan as a map of the "components of intervention, that is, determining which problems will be addressed, which outcomes will be sought, which interventions will be employed, and the order and sequencing of these components" (p.165).

To the extent possible, the practitioner should select intervention activities deliberately on the basis of available knowledge about types of social situations, problems, and persons, and evaluative information about probable outcomes. In

Step 2	Contract
Chapter 6	**Cover** • Priority target problems (three maximum) • Client's specific goals (accepted by practitioner) • Client's general tasks • Practitioner's general tasks • Duration of intervention sequence (time limits) • Schedule for interviews • Schedule for interventions • Parties to be included

FIGURE 6–1   Map detail

developing the treatment plan, she chooses from a range of alternative treatment components available. Planning requires judgment; therefore, treatment plans will vary with the preferences of the practitioner and the client, the style and requirements of the agency, and the obstacles, unforeseen events, and improvements that occur as treatment proceeds. Systematic work necessitates that planning be emphasized and formalized early in the process, but because of all the variations that occur in an actual case, planning takes place, in different forms, in all phases of the sequence.

THE ROLE OF ASSESSMENT IN PLANNING

The assessment acts as an instrument in decision-making about the contents of the plan. It suggests the probable limits and capabilities of the persons, the situation, and the resources. It also suggests the practical limits so that the plan adheres to the constraints as well as the possibilities of the realistic situation. From the assessment it is usually possible to derive the goals of the intervention sequence; that is, in view of the limitations and capabilities identified, the assessment suggests what is necessary to achieve in the intervention program.

Assessment goes on for the life of the case. The practitioner is always noting information, scrutinizing the situation, and evaluating what is going on. However, it is the essence of professional responsibility that a decision to act is made at certain key points.

The first key point is in the first step of the task-centered process, that is, at the point of target problem identification and definition. The rapid early assessment data are influential in helping the practitioner decide on a target problem. (See chapter 5.) By the time contracting and treatment planning are about to occur, the practitioner and client may have had one or more additional interviews, and possibly some information from collateral sources, that is, family members, other professionals, home visits, and the like.

Regardless of how much or how little additional information has come in, some time has elapsed and the practitioner has reviewed the situation in her mind. She might want to change some of the conclusions she made in the rapid early assessment—or she may not. Either way, the initial assessment should be reviewed at this point and put into as clear a form as possible given the natural limitations of the data. It is this second stage assessment, in which the rapid early assessment is evaluated, that now comprises the working assessment.

It is possible for the assessment process to become a barrier to helping people. It can be a costly ritual, contributing little to the efficacy or efficiency of treatment. Garfield (1986) points out that "prediction of therapeutic outcome on the basis of pre-therapy appraisals is disappointingly low with the average correlation ranging from 0.10 to 0.20." The rapid early assessment and its review should ordinarily suffice for making the treatment plan. An exception occurs when circumstances are obscure or baffling or when potentially critical issues require considerable study, consultation, and evaluation to be understood. In those exceptional instances case planning and contracting may be delayed as necessary, and the task-centered model should be applied flexibly to conform to the real life circumstances. Exceptions should be kept to a minimum and not be confused with the usual and expectable difficulties of case handling.

WRITTEN AND ORAL CONTRACTS: _____ ADVANTAGES AND DISADVANTAGES _____

Both written and oral contracts are used in practice. The written contract has an advantage if a high degree of explicitness is wanted, usually with intention to exercise control. The technical aim of the written contract in the task-centered approach is to make mutual agreement open and explicit. The aim may be to control quality so that the process conforms to standards and can be more readily monitored. The aim may be to control the client by suggesting the possibility or probability of sanctions should he fail to abide by the terms of the contract. The aim may be to control the behaviors of staff by holding them accountable for performance on the contract.

Written contracts are common in agencies that have many involuntary clients and reluctant participants. The control exercised by contracts under those circumstances is not necessarily negative. For the client the written contract may be a useful means for getting specific information about what the agency wants or intends, what it will do, who will do it, how it will be done, and with what expectations for final outcomes. For the agency the contract can be a way of monitoring performance, the client's, the practitioner's, and even the agency's own.

Although using the contract as a control is understandable, it poses ethical dilemmas. The contract mixes treatment, social control, and quality control. It opens avenues for manipulating the provisions of the contract to increase the appearance of good performance without actually achieving it.

Making a contract is a significant way to achieve clarity between client and practitioner. If well done, the client is an informed participant, in a good position to act independently in his own behalf, and a competent partner in the treatment enterprise. A client who has gone through careful discussion and planning should have a better understanding about what he has to do to reduce his problem effectively. Both client and worker will think twice about committing themselves to something that is not reasonable, not specific, and not feasible. The written contract is a barrier to a client's being misled about what he can expect, becoming confused, untrusting, or irate, and not getting available and appropriate services.

Although oral contracts should and can be specific, written contracts have a clear advantage in accountability (Maluccio & Marlow, 1974). Anyone can determine what actions were agreed to and finding whether those actions did or did not occur is potentially straightforward. A written document, with the participants' signatures, is an easy referencing for keeping track of what is supposed to be done and who is responsible. Clients, staff, supervisors, administrators, and consultants can use the written contract to make judgments about performance. When staff turnover is high, the written contract gives important information quickly to staff new to a case.

Written contracts have begun to be used only within the last decade. And though only a small amount of information has been gathered about the extent of the written contract's use and its effectiveness, the idea has caught hold in the field. What little evidence exists is positive. Clients have reported liking the specificity (Salmon, 1977). One study found that clients' willingness to develop and sign a contract was a good indicator of effective action to return children home from foster care (Stein, Gambrill, & Wiltse 1977). In juvenile delinquency cases and in foster care custody adjudications, judges have used written contracts to inform their decisions (Hofstad, 1977; Rooney, 1978).

Written contracts present a number of problems. For one thing, there has been no test of their legal status. We do not know if a client could sue a practitioner or an agency for failure to perform on a contract. We do not know if a contract is legally binding on a client and what, if any, sanctions can be applied legally if the client fails to perform. Furthermore, there may develop a trend toward evaluating staff performance, deciding to promote or not, and deciding to raise salaries or not according to the results of goal attainment (McCarty, 1978).

The problem with basing personnel decisions on clients' performance of contracts is that there is always uncertainty about the cause-effect relationship. Clients' failure to perform, as well as clients' success, can be related to personal and situational conditions that are uncontrollable. Although the basic idea of connecting client and worker performance is logical, making those connections probably exceeds our present technical capacity; that is, these connections probably cannot be made reliably.

As computerized management information systems continue to develop, contract items will be tracked. Interesting data, now largely unavailable, may then be obtained. However, the accuracy and meaning of such data depends on its quality: how good is the information in terms of appropriateness, relevancy, and accuracy? For instance, if staff members believe they will be judged by the quantity of performance, they will become skillful at contracting for easy, simple actions that can be readily performed and so produce a good performance "score." Staff workers may find themselves given poor performance ratings for failing to act because they did not know how and were not provided the training and resources.

It is conceivable that an agency performing maximally on all the easy, simple actions might provide many badly needed services. On the other hand, overemphasizing easy actions could lead to concentrating on trivia and avoiding serious problems that require risk taking. Since the reasons for poor performance on a contract are hard to discern and difficult to identify, contracts are not the only, or necessarily the best, data from which to judge performance. They are one source of usable data.

Involuntary clients are a cause of concern about contracts being misused. Involuntary clients tend to be vulnerable and powerless. They may agree to a contract that is not realistic for them and find themselves punished for failure: not getting their children returned to their custody, for example, when the resources for putting their situation in order were not available or not provided. Clients who are highly vulnerable—extremely ill, confused, very young, or imprisoned, for example—may lack the ability and the resources for making contracts on their own. If contracts can be made for them by caretakers, that would be a solution. On the other hand, caretakers may be unwilling or may enter into contracts with reservations.

Despite the problems of administering them, written contracts have merit. They can and should be used in the bulk of ordinary practice. However, written contracts should not be viewed as a remedy for all difficulties or as rigid machinery for pushing a case toward some hard and fast end. If a contract has been agreed upon and put into writing, it represents a degree of commitment to an arrangement worked out between the client and practitioner. This is a promising basis for positive movement. However, the contract is not permanent and could be altered at any time. It exists and remains in force at the discretion of the parties to it. The contract is a help to conducting a case process to a hopefully desirable result. But it has to be backed up by continuous work toward goal attainment. Although the contract is a technique for structuring the treatment process, it does not have a mechanical effect. Without mutual agreement and continuous work, the contract has little force for change.

Rothery (1980) has succinctly cautioned against mechanical agreements and ulterior agreements. The latter are hidden agendas created by unstated and possibly unperceived aims. Either the client or the practitioner may initiate a hidden agenda and cause it to be reflected in the contract. Or, it can be the case that both participants agree to provisions appearing appropriate on the surface but that are really pretenses. Such underlying assumptions may represent attempts to maneuver or manipulate the situation in the interests of one of the participants. This kind of practice is misleading and may spoil the honest working relationship.

An oral contract can be thought of as a gentlemen's agreement, a binding understanding between people who trust each other and have some real basis for that trust. An oral contract is a flexible agreement but lacks the sense of commitment if not negotiated as explicitly as a written contract is (or should be). The same discussions should precede the formulation of the oral contract as precede the written one. The fact is, however, that oral contracting allows for evading dealing with content, purpose, and consequences of treatment, hence may not be as straightforward as the written contract. Of course we can speak in a straightforward manner if we choose. In the end, whether a written or an oral contract is used, the choice is a matter of preference.

Oral contracts are more flexible, adaptable, and easier to handle than written contracts. Oral contracts are really semiwritten. In normal agency practice their substance should be written into the agency record, shown to the client, and at least initialed. The record of an oral contract can also serve for administrative control purposes, that is, for case accountability and client and staff performance measurement. Oral contracts, when written into the record, are about the same as written contracts, with the same advantages and disadvantages. What they lack is the appearance of firmness that is present in a written contract document.

———————— MAKING UP THE CONTRACT ————————

Contents of the Contract

The subjects to cover in the contract include:

1. Major priority problems—three at most
2. Specific goals
3. Client tasks: activities the client will undertake
4. Practitioner tasks: activities the practitioner will undertake
5. Duration of intervention: approximately how long the process is to last, or the time limits
6. Scheduling of interventions
7. Scheduling of interviews
8. Participants: who will take part
9. Location: where the sessions will occur

These nine items can be thought of as the basic structure of the intervention plan. It is the aggregate of the elements of the plan and shows a planned relationship among the parts.

Interviewing Technique during Contracting

Interviewing during the contracting should be conducted in a manner that achieves (Epstein, 1985):

☐ as much participation as possible from the client in making suggestions for the contract
☐ complete and detailed explanations from the practitioner about her suggestions and recommendations
☐ adequate opportunity for the client to raise questions, give reactions, and ask for and receive clarification

Contract discussion begins discursively. There is circling around the subject, exploring what the client thinks and believes the priority target problems should be, what would help most, what should be done first, and what should follow.

The practitioner shares her opinion with the client. If the practitioner thinks the client's formulation is mistaken, she should try to convince the client to make a change. That is done through discussion, exploration, explanation, and clarification. Many clients adopt a practitioner's recommendations to a greater or lesser degree because they respect the professional's qualifications as an expert. The practitioner's attempts to influence the client may fail, however, if the client considers the practitioner's opinion to be wrong, or if the professional opinion contradicts strongly held beliefs and values of the client.

Should the client be strongly opposed to the practitioner's opinion and should he not be convinced by an ordinary amount of back and forth exchange of views, an impasse will occur. The task centered approach recommends that the practitioner accede to the client's choices unless those choices are (extremely rarely) unethical, immoral, illegal, or so clearly impossible that she must refuse to go along with them. The idea is to achieve some gains, even modest ones, for the client. Most people do not easily change their minds about what they want. If the practitioner is unable to convince the client to follow a recommendation, she can still concentrate on developing a program of work that is congruent with the client's stated concerns.

If the practitioner feels unable to comply with a request, she should tell the client the reason, that it is not out of unwillingness to help but because she knows there is no way to do what the client asks. In addition, the practitioner should thoroughly "walk through" the specific circumstances in order to show what cannot be done, why, and what would be the probable consequences of pursuing the client's idea. The practitioner should fully state and explain her reservations. The major communication to facilitate reaching an agreement on what to do is this: *What acts, if done first, will help most?*

Stating Priority Target Problems

The contract should state at least one and no more than three target problems. This can be done after the array of problems has already been elicited in the first step of the task-centered process. Problem statements should be prioritized, preferably by the client. The practitioner helps the client decide on priorities and may discuss the appropriateness of the client's selection or recommend priorities if necessary. The farther away one gets from the client's own real interests, the more difficulties may arise. If there is a mandated problem from a powerful source, this problem should be among the priorities.

Guidelines for selecting priorities

First action   In step one, the initial problem-defining phase, the discussion should have elicited from the client an array of problems as perceived by the client. Taking up that array, the first action is to *group the problems into classes or categories to depict the problem as an umbrella for a group of subproblems.*

Second action   Proceed to select priorities as follows.

1. *Assign priority to the problem that the client asserts is of the highest interest, that most needs to be taken care of, and that will make the most difference to improve the situation.* This choice has a high probability of success because it is congruent with client motivation. However, the client's decision may not be well-advised, in which case the practitioner should undertake to influence the client to make a more appropriate decision.

2. *Assign priority to the problem according to a judgment made mutually between client and practitioner.* This choice is not as likely to produce as good results as the client's spontaneous selection, nevertheless, it is likely to produce satisfactory results if the client has been genuinely involved in arriving at the decision.

3. *Setting priorities may be postponed for a short or a long time, during which the participants explore questions from a number of perspectives.* This tentative posture on priorities is appropriate when an issue is obscure. The client's commitment may be ambiguous, or the client may be perceived as needing more time to become secure in the helping situation. By postponing the selection of priorities, however, the impetus for work is almost certain to be slowed, causing the helping process to become inefficient. This option should be used sparingly and reserved only for the most obscure situations.

Guidelines for stating problems in a contract

1. Grammar of statement

Subject	**Active Verb**	**Object**
Client	*is having*	*stated deficit, excess, conflict or dissonance.*
Mrs. A ⟶	is lacking ⟶	adequate child care.
John ⟶	is fighting ⟶	too much with his mother.
Mr. and Mrs. B ⟶	are ⟶	in continuous and serious discord about his jealousy of her.
Mr. and Mrs. C ⟶	are clashing ⟶	seriously over the budgeting of their income.

Sample Shortened Contract Statements

☐ Mrs. A lacks adequate child care.
☐ John fights too much with his mother.

☐ Mr. and Mrs. B are in conflict about his jealousy.
☐ Mr. and Mrs. C are in conflict over budgeting.

2. Parsimony of statement. Avoid long phrases that purport to explain the problem. Explanations are not necessary in the contract.

Stating target problems in a multiple-person case
When more than one participant are involved, it is possible to state the three problems from the viewpoint of each person. Normally the viewpoints of the different participants will be related. When several people in multiple-person cases participate, the firmer the formulation of the target problems of each, the better. For example, when dealing with a whole family or a part of a family, it is preferable to interview each person alone to elicit his views about the target problems. When the group meets together later, the separate statements are made to the group. Differences of opinion can be aired at that time and negotiated to the extent possible before the contract is set. Because of lack of time or because of other logistics such as distance to be traveled to come together, it is not always feasible to conduct separate interviews with each participant. In that case, the practitioner needs to spend time and give each individual as much leeway as possible to give his or her viewpoint when the group meets.

It is to be expected that there will be differences when the target problems of the individuals become public in the group. These differences are to be negotiated in the group session. Some differences seem so extreme that they become, for all practical purposes, nonnegotiable. Some members may state problems that seem unrelated to those that the others have brought up. Some differences that seem unrelated are not. Rather, they are mirror images; that is, the problem statements of two persons in conflict are opposite, but the connection is that they are about the same condition. The disjunction is that the different clients seek different solutions.

Reducing a long array of problems in a multiple-person case
To reduce the problems stated in a multiple-person case to three, the practitioner has three options.

1. *Settle on the three problems about which there is the most agreement.* These are three problems for all participants together. Hold the remainder for later consideration, after work has begun on the three agreed-on problems.

2. *Settle on up to three problems, with or without agreement among the participants.* All participants will have separate lists (as in Example 6–3, which describes the case of Rick and his mother) that will be interrelated but not identical. This option makes for a complex situation because time has to be allotted to give proper consideration to each participant's work, often by interspersing individual sessions between group sessions. This second option reflects the most common practice in multiple-person client sequences.

3. *In case of extreme disagreement, settle on up to three problems to be dealt with in group sessions, and provide additional individual or subgroup sessions.* This option can be used alone or together with the other options.

Stating Goals

The contract should state the goals of the intervention from the client's standpoint, not the agency's or the practitioner's standpoints. This would normally legitimate the client's motivation and serve as a criterion statement against which to evaluate results.

The number of goal statements should be few and address the priority target problems. It should be possible to show a direct connection between the problem and the goal.

If the agency has use for recording its own goals, distinct from those of the client, these should be labeled as agency goals or agency service objectives and recorded separately. Caution is called for to avoid imposing agency goals on clients. Agencies will often want to keep tabs on their own organizational goals in a given case to evaluate themselves and to conform to requirements of legislative and funding bodies.

Here are some examples of right and wrong goal statements.

Right: Temporary foster care home is to be available on 24-hour notice in case Mrs. A needs to enter the hospital.

Wrong: Family assessment.

Right: Cut down the frequency of John's fights with his foster father 50%.

Wrong: John is to report for counseling.

Planning and Stating Tasks: Client and Practitioner

Tasks are particular kinds of problem-solving actions, planned by and agreed on between practitioner and client, and capable of being worked on by the client and the practitioner outside, as well as inside, the interview. *Client tasks* are actions clients intend to take that are expected to reduce the target problem. *Practitioner tasks* are actions practitioners take on the client's behalf to reduce the same problem.

The way tasks fit into the problem-solving paradigm can be diagrammed in the following manner.

Problem-solving paradigm	Task-centered model
General orientation	Problem explored
Generation of alternatives	Task possibilities developed
Testing and implementation	Tasks tried out
Verification (evaluation)	Results tallied

Types of tasks

There are two broad types of tasks—general and operational (Reid & Epstein, 1972; Reid, 1978)—and numerous types of subtasks. These classifications are heuristic and help in thinking about how to formulate actions. They have no particular virtues or purposes other than planning aids. One should not worry about how to classify tasks, only that tasks should be sensible and capable of being put into action with help as needed.

General tasks   *General tasks* state the direction of an action but do not spell out exactly what is to be done. General tasks always imply the client goals. Often a general client task and a client goal are the same. They refer to two aspects of the same phenomenon. The general task says what is to be done, and the goal says what the condition ought to be when the task is done. They may converge. It is necessary to get both stated and understood. For example,

> *Right:* Ray is to enroll in the Adjustment Training Center. (specific)
>
> *Wrong:* Job training (broad, complex, not specific)
>
> *Right:* Ray is to find and maintain living arrangements near the Center. (specific)
>
> *Wrong:* Independent living (broad, complex, not specific)

A general task consists of a package of separate or separable actions that together form a whole action recognizable as a unified thing, for example, "To obtain medical care." The definite separate sections of the general task can be thought of as subtasks. For instance,

> Mrs. A will phone the doctor tomorrow.
> She will get an early appointment.
> She will explain her health problem to her children before her next medical appointment.

Subtasks come and go as client and practitioner work to achieve the general tasks. The contract should not be encumbered with stating lists of subtasks, which they are part of the regular give and take between practitioner and client as they work together to accomplish something. If significant, subtasks can be mentioned in the running record or log.

Operational tasks   *Operational tasks* state the specific actions the client is to undertake. They are a type of subtask because they contain information about definite actions. Operational tasks are often broken down further into subtasks. For example,

> *Right:*   Fill out and submit an application to the Center.
> Visit the Center.
> Keep an appointment for psychological tests.
> Have an interview with a public information officer to get an advertisement placed in the newspaper to locate a boarding home.
> Visit boarding homes.
>
> *Wrong:*   Come for regular counseling.
> Obtain psychological and social assessment.

Note that the wrong statements are too complex, broad, and vague.

Other types of tasks   For purposes of analysis, subtypes of general tasks can be classified. In real practice these types are fluid, become combined with one another, and drop in and drop out as practical. Classifying tasks has no particular operating use and is of value only for thinking carefully about the processes.

1. *Unique tasks.* Planned for a one-time effort, for example, "Mrs. A is to see the foster home finder Tuesday."
2. *Recurrent tasks.* Planned for repetitive action, for example, "Mrs. A is to talk to her children each day to explain how she feels and what she is doing to regain her health."
3. *Unitary tasks.* A single action requiring a number of steps: "Mrs. A is to arrange for her hospitalization."
4. *Complex tasks.* Two or more discrete actions that are closely related, for example, "To discuss with her physician the several possible types and effects of surgery and consider what each would do to her ability to work and to care for her home and her children."
5. *Individual tasks.* To be carried out by one person.
6. *Reciprocal tasks.* Separate but related tasks to be worked on by two or more persons; usually exchanges (e.g., "Mrs. B will refrain from yelling at Arthur and Arthur will tell his mother what worries him instead of running out of the house").
7. *Shared tasks.* Two or more persons doing the same thing (e.g., "Mrs. B and Arthur will talk to the psychiatrist together").
8. *Cognitive tasks.* Mental activities, for example, "Mrs. E is to think about what exactly she likes, dislikes, and is uncertain about in her marriage." Care must be used that cognitive tasks do not degenerate into unproductive ruminations that have no references to present problems. At the same time, being aware

of and understanding what he wants, needs, and deserves can clarify the client's priorities and help him make choices and decisions (Ewalt, 1977).

Interrelations between task types Ordinarily, operational tasks flow from general tasks. They are a prominent part of Step 3, task achievement. Operational tasks are started as a result of making the contract. However, they do not need to be written into a formal contract because they change frequently. Operational tasks usually begin as an immediate result of the contract. They continue as a major activity into the problem-solving, task-achievement stage to be discussed in Chapter 7.

How to plan tasks

Task planning starts after target problem specification. It consists of generating alternative tasks in discussion and crystalizing a plan of action or strategy. Tasks are agreed on, and task implementation is planned. The whole strategy is summarized.

Task planning starts with the contract. It continues into the next steps as often as necessary, that is, any time client or practitioner is uncertain or lack information about what to do next. However, to keep up momentum, tasks should be planned to take care of major actions. Minor or peripheral matters should be handled in a commonsense, helpful way without subjecting them to a full-scale process. In other words, the idea of the sequence is to help the client along, and the steps of the process are to be used for that purpose. Overplanning and overmechanizing the process will simply clutter the works.

"Piecemeal" planning A task plan may be made in one session, following the problem specification, but it is more usual for tasks to emerge piecemeal, during several phases of a single interview or over two or more interviews. Whereas target problems tend to remain stable over the life of the case, tasks change often. Tasks change because they are done, are not done, or cannot be done. Completed tasks are dropped. Tasks not done are analyzed to obtain information about the barriers to task achievement. They are then revised or dropped.

Sources of information for task planning

The sources of information about reasonable tasks to reduce a problem include:

1. *The clients' own experience (the basic source)*. The first step in planning a task is to find out from clients what they think they could do to cut down their target problems. Most clients have sound ideas on this subject once they are convinced that it is safe to state their own ideas and that their ideas will be respected. The practitioner is responsible for clarifying and molding clients' suggestions and introducing tasks for consideration to clients who do not readily generate their own ideas.

2. *Expert knowledge about reliable or reasonable problem-solving actions.* It has been common for service workers to depend on familiarity with a few general treatment methods for knowledge to use in their cases. Selective information from general reading and conferences and advice from supervisors and consultants is used. It would be preferable for a practitioner to have access to knowledge that is directly related to particular case problems, but getting that information is often difficult and time consuming. The literature is spread out in university libraries; rarely do agencies have sufficiently complete and up-to-date libraries that can provide practitioners with quick access to the latest and best quality information. Since practitioners do not have time to run down this knowledge for themselves, resource people on the staff, cooperating specialized agencies, and consultants must secure this information for them. The time is coming when much more information will be available via computerized information systems and will be organized in practitioner-friendly systems.

3. *The practitioner's own experience.* Practitioners should not hesitate to draw on their own practice and personal experience to suggest client tasks. If we have had a similar experience ourselves, we have ideas about actions that failed or succeeded. Especially pertinent is a collection of previous practice experiences with similar situations.

Formalizing tasks

After task alternatives have been generated with a client, the next step is to reach an explicit agreement about which ones will be undertaken. Then details of implementation should be discussed. This means client and practitioner agree on what is to be done, when, with whom, where, under what specific conditions (if any), and how. The client should emerge with a clear idea, a blueprint to help him accomplish the tasks.

Each task agreed to must have discussion of how the task is to be started up and pursued. The client needs only to have a brief review of the expected actions for tasks that involve familiar actions. Tasks involving novel actions for the client require detailed step-by-step discussion, including alternative actions in case of unexpected developments. All task agreements should be briefly summarized at the end of a session.

Review: how to plan client tasks

1. Generate alternatives
2. Agree with client on tasks
3. Plan details of implementation
4. Summarize

Practitioner tasks

Practitioner tasks are actions that the practitioner is committed to do on the client's behalf between sessions. Practitioner tasks supplement the client's actions and should facilitate the client's work. Negotiating and conferring are the practitioner's chief tasks.

Negotiating and conferring include working with agency and community officials and with collaterals such as neighbors, friends, and family. Negotiations are conducted to transfer resources, services, and good will from the organization to the client; to package or design those resources, services, and good will in a way to reduce the client's target problems; and to satisfy the official terms and conditions as well as powerful mandates held by the organization. Conferring resembles negotiating but emphasizes transferring helpful or needed information and personal relations.

Guidelines for negotiating with agency and community officials

1. Identify the terms and conditions the agency requires the client to meet.
2. Specify what persons must or should participate.
3. Specify what documents must be produced, by whom, and where they are to be delivered.
4. Specify the authority for the requirements or expectation, that is, what legal, judicial, professional, or customary authority exists to justify the expectations.
5. Elicit a clear and concrete understanding of an agency's or official's intentions and plans.
6. Secure information possessed by the agency or official about the problem.
7. Secure information about the agency's special knowledge concerning a client and a problem area.
8. Secure information about what agency resources are available to the client.
9. Reach agreement on resources and services to be supplied by the agency or official.
10. Influence the agency to take a positive attitude towards the client to ease his entry into its system and to encourage his participation.
11. Request that the agency or official report, confirming or revising agreements.

EXAMPLE 6-1

Sample Memorandum Recording for the File of the Results of a Negotiating Session with Other Agency Officials*

(1) Required terms and conditions
(4) Authority
(5) Agency intentions and plans

*(Numbers in parentheses refer to guidelines for negotiating, and are shown only for reference.)

Met with 24-year-old Mark Jones' probation officer and his supervisor. The Court ordered Mark to report for psychiatric counseling while on one year's probation. The probation department referred him to our clinic. The probation department staff thinks it is probable that Mark's repeated traffic offenses (driving without a license, speeding, failure to pay parking violation tickets) are due to psychological problems for which he should be treated. The court staff sees Mark as an intelligent and agreeable person who could benefit from treatment that would "straighten him out", by which they mean clearing up his troubled relationship with his girlfriend with whom he has a child, getting regular employment, paying regular child support, getting married. Along with such improvement in the organization of his life, the court wants him to get driver training and a license. The court does not want to sentence this man to imprisonment and hopes for a better outcome through therapy.

(6) Securing information
Mark's history contained problems. He was thought to have been physically abused by his parents when he was a young child. As a result of the investigation at that time, Mark was placed in a foster home for several years. He ran away several times and associated with youth known to be involved in theft and drugs. But Mark himself seemed to behave within the law. He graduated from high school and is now employed irregularly as a garage mechanic. For four years he has been living with his girlfriend. She is a secretary whose mother provides child care for the couple's son. When they are together, there is continual fighting and sometimes there are drinking bouts. Mark can give no coherent explanation of what he and his girlfriend fight about or what the source of their difficulties is.

(2) Required participants
The court requires only Mark to be in treatment. They would like to involve his girlfriend but realize that her participation must be voluntary even though they know the couple have much conflict.

(8) Available agency resources
The probation officer will see Mark once per month for a checkup interview. This is expected to remind Mark that the court has authority over him and that he could go to jail if he fails to cooperate.

(9) Agreement on resources and services
We agreed on the probation plan stated above (monthly checkup by probation officer).

(10) Influencing the agency
We agreed that the probation officer will be receptive to Mark's complaints and distress about being required to go into treatment and that the officer will take a supportive and clarifying attitude toward the treatment. For ourselves, we did not think we could predict how Mark would react to treatment. The probation personnel indicated that they were realists and expected only that we try our best.

(11) Reporting
We confirmed that this summary represents the sense of our interagency understanding of each other's roles, but that we would check with each other at the end of each month to see how we each were doing with Mark and determine if our understanding still held or needed revision.

Not applicable
(3) Documents
(7) Agency special knowledge

Conferring with collaterals

Conferences held with the client's family, friends, teachers, physicians, a state's attorney, and so forth. The major purpose of these conferences is to win these other interested parties over to take one or more actions to reward, legitimize, respect, teach, or help the client. Actions taken by collaterals should fit the plan for task achievement and be specific. Conferences often give the practitioner an opportunity to solicit information that will be of help in assessing the situation and weighing alternatives for intervention. (See Example 6–2.)

EXAMPLE 6–2

Sample Record Note on Conference with Mark's Employer

I met with J. Battleman, with Mark's agreement, and after he had discussed with Mr. B that I would call and got his okay. Told Mr. B that I knew that he was aware of Mark's problems and that Mark had been unreliable in his work. I was there frankly to intercede for Mark who saw the handwriting on the wall and understood he was finally going to be fired. I said I understood Mr. B's frustration and also that Mark was an expense at present and that Mr. B was not getting his money's worth out of Mark. Mr. B was quite resentful about my interceding for Mark and let me know he thought it was pretty outrageous. Standing my ground, I explained that I thought and the judge thought that Mark could straighten out but needed time. That was all I wanted—some time. Both Mark and I were ready to work to get him to work regularly and on time. Mr. B said that was the problem. Mark got him into all kinds of trouble with customers by not showing up, showing up late or drunk, or both. And that crazy business about Mark's driving his car without a license! In the end, Mr. B agreed to a one month-probation, to give Mark and me enough time to get started on a treatment program.

Providing resources

The contract should state what resources are planned for inclusion in the service to the client and describe the general means for their procurement. These resources may be tangible and material, for example, cash, food stamps, medical care, clothing, housing, education; or they may be counseling services, for example, psychotherapy or interpersonal skill training. The resources provided may be controlled by the agency or may need to be procured from another agency through prior agreements about division of services, referral, advocacy, or purchase of care.

Selecting and Scheduling Interventions

Selecting tasks and selecting interventions are intertwined. Professional usage does not clearly distinguish between these two terms; both are relatively new, nontraditional, technical terms whose meanings are still evolving.

The term "intervention" is used to describe something that occurs and comes between various interests in a discordant situation, for example, interference with or mediation of conflicting interests. "Intervention" usually refers to some preassembled group of techniques that have been conceptualized in a coordinated manner and have achieved recognition in publication or another official medium. Tasks are small units of intervention that are individualized and not permanent features of the sequence of intervention or treatment. "Intervention" has come to be a synonym for treatment and is used by practitioners and theoreticians who prefer not to associate themselves closely with the implication of medical practice that is implied by the term "treatment."

A feature of contemporary practice is that new and revised intervention programs are constantly being designed and disseminated. In addition, it is characteristic of practice that individual practitioners continually invent interventions out of their own experience and as a product of their interaction with particular clients and settings. It is not possible to be up-to-date on all the sources of information about intervention. However, the most efficient sources are

☐ Computerized data banks, provided that they can screen and analyze the detailed information that is provided;
☐ Professional journals
☐ Conferences, workshops, continued education, in-service training
☐ Formal university-based professional education
☐ Synthesized and summarized literature reviews
☐ Supervision and consultation

Selecting interventions tends to be more art than science and depends on habit and preference. To increase the realism and objectivity of the process, certain guidelines make sense (Gambrill, 1983; Thomas, 1984).

Guidelines for selection of interventions
Interventions selected should

1. Have a credible record of success in similar cases.
2. Be acceptable to all participants.
3. Be efficient and capable of being implemented with reasonable cost and time.
4. Be as nonintrusive as possible, minimizing the amount of change needed to put the intervention in place, thus probably decreasing the risk of negative side effects.
5. Have a positive orientation.
6. Be likely to generalize and be maintained, and enhance problem-solving skills (see Chapter 8).
7. Be individualized, taking account of unique situational and individual differences that necessitate adapting recognized interventions to fit the present case.

Interventions should be scheduled in an organized way, avoiding depending on momentary flashes of insight to show the way. This is not to say that if some very good idea emerges out of the blue we should not catch it and run with it—we should—but we cannot rely on such luck to see us through the hard work of planning and implementing problem solving. Some programmed intervention packages recommend the order of the interventions. Some suggest stages that clients can go through and suggest stopping at the stage that accomplishes the desired results. Most intervention scheduling is flexible and follows the conventional logic of beginning, middle, and end. The most important guideline for scheduling is this:

> The plan should provide and the contract should include a decision reached with the client and any other important participants about what interventions will start the process, what effects are expected to follow, and approximately when the intervention will end.

Taking the target problem priorities as a guide, the schedule of interventions should start with itemizing what is to be done first, second, and third, roughly at the beginning, middle, and end. Interventions have a way of losing specificity and order as they progress. The chain of events they start is not capable of being fully anticipated. Many actors and actions get involved that influence the interventions.

Intervention schedules should be definite. However, they should be changed readily in the face of obvious need. Their purpose is to push and to get movement in the intervention program.

Scheduling Interviews

The preferred way to schedule interviews is to establish specifically how often they will occur, where and when they will be held, and how long they will last. These specifics can be changed later if they prove to be inconvenient. However, to start off without a systematic schedule is to invite uncertainty, inattention, and misunderstanding. A fluid and diffuse mode of scheduling time invites drift.

Setting Duration, Or Time Limits

A review of current literature reveals considerable variation and disagreement among authors about what time limits to set for interventions. Absence of research evidence only adds to the lack of consensus. A recent exploratory study concluded that criteria for planning duration of treatment were primarily idiosyncratic (Fortune, 1985). Other writers have attempted to develop theoretical positions about the appropriateness of time limits (Kanter, 1983). Given this state of affairs, the guidelines in the task-centered approach should be construed as practice-based information to be used in a flexible and commonsense fashion until robust information is generated. A number of general rules can guide practice in defining time limits for a particular case.

1. Task-centered intervention should be planned to take place in eight to twelve in-person interviews with the clients, spaced out in a regular schedule over a two- to three-month period.
2. Negotiations and collateral conferences in any number can be included or excluded, depending on need.
3. The planned number of interviews should be noted in the contract, together with the planned dates and times.
4. The number of interviews may be reduced or extended to fit any natural time limits inherent in the problem situation; for example, if Mrs. A is to be incapacitated for only four weeks, the time limit for the intervention could be one month.

There has been no research to study what time limits are "best" for any particular problem, age group, or personality type (see Chapter 3). Agencies develop practice styles about how they apportion time and make time limits on the basis of their judgments. Some agencies set numbers of interviews on the basis of an administrative decision. Available staff time may also determine time limits. Experience develops practice knowledge about what time allotments seem appropriate. Where third-party payments are made, it is customary to set the limit to equal the amount of service that will be paid for or reimbursed by another agency or an insurance company.

Rule of thumb

The experience of the research projects on which the task-centered approach is based suggests a "rule of thumb"—eight client interviews plus any number of agency negotiations and collateral contacts, over a two- to three-month span. The contract for an eight-interview sequence can be shortened or extended.

Reasons for time limits

Time limits appear to mobilize effort. Like any deadline, they set an objective towards which clients and practitioners can organize energy and expectations. Time limits create a push that gets things done.

Rarely do clients object to time limits. Those who do object often have been habituated to an open-ended style as a result of previous treatment experience. Or they may have adopted the view that long-term treatment is a status symbol or an interpersonal security situation. Occasionally, clients seem to pick up nonverbal cues from practitioners who feel anxious about using time limits. No deleterious effects from time limits have been reported except the occasional verbal anecdote about a client who develops a severe separation anxiety that a practitioner new to short-term treatment attributes to time limits. (Actually, the client's anxiety might have been induced by any number of other things.) In fact there appears to be a significant decrease in dropouts when explicit, time-limited sequences are compared to open-ended sequences. Time limits also put the client-practitioner relationship on a work basis, cutting down on the development of unnecessary client personal dependence on the practitioner.

Special conditions for time limits

There are a number of conditions where special time limit conditions pertain: children and adults in foster care, chronic care, or long-term care; children or adults in legal custody or under court ordered treatment; children or adults receiving medical or mental health treatment; young children in direct treatment; or parents learning new child care skills.

1. *Clients in foster care, chronic care, or long-term care.* In foster care or chronic care, living arrangements are provided that are separable from counseling. The counseling should follow the usual rules for task-centered intervention addressed to specific target problems and include time limits. The contract for living arrangements is distinct. The living arrangement contract can be open ended if that arrangement is intended to be permanent or indefinite. If this is not intended, the plan should specify the expected duration of the living arrangement, the discharge plan, and the alternative plan. While the particular living arrangement exists, there may be a series of separate task-centered sequences. Critical points in settings that would normally call for such sequences are admission, personal crises, changes in living plan, and discharge.

2. *Children or adults in legal custody with court-ordered requirements.* Typical incidences of legal custody with court-ordered requirements include children who are wards of the court and ordered to be in foster care, children or adults on probation or parole, and persons legally declared incompetent who have a court appointed guardian. The terms of the court order may exceed the task-centered model's normal time limits. The contract for intervention in such cases should follow the normal task-centered time limits. Thereafter, additional sequences can be contracted for, if advisable, or the situation can be placed in a monitoring status. (See chapter 8.)

3. *Children or adults receiving medical or mental health treatment.* Clinics vary a great deal in their expectation that medically supervised or medically oriented treatment will be open ended or time limited. Because of side effects and legal requirements, the provision of medication almost always requires continuing medical supervision. Medical and psychiatric care may involve some regular checkup or monitoring to observe the development of a chronic health condition. When the medical or mental health agency opts for extended time and the social welfare agency agrees, the intervention plan proceeds according to the medical recommendations. Interventions concerning the problems in living, however, can be restricted to one or more task-centered sequences. (See chapter 9.)

4. *Young children in direct treatment.* Young children have relatively short attention spans that need to be considered when planning the eight-session interviewing schedule. Young children may be interviewed in short segments of time, with two short segments counted as one for purposes of the interview scheduling.

5. *Parents being reeducated in child care skills.* Evidence suggests that parent education is an effective activity to reduce parent-child conflict problems and modify child-rearing practices (Levenstein, Kochman, & Roth, 1973; Pinkston, 1979). There is also some evidence that frequent contact and service beyond the usual two to three months characteristic of task-centered intervention—up to one year—enhances effectiveness in dealing with these types of problems (Sherman, Neuman, & Shyne, 1973). In view of this evidence, it would be appropriate to contract for extended duration if doing so accords with the practitioner's judgment and the client's interest in particular circumstances. The extremely important proviso is that cases be kept open *only* when definite plans and implementation are actually desired by clients who also show credible evidence of improvement and *only* if appropriate services actually exist and can be provided.

Extensions
When convincing evidence exists, there should be no artificial barrier to extending time limits. But lacking that concrete evidence, extending a contract on some general belief that more is better has no known value. It would be better to conclude with the completion of the planned brief intervention sequence. There should be no bar to reopen cases if requested to do so or if an involuntary client is referred again.

The reasons some cases continue for long or very long periods of time are varied. There are economic advantages to providers of long term interventions. Some types of medically supervised interventions are established to continue over long periods of time, partly because of habit and style, partly because of what is known or believed about stages of development in diseases. Interventions that involve large investments in reeducation of children and adults may justify long-term intervention. The fact is that the state of knowledge does not justify any hard and fast conclusions about the conditions under which long-term intervention is or is not justified.

The present tendency is to curtail the length of time used in interventions. Especially when cost is important and when effectiveness is doubtful, long-term interventions are not justifiable. The number of people who benefit from brief, focused interventions is large and potentially larger.

Deciding Participants

The universe of persons who can be involved in an intervention sequence is closed. Only certain categories of parties may be included: family members, peers, nonfamily persons in the household, a relevant group (interest group, age group, neighborhood or civic group, for example), or immediately influential authorities (teachers, doctors, caregivers, for example). If possible and if feasible, those who are an immediate part of the problem and its solution should be included in the contract, but only if they are available and have expressed a willingness and ability to participate.

Some people, such as parents of minor children, can be included because their social role commands their involvement. Persons can be deemed an immediate part of the problem and its solution if they are in a continuing, current relationship with the central client and if they occupy a position that seems to precipitate, exacerbate, maintain, or restrain the problem. Persons whose social role commands their involvement are those who exercise direct care of and give financial support to the central client.

In deciding which parties are to be included in the contract, the crucial factor is their willingness. Rarely do persons of potential value to the success of an intervention agree to total involvement. They have their own agendas, which come first. It is not uncommon, however, for a married couple or parents and children to agree to joint interviews. It is sometimes the case that whole families will come together for interviews or that men and women friends will attend together. Mostly, however, persons other than the central client will take a lesser degree of responsibility. They can contract for moderate or minimal inclusion. They may be prepared to attend once or only occasionally, or they may participate by telephone contact. The degree of involvement of persons close to the client is not crucial. What is crucial is that there be discussion with them to find out what they are ready to do and to commit them to specific actions.

Location

Where interviews are to be held is a matter of custom, convenience, and expediency. Interviews in the client's home offer observations and interactions with real living conditions and excellent opportunities for assessment. However, they may be subject to interruptions, lack privacy, and in certain circumstances (for example, in high crime neighborhoods) pose security problems. Office interviews are most convenient for practitioners and are also less costly than home interviews, but some clients are much less comfortable in the agency's office than in their own home and neighborhood. Interviews are sometimes held on the street and in public buildings depending on purpose and on what is practical and prudent. The important thing for making a contract is that there be a plan for the place to hold interviews and a schedule of interviews and collateral contacts.

EXAMPLE 6–3

Example of a Contract

Rick is a 15-year-old black youth in foster care. He is an only child being reared by his mother who was deserted by his father when Rick was only 4 years old. He came into foster care one month ago with his mother's reluctant approval after having been picked up by the police twelve times within the past year for running away, fighting, and belonging to a gang. The practitioner is employed in the state child welfare agency and regards both the mother and Rick as clients.

Contract Topic	*Specification*
1. Major priority problems	*Rick*
	• Too many people are trying to raise me.
	• My mother pays too much attention to my aunt's advice.
	Mother
	• Rick does not go to school.
	• He stays out too late at night.
	• He keeps bad company.
	Mandated
	• *By court:* Minor in need of supervision.
	• *By agency opinion:* Mother too strict.

Contract Topic	*Specification*
2. Goals	*Rick*
	• To be discharged from foster care.
	• To return home and enroll in school.
	Rick and Mother
	• To set up a curfew plan.
	• To stop aunt's interference.
3. Client tasks	*Rick*
	• To decide what vocational training he wants
	Mother
	• To decide on latest possible curfew time
	in exchange
	Rick
	• To advise Mother of a plan for reporting lateness to her.
	Mother
	• To put limits on aunt's interference
4. Practitioner tasks	• To arrange vocational testing for Rick
	• To get and deliver to Rick and Mother all available information about work training programs
	• To confer with aunt about her role in mother-son conflict
	• To prepare recommendation for court about plan for Rick's discharge from foster care
	• To negotiate Rick's renrollment with school official
5. Duration	Two months
6. Intervention schedule	*Sessions 1, 2, 3*
	• Decrease aunt's interference
	• Start decrease in Rick's performance problems in school and gang membership

Contract Topic	Specification
	Sessions 4, 5, 6
	• Prepare return home, re-enrollment in school, how mother and son are to interact re: curfew, friends, and other Rick's interests.
	Sessions 7, 8
	• Review, evaluate, plan forward.
7. Interview schedule	October 6, 13, 20, 27; November 3, 10, 17, 24
	4 P.M.
	Two months
8. Participants	Rick, mother, aunt, foster parents
9. Location	Agency office

REVISING THE CONTRACT

The written contract tends to become solidified and amending seems difficult. However, a written contract should be amended when it becomes more or less irrelevant. Revisions are needed when a good deal of change has taken place or when understanding of the situation has changed in some major way. Amendments can be made easily if the contract sticks to major items rather than great amounts of detail. For example, a contract should state that "Lester is to look for and rent housing," rather than "Lester is to read the housing advertisements in the *Daily Express* on Monday, Wednesday, and Friday, at 8 o'clock after breakfast." It is unnecessary, artificial, and burdensome to revise contracts for details.

OTHER CONTRACTUAL ACTIVITIES

In view of the endless possibilities that arise in real life, it is always necessary to take into account activities that need to be done but are not included in the basic contract recommendations of this book. The contract is a living document that is only useful to help organize, plan, and monitor the ongoing interventions. Many activities not specified here may need to be and should be included.

SUMMARY: BASIC ACTIONS

The contract is an agreement to work toward the reduction or alleviation of stated personal problems. Rapid early assessment can be used to make a practical working identification of the problem and the probable and feasible alternatives that could be expected to alleviate it. Contracts may be written or verbal, according to preference, although the written contract makes for a tighter planning process.

The contract covers major priority problems, goals, tasks, duration, schedules, participants, and location. The major communication to facilitate reaching an agreement with clients on what is to be done and thus included in the plan is: *What acts, if done first, will help most?*

There are numerous types of tasks. Their selection is a matter of individualization plus information about successful interventions from various professional sources and experience. Successful tasks tend to be those to which the client has a great deal of commitment and in which he has been as fully involved as possible in selecting and planning. Practitioner tasks are those the practitioner is committed to perform on the client's behalf. Client and practitioner tasks are stated in the contract.

Tasks should have a credible record of success in similar cases, be acceptable to all participants, and be efficient and as nonintrusive as possible. There should be a likelihood that the improvement obtained from task performance be generalizable and maintainable.

Task-centered sequences should be planned with time limits of two to three months. The number of interviews can be revised if necessary. Extensions should be made not whimsically but based on evidence of need and evidence that results can be reasonably anticipated.

REFERENCES

Epstein, L. (1985). *Talking and listening: A guide to the helping interview.* Columbus, OH: Merrill.

Ewalt, P.L. (1977). A psychoanalytically oriented child guidance clinic. In W. J. Reid & L. Epstein (Eds.), *Task-centered practice* (pp. 27–49). New York: Columbia University Press.

Fortune, A. E. (1985). Planning duration and termination of treatment. *Social Service Review 59*(4), 647–662.

Gambrill, E. (1983). *Casework: A competency-based approach.* Englewood Cliffs, NJ: Prentice-Hall.

Garfield, S. L. (1966). An eclectic psychotherapy. In J. C. Norcross (Ed.), *Handbook of eclectic psychotherapy* (pp. 132–162). New York: Brunner/Mazel.

Hofstad, M. O. (1977). Treatment in a juvenile court setting. In W. J. Reid & L. Epstein (Eds.), *Task-centered practice* (pp. 195–202). New York: Columbia University Press.

Kanter, J. S. (1983). Reevaluation of task-centered social work practice. *Clinical Social Work Journal, 11*(3), 228–244.

Levenstein, P., Kochman, P., & Roth, H. (1973). From laboratory to real world: Service delivery of the Mother-Child Home Program. *American Journal of Orthopsychiatry, 43,* 72–78.

Lidz, C. W., Meisel, A., Zerubavel, E., Carter, M., Sestak, R.M., & Roth, L.H. (1984). *Informed consent: A study of decision-making in psychiatry.* New York: The Guilford Press.

Maluccio, A. D., & Marlow, W. D. (1974). The case for the contract. *Social Work, 19,* 28–36.

McCarty, L. M. (1978). A protective service caseworker performance scale. *Child Welfare, 52*(3) 149–155.

Pinkston, E. M., Friedman, B. S., & Polster, R. P. (1981). Parents as agents of behavior change. In S. P. Schenke (Ed.), *Behavioral Methods in Social Welfare.* Hawthorne, NY: Aldine.

Reid, W. J. (1978). *The Task-centered system.* New York: Columbia University Press.

Reid, W. J., & Epstein, L. (1972). *Task-centered casework.* New York: Columbia University Press.

Rooney, R. H. (1978). Prolonged foster care: Toward a problem-oriented, task-centered practice model. (Doctoral dissertation, School of Social Service Administration, University of Chicago).

Rosen, A., Proctor, E. K., & Livne, S. (1985). Planning and direct practice. *Social Service Review, 59*(2), 161–177.

Rothery, M. A. (1980). Contracts and contracting. *Clinical Social Work Journal, 8*(3), 179–187.

Salmon, W. (1977). A service program in a state public welfare agency. In W. J. Reid & L. Epstein (Eds.), *Task-centered practice* (pp. 113–122). New York: Columbia University Press.

Sherman, E. A., Neuman, R., & Shyne, A. W. (1973). *Children adrift in foster care: A study of alternative approaches.* New York: Child Welfare League of America.

Stein, T., Gambrill, E., & Wiltse, K. T. (1977). Contracts and outcome in foster care. *Social Work, 22*(2), 148–149.

Thomas, E. J. (1984). *Designing interventions for the helping professions.* Beverly Hills: Sage.

CHAPTER
7

THIRD STEP

Problem Solving, Assessment, Task Achievement, and Problem Reduction

| Step 3 | **Problem solving: task achievement, problem reduction. Select as needed** |

Chapter 7

DEFINE AND SPECIFY TARGET PROBLEM (THREE MAXIMUM)

Restate and name the problem: the particular conditions and behaviors to be changed

Assess (related to target problem and goal)
• Target problem
  How often it occurs (frequency)
  Where it occurs (site)
  With whom (participants)
  What immediate antecedents (forerunners)
  What consequences (effects)
  What meaning (importance)
• Social context (social conditions precipitating and maintaining the problem)
  Work-school circumstances
  Economic status
  Family organization
  Peer group organization
  Housing state
  Cultural/ethnic background
• Cognitive-affective circumstances
  Client characteristics
  Mode of functioning
  Personal resources
• Other assessments

GENERATE ALTERNATIVES
• Find out and identify a feasible range of possible problem solving actions

NEGOTIATE SUPPORTIVE AND COLLABORATIVE ACTIONS OF OTHER PERSONS AND AGENCIES

DECISION MAKING (confirm goals, select what will be done, and design details of the intervention strategy)
• Re-affirm contract and goals
• Determine basic interventions
• Plan timing and sequence
• Select participants
• Get client agreement and understanding (informed consent)

FIGURE 7–1 Detail of map

• Get agreement and understanding of others

IMPLEMENT (carry out strategy)

Develop tasks

• Formulate tasks
• Get client understanding and agreement to tasks
• Get client understanding of rationale and incentives for tasks
• Summarize tasks
• Review expected difficulties
• Devise plans for client task performance
• Summarize tasks
• Devise plans for client task performance

Support task performance

• Review number of sessions outstanding
• Obtain and use resources
• Find out obstacles to resource provision
• Give instruction
• Give guidance
• Do simulations
• Do role plays, simulation, and guided practice
• Accompany client for modeling and/or advocacy
• Other
• Find out obstacles to task performance
  In the social environment: lack of resources, stress, discrimination, structural problems
  In the interpersonal transactions: deficit and conflict, lack of cooperation
  In the psychological state: fears, suspicions, lack of knowledge
• Plan actions to remove, reduce, alter obstacles
• Remedy practical barriers to task performance, e.g., lack of skills, lack of cooperation and support from others, and lack of resources
• Alleviate cognitive barriers to task performance: discuss fears, suspicions, lack of knowledge, adverse beliefs
• Plan and state practitioner tasks: inform client of practitioner tasks, review implementation of practitioner tasks, review problem state

Verify (check, test, confirm, substantiate probable effects of interventions) and
Monitor (record problem status regularly—use structured notations, charts, graphs, plus brief, succinct narrative comments)

FIGURE 7–1, continued

> **Revise contract,** or some parts of it, if:
> • Progress unsatisfactory
> • Progress exceeds expectations
> • New problems emerge
> • Problem takes on different characteristics
> • Tasks not performed, or poorly performed
> • Supports and resources ineffective
> • Practitioner tasks ineffective or not feasible

FIGURE 7–1, continued

This chapter will set out ways to put into effect ideas that have already been stated in theory in previous chapters. In Chapter 2, we described and discussed the nature and characteristics of individual and family problems. Chapter 3 explored a variety of approaches to problem solving. Chapter 5 dealt with methods for identifying problems and constructing the focus for problem solving attention. Chapter 6 explained how to construct plans and contracts that focus on problem reduction. This chapter depicts actions to achieve a reasonable amount of problem solving.

Most experts believe that corrective experiences during treatment develop problem-solving skills (Brown, 1977). Spivak, Platt, & Shure (1976) suggested that Jahoda (1953) made the earliest statement in the contemporary professional literature about the probable relationship between problem-solving thinking and personal adjustment.

It is widely assumed that intervention in human problems is problem solving. The idea of problem solving as the theme of intervention is not only useful but has achieved almost universal consensus. The task-centered practice model can be interpreted as a set of problem-solving techniques. The term problem solving is a neat way of capturing the theme of intervention. This term, *problem solving,* as used in this book, means a process of decreasing the frequency, quantity, and intensity of problems, or *problem-reduction* or *alleviation.*

Problem-solving should always take into account that increasing material or social resources activates and perpetuates problem solving; and, except in the most unusual circumstances, increases well-being. A single-minded concentration on psychological conditions in isolation or divorced from the social context is always inappropriate. The reverse, that is the single focus on the environmental and social context, is also wrong but is an error only infrequently made. It is wrong to attend only or primarily to what a client feels about a problem unless at the same time we find out and say what the problem is in the real world. It is wrong to lead a client into talking that does not connect to and does not result in some burdens lifted, some straightening out of lifelines, or some concrete benefit.

PROBLEM-SOLVING PROCESSES IN
_____ COMPLEX, NATURAL CIRCUMSTANCES _____

A basic framework for problem solving can be visualized in five parts.* Although these parts represent stages, the parts overlap continuously. However, they have a logic that is sequential. One part will tend to dominate at each sequential phase.

1. *General orientation.* The general orientation identifies the particular stresses that generated the problem: its social context; its environmental, interpersonal, and personal features; the beliefs, attitudes, feelings, meanings attributed to the problem; and the goals and resources available for problem reduction.

2. *Problem definition and formulation.* Problem definition and formulation refer to the detail and outline of the problem circumstances and actions and the statement of the problem in clear, concise language.

3. *Generation of alternative problem-solving strategies.* Generating alternatives means producing ideas about lines of action. The particular ideas called for are those that will probably reduce the problem.

4. *Decision-making selection of intervention strategy and tasks.* Decisions are predictions made based upon information and judgment. Decisions lay out the probable course that will be taken to achieve the desired goals and are necessary judgments in order to achieve movement in a case.

5. *Implementation.* Implementation means carrying out the strategy and verifying its outcome. This chapter concentrates on implementation.

_____ **IMPLEMENTING THE TASK-CENTERED MODEL** _____

The overall objective of the task-centered model is to put effort on those problems likely to be influenced by presently known methods. With the best will in the world, many human problems evade reduction. We do not know the answer to many problems. At the present level of knowledge, some problems are intractable.

In the task-centered model, the implementation phase (Step 3) uses most of the time. In the usual circumstance, implementation occurs during the time when interviews two through seven take place, assuming an eight-interview sequence. In a longer or shorter sequence, the implementation phase is the middle of the time planned for the case. The major objective of implementation

*Adapted from D'Zurilla & Goldfried, 1971; and Brown, 1977.

is to help clients achieve tasks. Problems are usually reduced and alleviated as tasks are achieved.

Refining the Problem

Implementation often starts with refining the problem definition and specification. This process is most likely to occur at the start of the third step and may be taken up periodically if the problem becomes vague or confused for either the practitioner or the client. Refining attempts to improve the target problem definition and specification by pruning and polishing, introducing subtleties and distinctions. Refining serves to confirm what has already been decided. Care should be used to confine exploration of the problem only to the extent that it will clarify exactly what problem is being worked on. If the matter is already sufficiently clear, more exploration is unnecessary.

_____ ASSESSMENT IN THE THIRD STEP _____

Characteristics

Previously we have discussed rapid early assessment in the first step (Chapter 5) and working assessment for contracting in the second step (Chapter 6). These assessments are sufficient to launch the case and may be sufficient to anchor the third implementation step. Nevertheless, in complex, natural circumstances aspects of a case may appear enigmatic, equivocal, or obscure. Rather than engage in broad extensive exploration, it is preferable to conduct a planned and bounded exploration (if deemed necessary) constrained to the present problems for which the interventions are to occur.

Assessment is a judgment of use to practitioners and may have considerable effect on clients. It may result in a more knowledgeable and expert professional understanding that will help a practitioner design the most productive interventions. Assessment can be a positive experience for a client by sifting out and clarifying what are the parts of the problem situation and how that situation exerts its influence on her. Assessment that is overly concentrated on only one aspect of a situation, ignoring other potentially important aspects, will be distorted.

Assessment and Diagnosis Compared

Assessment is a judgment, an opinion, or an appraisal of the problem made for the purpose of understanding and interpreting it. Diagnosis may include the same information, but it is primarily concerned with recognizing disease from its symptoms. In many practice settings we are not dealing with disease, but rather with routine to extreme problems in living. Illness may or may not be present, and it may or may not be a focus of intervention. Present-day culture tends toward belief in psychic determination, interpreting problems in living as symptoms of disease, identifying those problems as mental illness, developmental arrests, deficits, disorganization, emotional turbulence or disorder. There is overlap in the concepts of assessment and diagnosis. Their differential use is related to whether or not we view problems in living as medical issues, or the degree to which we medicalize social deviance and disadvantage. Both the assessment intent and the diagnosis intent are present at the same time in many case situations.

Ordinarily, neither an assessment nor a clinical diagnosis will indicate what the treatment or intervention should be. Clinical diagnosis of psychopathology does not prescribe treatment. It defines and describes disease. Both assessment and clinical diagnosis provide some explanations of the problem and imply some or a range of interventions that may be appropriate and others that may be irrelevant or contraindicated.

Target Problem Assessment

Some regularly recurring circumstances suggest elaborating assessment in the third step. The target problem may seem to slip or slide out of place in the focus. The details may become vague, contradictory, inconsistent, or not properly connected to the intervention plan and tasks. There may develop an uncertainty about how to proceed with the problem and/or situation. The problem may be defined as mental illness or social dysfunction and become subject to mental health intervention or medical diagnosis and classification. Given any or all of these circumstances, a prudent judgment would be to conduct limited and focused elaboration of the existing assessment with concentration on tightening up the details, meaning, and ramifications of the target problem. The kind of assessment that has been useful for understanding the client's problem in task-centered practice answers the following questions:

- ☐ *What is the target problem?* The problem identification, description, specification, name
- ☐ *What is the frequency?* How often does the target problem occur? When does it occur?
- ☐ *With whom?* Who are the participants?
- ☐ *Where?* What is the site?
- ☐ *With what antecedents or consequences?* What happens before and afterward?
- ☐ *In what context?* What are the significant conditions?
- ☐ *In what cognitive-affective situation?* What is the mental state of the person?

EXAMPLES OF ASSESSMENT

Mrs. F

Mrs. F found a lump in her breast four weeks ago. She became afraid she might have cancer and need surgery. She worried constantly and could not rest or sleep well, regardless of who was with her or where she was. She became fatigued, overwhelmed, confused, and anxious. She procrastinated for two weeks, trying unsuccessfully to ignore the matter. She finally saw a doctor who confirmed her worst fears. While not definitely making the diagnosis of cancer, the doctor recommended that Mrs. F enter the hospital for a biopsy. Mrs. F is a single mother who supports herself and two young children doing low-skilled sales work in a local grocery. The work is physically exhausting with long hours and compels her to make precarious child care arrangements that are too costly for her meager income. She has been so tired and chronically overwhelmed that she has no personal life or social life to speak of, having little to do even with her mother and sisters who live in the same city but at quite a distance. Her affections are totally directed to her two children and she is an excellent mother. She attends church but is not involved in activities; she has made a few acquaintances but no friends. The co-workers at the store are her real support group, but her relations with them are confined to the workplace and do not extend into her personal or home life. Mrs. F is a hardworking, decent person with limited education and narrow interests. She is a sturdy problem solver in ordinary mundane matters. She was deserted by an alcoholic, brutal husband three years ago and picked herself up, found a job of sorts, and has made do. Faced with the terror of a life-threatening cancer and a significant bodily mutilation, she has become thoroughly disorganized and depressed.

☐ ☐ ☐

Mrs. G

Mrs. G is worried and resentful that her only son Arthur, 12, hits her in the stomach and on the face. In the past year he has done this about six times, always when they are at home alone. The last time was a week ago. Arthur hit his mother right after she yelled at him to stop being so curious about a girl. She ran into her bedroom and slammed the door after this last incident, and Arthur ran out of the house. Mrs. G is excitable, speaks in a loud, frenetic tone of voice, and is probably given to exaggeration. She says, for example, that Arthur is "always" and "constantly" hitting her when in fact these attacks are infrequent but very disturbing. Mrs. G is extremely perturbed about Arthur's developing a strong interest in girls and regards this as a bad sign. Her husband vanished years ago. She has no relatives locally and is estranged from her siblings in a distant city. She is not a churchgoer. She receives support from the

welfare department, has no skills, does not work, and has never worked. She
seems to have no interests except Arthur, but she is very worried about him. He
does poorly in school and is inattentive, but he plays satisfactorily with the other
boys his own age in the neighborhood. Lately he has become sullen and
constantly alert to girls, making lewd remarks about them, and Mrs. G has no
idea where this behavior comes from. She is really frantic about what to do with
Arthur.

Baselining and Assessment

Baselining helps to understand the problem in detail and design relevant
interventions. The techniques of baselining have been developed in the field of
behavior modification and are thoroughly explicated in its literature such as the
recent text by Gambrill (1983). Getting a baseline is getting an accurate account
of the frequency, intensity, and characteristics of the problem. A baseline can
answer many assessment questions. A baseline is a necessity if there is to be an
empirical evaluation of progress or change.

Ordinarily, baseline information is obtained after the problems have been
decided on and the contract has been made. The baseline may be the first
implementation act. However, a baseline can be taken earlier if it will help make
the target problem more specific. Baselines may be current or retrospective. For
the current baseline to be concrete and useful, it should give accurate
information about how things are.

The common ways of getting current baselines are direct observation and
logging. *Direct observation* requires the practitioner to be present when and
where the problem occurs and to keep a record of observations in a systematic
way. If it is possible for another reliable person to make observations, the
objectivity of the information may increase. *Logging* involves the practitioner,
client, or outside observer keeping a record. Logging one's own situation can
shed light on a problem and often leads a client to generate a change strategy
quickly.

To generate a retrospective baseline, the practitioner leads a client to think
back in time and to offer examples from memory about frequency, site,
antecedents, consequences, and meaning of the problem. A retrospective
baseline imposes some form on the assessment and at times may be the only
information available. People are not necessarily accurate informants about
details of their problems. Their information is influenced by lapses and
distortions of memory, their moods, and their beliefs about the kind of
information a practitioner and agency think is acceptable. Retrospective baselines
may be improved by collateral information from other sources. Although those
sources may be biased and inaccurate, a retrospective baseline is probably better
than none.

EXAMPLE

A Baseline in a Natural Setting: Tina

Tina, a 22-year-old woman, has two children, four and six. She has no husband and is on welfare. The agency provided her with training as a typist. For two months she has been employed in a large firm as a clerk-typist, her first job. The agency secured daycare for the 4-year-old. Tina's mother provides after-school baby-sitting in her own home for both children.

Tina gets up at 5 A.M. to do housework, prepare meals, take one child to the daycare center and the other to her mother's. Then she travels 45 minutes to work. She is already frazzled when she gets there. After work she picks up the children, eats, puts on the TV, and collapses.

Tina's supervisor reported to the job program office that Tina is in danger of being fired. The work she does is satisfactory, but she is not energetic and she causes trouble. Called in by the counselor, Tina disposes of the lack of energy problem; there is nothing she can do about it because she is legitimately exhausted by her schedule. Tina does not want to be fired. She admits that she cannot restrain herself from insulting her supervisor and fellow employees. This is the trouble she causes. She says she is "too mouthy," and she would like to cut that out. The goal of the contract is to reduce the frequency of her insults to her supervisor and the others.

Initial exploration and retrospective baseline information result in complications. Tina says that her boss and the others treat her as if she were "invisible," meaning unworthy. Meanwhile she observes other employees making mistakes and goofing off. That gets her goat because she tries so hard. Her boss does not like her because she fails to "con" her with compliments and gratitude the way the others do. She does not think her supervisor has very good judgment.

She suspects the supervisor holds her job because of friendship with "big-wigs" in the company. Tina is always so tired and so offended that she constantly blurts out insults to all of them. She rages inside about their disrespect toward her.

At the start of Step 3, Tina agreed to keep a log daily, for 10-minute intervals at critical times in the day's work flow from 8:30 to 8:40, from 10:15 to 10:25, from 1:30 to 1:40, and from 4:00 to 4:10. (See Table 7-1.)

Her log showed that Tina insulted two people and did not insult two. Each insulting statement was preceded by a need to work on someone else's papers. With this assessment, the problem was cut down to size. Being "too mouthy" became "mouthing off at certain people who usually give me bad work to follow up."

TABLE 7–1 Tina's log (simplified)

Time	What I said	To whom	Where	What happened
8:30–8:40	Your papers are illegible.	Corinne	Corinne's desk	She cried and complained to other workers.
10:15–10:25	Talked about TV show.	Betty	Coffee room	She was nice.
1:30–1:40	Bad food at lunch	Betty	My desk	She sympathized.
4:00–4:10	Corinne and Helen don't fill out forms right.	Supervisor	Supervisor's desk	She glared; said I should mind my own business.

Usefulness of baseline information

A baseline gives an estimate of the frequency, magnitude, duration, antecedents, and consequences of specified events and behaviors. It reveals whether or not a problem is sufficiently important to warrant intervention, and what is important about it. It provides data from which to measure change or nonchange.

Baselining in complex problem conditions

A baseline can be obtained when the target problem is a person's behavior, for example, insulting the boss, fighting with other children or a spouse. There are, however, no techniques for baselining a many-faceted problem condition. Many target problems are bad social conditions; for example, a mother does not have custody of her children; an elderly person does not have an adequate home; someone has been refused care at a mental health clinic; or a parent has been refused privileges to visit the children. These conditions call for accurate identification of the problem condition, that is, the negative combination of circumstances or state of affairs.

Some complex conditions containing many parts and many persons acting in relation to one another can be baselined by selection. If some crucial behavior can be isolated and if changing this behavior can alter the situation, then a baseline can be taken. If the condition is too complex for taking a baseline of distinct behaviors, exact information should be obtained about the important facets of the condition.

Assessment of Social Context

The social context is comprised of the physical environment, the social network, the socioeconomic condition, culture, ethnicity, neighborhood and community, and macrosystems such as the national economy and the driving priorities of the politics of the time. All these elements should be considered together in relation to what impact they have on the client, how they influence what the client thinks, believes, values, and wants, and what opportunities and deprivations are the client's lot because of her particular niche in the social system.

Many unsolved technical problems seriously impede the ability of the helping professions to adequately incorporate assessment of social context into a practical and useful assessment. The variables seem too numerous and too diverse; there are too many varying definitions of concepts and development of theory is uneven. However, particular segments of the social context can be judged to be precipitating and maintaining problems. If these influences can be identified and understood, they can then pinpoint an area or areas of the social context amenable to change that can improve the client's situation directly. A gross appraisal of the social context often suggests a relevant selection from among all the conditions and actors. Only those sectors that are judged most relevant to the problem should be selected for a focused exploration.

Here is list and brief characterization of the conditions that are highly important in analyzing the social context of a client's immediate problem. A full exposition of meaning and issues involved in the social context is beyond the scope of this book, and the reader is well-advised to consult specialized works usually classified under the field of "human behavior and the social environment" (Anderson & Carter, 1984; Berger & Federico, 1982; Johnson, 1980).

1. *Work-school circumstances.* Work is central in the lives of most adults because it provides economic independence, status, family stability, and the opportunity to interact with other people in the most basic activity of society. Unemployment restricts or eliminates work opportunities, and dissatisfying work incurs severe negative repercussions in individual lives and in the social order. School plays the same role for children and youth as work does for adults. If school is repugnant, frightening, uninteresting, and unattractive, school problems will emerge and do a good deal of damage.

2. *Health care circumstances.* Ill health and inadequate health care undermine the well-being of many people. Illness itself creates immense problems that are compounded for those who may not have access to good care or who may not know how to negotiate their way through a cumbersome system for locating and funding health care.

3. *Economic status.* Educational attainment, occupational pursuit, family income, and occupational background of parents combine to depict economic status or, more properly, socioeconomic status. An individual's place in society cannot be characterized adequately by reference to any one single feature of this group of conditions. Nevertheless, lower levels of socioeconomic status are often closely associated with individuals having less control over their environments and living conditions and give rise to disaffection and an absence of well-being.

4. *Family organization.* It is widely believed that individual problems can be understood in relation to the nature and organization of the family system in which the individual is embedded. It is frequently possible to note and intervene in dysfunctional family relations that maintain a problem. Indicators of trouble in the family can be located by observing or becoming informed about power arrangements, hierarchies, communication patterns, exploitation and abusive patterns, dependence and independence, financial arrangements, handling of conflicts and crises, and problem-solving patterns.

5. *Peer group organization.* The circle of a person's friends provides support and nurture, help and intimacy, and closeness and comfort. An individual's social circle can also be an embarrassment, a source for envy and jealousy, for undermining one's strength and ambition, or for acquiring destructive modes of living such as excessive use of drugs and credit cards.

6. *Housing state.* Decent housing is a source of comfort and strength. Living in unsanitary conditions, in ugly or overcrowded surroundings, or in unsafe and unsavory neighborhoods is an inducement to poor mental health.

7. *Cultural/ethnic background.* A client's cultural and ethnic background is a major determinant of her values, norms, expectations, and reactions to crises and other problems. Substantial personal, interpersonal, and political turbulence today stems from varying culturally determined beliefs, from differential access to wealth and power, from unemployment and lack of opportunity. These areas are sources of considerable maladjustment in personal lives.

Starting from the gross exploration of the social context, the assessment of social context attempts to judge what factors in the environment and in the problem situation are precipitating and maintaining the problem. However, the social context is a source of strength and help as well as often a source of trouble. The positive elements should be identified as carefully as the negative ones. A comfortable apartment or house, moderately understanding relatives and friends, interested teachers and authorities, moderately good health, basically adequate income with health insurance and access to credit, individual talents and interests—all these add up to opportunities, latent or overt, that can be called on to aid problem solving.

Proceeding from the earlier exploration of the gross features of the social context, assessment at the start of the third step helps make a more specific judgment and is thus an aid to intervention. The practitioner may conclude that some feature of the social context is precipitating or perpetuating the problem.

This assessment leads to the development of an intervention strategy that will concentrate on influencing and changing the conditions of the social context. Having such a social context assessment gives the practitioner the ability to give advice and make recommendations about actions to the client, referral sources, family members, and other agencies. On the other hand, an assessment of the social context can lead to the conclusion that the social context factors cannot be changed. That judgment is also the basis for advising the client and attempting an alternative strategy.

Assessment of Cognitive-affective Circumstances: Client Characteristics and Mode of Functioning

The client's personal resources and cognitive-affective traits are summed up and revealed in her presentation of herself to others and her perception of herself within the privacy of her own mind. These characteristics make the statement about who she is and where she came from. A client's personality and modes of functioning are shaped by her biological equipment, upbringing and education, habits, and expectations and views of herself, other people, and social institutions arising from ethnic background, culture, social class, personal traits, values, and circumstances. Personal resources and traits reveal themselves in such attributes as mood, intelligence, affective life, and modes of thought.

An assessment of the client and her functioning can be organized by using the observations made about the client during the initial exploration (Step 1, Chapter 5) and adding other related information. The practitioner draws a conclusion and makes a judgment about the client's talents and capabilities, personal inadequacies, and style or pattern of conduct. This assessment gives a practitioner some clues to understanding what the client may do to precipitate or exacerbate the problem and what potentials and limits there are for personal change, that is, change in the client's characteristics, traits, life style, patterns of interpersonal relating, problem solving, and cognition.

The personal assessment process lends itself to overuse of psychiatric examinations and psychological tests. Such examinations and tests are required in many settings and may produce informative, valuable, and useful information. The criterion for referral for specialized diagnosis is that the client's actions are extremely odd or not understandable, or show sensational contrasts or striking incongruities. Such clients may be helped or protected by being directed into the psychiatric treatment stream of intervention. If there is a real possibility clients will be helped or adequately protected, such resources should be used. A clinical diagnosis may help the practitioner design an intervention strategy. The service delivery system may require extensive use of psychological and psychiatric assessment procedures because of the increasing tendency for treatment resources to be concentrated in the mental health stream of services.

Other Possible Assessments

Other areas, in individual instances, may be helpful in rounding out an assessment.

Causal explanations

In our science-oriented society we seek causal explanations. Real knowledge about causation of social and behavioral events is weak. Various theories try to identify causation, but ordinarily these theories are difficult to apply to problem-solving undertakings. The American Psychiatric Association's *Diagnostic and Statistical Manual of Mental Disorders* (*DSM III*), for instance, explains that it adopts a descriptive rather than an etiological approach to describing diagnostic entities because for "most of the *DSM III* disorders the etiology is unknown" (1980, pp. 6–7).

Nevertheless, people often want explanations of the origin or fundamental basis of their problems to obtain a cognitive map of their lives, to provide boundaries, to simplify a condition, and to reduce it to manageable proportions. A working explanation of causation can be obtained from the client's reflections and from the practitioner's and agency's knowledge and experiences. Although underlying problems are sometimes apparent or discernable, they are often obscure, and explanations are based on ideological grounds. An explanation of problems based on common sense, experience, or up-to-date research, if available, provides usable explanations. A rough working explanation is what is needed. People who want a greater self-understanding should locate practitioners rigorously trained in the art of developing self-understanding: psychoanalysts, advanced social workers or other therapists with special expertise, philosophers, or wise religious people.

Past problem solving explanations

A moderate amount of information about what the client has recently done to try to solve the problem can be helpful, providing history taking of too broad scope is avoided. Recent past problem solving provides information about possible tasks to do and to avoid. If a target problem is chronic, the past three to six months provides adequate information on which to make an assessment.

Past history

The history of how the problem developed may be limited to broad information about prior occurrences, duration, and fluctuations in its course. Ordinarily the history of a problem is of interest in explaining a problem but does not contribute much to organizing present problem-solving tasks. That the problem is old does not by itself predict the difficulty of present problem solving. However, an old and obdurate problem will have established habits in the client, in her social network, and among social agencies that are hard to change.

_____ **GENERATING ALTERNATIVES** _____

As we buckle down to serious focused work on reducing the problems, we need to find out and identify a feasible range of possible problem-solving actions. The source of alternative actions or tasks are the client's own experience, the practitioner's personal and professional experience, and professional and technical literature and other expert information.

Practitioner and client develop alternatives in discussion that is open ended at first and narrowed thereafter to get one answer, or preferably several answers, to two questions.

The first question is addressed to the client: *What kinds of things could you do to tackle this problem?*

The second question is addressed to the practitioner: *What can I do to help the client tackle this problem?*

The practitioner has to clarify and shape these alternatives into understandable form. Important persons and officials in the client's social network should also be asked what actions they should, can, and will take. As far as possible, what these other persons and agencies suggest should be pinned down and discussed with the client.

NEGOTIATING SUPPORTIVE AND COLLABORATIVE _____ **ACTIONS OF OTHER PERSONS AND AGENCIES** _____

In Chapter 4, which discussed the start-up phase, negotiating strategy for achieving consensus among collaborating agencies was recommended. In the implementation phase of the task-centered model, there may be need to renegotiate with agencies because the original agreement may have deteriorated or because new developments may have recast the situation. The implementation phase may also require the practitioner to actively negotiate with private individuals who seem to be in a position to help the client perform tasks through instruction, direction, modeling, encouragement, clarification of situations, and other innumerable types of support. Individuals in potentially supportive positions include relatives, friends, neighbors, teachers, physicians, ministers, landlords, and employers.

It is not easy to construct supportive networks among others who are busy and preoccupied with their own lives or who are fearful of getting involved because of potential deleterious effects. On the other hand, their friendship, advice, encouragement, and relief of pressures may be valuable to the client. This is particularly the case if one or several of these persons are the source of pressure being felt by the client who needs and may deserve relief. The direct intervention of the practitioner may have beneficial effects beyond what the client can do for herself.

Practitioners can consult in person with those involved in conflicts related to the target problems. This may successfully decrease pressures, particularly by locating what it is about the client that is precipitating and maintaining the interpersonal problem. If a process of reciprocity can be started, and if the significant other persons can perceive a potential personal benefit to accrue from helping the client, it may be possible to negotiate a series of exchanges in which the client makes certain desired concessions in return for what he can get from the other. The reverse process may also obtain; the client may give in certain areas in order to get the obvious benefits from the other person.

____ DECISION MAKING: GOALS AND INTERVENTIONS ____

The preliminary decision making will have been done already in the making of the contract. (See Chapter 6). At this stage, those understandings should be confirmed and changes made if necessary. Discussion of the preliminary decisions often will produce commitment on some aspects of the contract. In some areas, however, new and revised goals and actions may be considered and approved. Out of the alternatives generated, choices should be made. The choices are the result of considering what is known to be an effective or reasonable program to reduce the target problem, what is within the resources of the client and agency, and what is perceived by the client to be most suitable. The ability to identify the most promising interventions is the result of professional study, practical experience, supervision and consultation.

The assessment information indicates what is within the client's social and personal resources. Agency rules, regulations, expectations, and norms outline what resources the agency has or can readily acquire. What is perceived by the client as actions in her interest for which she is willing to work is known already from the first and second step discussions, that is, from the initial targeting of the problems and the initial contracting.

Substantial clarity is needed to ascertain that the goal is feasible, meaning capable of being done or carried out. The goal should follow the results of assessment in being within the client's abilities and resources and within the agency's ability, mission, and style. There must be a body of practice knowledge that explains and directs intervention. At the same time, care must be taken not to select trivial goals because they are thought to be easy or mechanical goals because they are thought to lend themselves to concreteness. Goals have to be significant for affecting the client's situation in thoroughly meaningful ways.

The product of these choices is the intervention strategy, which consists of a list of actions to be taken, when they should be taken, in what order, and by whom. It is of the highest importance that the client know and understand the strategy. It is equally significant that important others be well-informed so that their reluctance is neutralized and their support obtained.

—————————————— INFORMED CONSENT ——————————————

The doctrine of informed consent holds that practitioners of the helping disciplines should disclose to the client information about the content and probable consequences of interventions, as a matter of right, as an ethical act, and as a means for promoting individual autonomy and encouraging rational decision-making. Research evidence suggests that well-informed clients who participate maximally in decisions about their treatment are likely to be those who make the most effective use of treatment.

In the practice of medicine, the doctrine of informed consent is so well-established that it is sometimes possible for clients to sue and collect damages if the procedures for informed consent were not appropriately followed. In the practices of helping professionals who are not physicians, the legal implications are not definite. However, the nonmedical professions are attracted to the doctrine of informed consent on ethical grounds and because of its value in motivating genuine client participation. The process of pursuing informed consent consists of

☐ providing the client with ample and adequate information about what will be done and why
☐ providing ample opportunity for the client to ask questions, get answers, and discuss concerns in a serious and responsible atmosphere
☐ repeating, amplifying, or correcting the information as needed

Lidz et al. (1984) published the first comprehensive empirical study of decision making among psychiatric patients in three distinct psychiatric settings—an outpatient clinic, an inpatient hospital, and an evaluation center. Although the findings varied somewhat from setting to setting, overall actual practice showed that the doctrine of informed consent was only slightly in evidence.

It appeared that staff communicated information not so much to ensure that clients were well informed but rather to gain their compliance with decisions that were already determined by the nature of the service delivery system and the particular training of the professional groups involved. The research also revealed that patients were not inclined to be the primary decision-makers in these circumstances.

The work reported by Lidz et al. shows that there are many issues about the processes of securing informed consent. Routine signing by clients of abstract and obscure expectations without clear notions of their practicality and the means of their achievement probably represent the form but not the substance of informed consent. Clearly, more attention needs to be paid to this subject by the professions and agencies. The values involved are fundamental ones that have important consequences for achieving successful intervention.

OVERLAP OF PROCESSES

The third step overlaps with the first step (target problem identification) and with the second step (contract and planning). Studies of the processes of task-centered practice reveal that practitioners do in fact overlap these steps through a process of repeating the initial exploration (Basso, 1986; Reid, 1978; Rzepnicki, 1982). For the sake of efficiency, the overlap of processes should be minimized, but not at the expense of clearing up important questions. There should be no hesitation about overlap if needed to clear up uncertainties.

IMPLEMENTING THE INTERVENTION STRATEGY

Developing Tasks

The basic rules for planning tasks were explained in Chapter 6 in connection with the initial statement of general tasks for the contract. During the middle phase, implementation, new tasks can be expected to be developed as movement or its absence occurs. In evolving and expanding tasks, the basic rules in Chapter 6 continue to apply. In addition, additional work is done so that the client gets as much help as possible in carrying out her tasks. The object is to develop tasks that have a reasonable possibility of being performed.

Supporting Task Performance

A great deal of the implementation is devoted to supporting task performance, that is, to obtaining and using resources, showing the client how to accomplish the tasks, finding out what obstacles are in the way of good performance, removing, reducing, or altering those obstacles, finding remedies for practical barriers to task performance, alleviating cognitive barriers, and judiciously using practitioner tasks to move the activity along. Guidelines for increasing the probability that a client will carry out tasks include: ensuring the client's understanding, establishing incentives, establishing rationales, anticipating difficulties, summarizing tasks, and devising concrete tasks.

Client understanding   Enough discussion time needs to be allowed to ensure that the client understands and agrees to the tasks. Tasks should not be assigned without a discussion that obtains genuine, or at least tentative, consent. It is common for the practitioner to suggest tasks; however, good client performance can be expected only if the client is committed to the actions.

Clients can be directed when they ask what to do, and clients do ask this question often. If the practitioner knows what the clients should do, he may say, for example, "What I suggest is . . . ." Clients can be expected to change or contradict these suggestions.

Incentives Establish incentives for task completion. The client needs to believe that the effort is worthwhile and that it will alleviate the problem. For example, "Talking to the children about your health problem will be stressful, but it will calm their imaginary fears."

Rationale Establish the rationales for the task work. There must be an understanding of a compelling reason why the difficulties of task work should even be attempted. For example, "I have to do these things in order to live through the distress of my illness and be in a position to resume some kind of normal life later, even if I am left handicapped and disfigured."

Expectable difficulties Anticipate expectable difficulties. Raise, discuss, and elicit the client's fears about obstacles that she will encounter working on tasks. Sift out what is probably real and not real. Reassure the client maximally but do not mislead her.

Summarize tasks At regular intervals, particularly at the conclusion of an important discussion or at the end of an interview, summarize briefly and concisely what exactly is going to be done in the next immediate time period. This process seems to be beneficial in pinning the tasks down in memory and attention.

Devising plans for client task performance Discuss plans in a manner as detailed as necessary to make concrete outlines of what the client needs to do, when, where, and with whom. With some clients and some tasks, the client's own capability and initiative will make it possible to be brief about this step. However, when the client lacks information and is fearful and inexperienced, this step may need to go into exhaustive detail.

Provide resources

Weissman's (1976) research on linkage technology offers a methodology for linking clients with resources. This methodology can be outlined as follows.

Locate and select the appropriate community resources To accomplish this activity, an agency must have extensive up-to-date lists of available resources. Knowledge of the caliber of those services is also needed. The practitioner needs to be able to describe and explain to the client the characteristics of the resources and how the particular agencies operate. He should also provide the client with an evaluation of the quality of the resources. The client is then in a position to make an informed choice among the possible resources and to have some idea of what can reasonably be expected. Weighing the advantages and disadvantages of either course the client may also opt for not using the resources. Most often, the client will seek and should be given the practitioner's opinion of the usefulness and drawbacks to using the resource.

Connect client to resources firmly   Obtaining a good connection between client and resource is where many such efforts fail (Kirk & Greenley, 1974). It is often assumed that there is or should be a fit between what the client needs and what the resource can do. This assumption, however, is often illusory. Various connection techniques have been described.

1. Simple directions: Directing means writing out the name and address of the resource, how to get an appointment, transportation directions, and basic expectations about what the resource can be expected to provide. Simple direction appears to effect a connection when clients already know what they need but have not known how to locate the resource.
2. Directions plus a name: This technique adds to the directions the name of a person to contact.
3. Providing a letter of introduction: The practitioner can add a brief written statement, read and approved by the client, describing the problem and what the client would like done.
4. Facilitating with phone calls: In addition to or as a substitute for the foregoing, the client makes the phone call to contact the resource from the referring practitioner's office. The practitioner assists, if necessary, by making the call and turning it over to the client.
5. Facilitating in-person contacts: The practitioner may accompany the client to the other agency or may request a relative or friend to go with the client.
6. Cementing the connection: These are techniques for assuring that the connection will get results.

☐ Check-back. The client reports back to the practitioner on the effects of contact with the resource immediately after the initial connection.
☐ Persisting. The practitioner contacts the client at frequent intervals to find out what is taking place.
☐ Interspersing. The referring practitioner has an in-person contact with the client both before and after interviews with the resource.
☐ Monitoring. The referring practitioner monitors the resource provision at interviews scheduled for that purpose or during regularly scheduled interviews.

Weissman's preliminary findings in his study of the effectiveness of these techniques suggests that most referrals in the setting studied (industrial social work) were successful. The simpler techniques were effective when the target problems involved obtaining legal, financial, and health resources. Complex social-environmental and mental health problems required the most elaborate of the techniques.

Find out obstacles to providing resources   Obviously some resources are in short supply and not easily obtained. Slowness of resource procurement and meagerness of resources can create substantial obstacles to task performance. The best substitute available will have to be used. Clients sometimes need advice, instruction, and guidance in how best to use resources, once obtained.

Showing clients how to do tasks: Teaching through instruction, simulation, and guided practice   The practitioner should inform the client about conditions she does not know about or understand, the people she will be dealing with, the expectations of others, the location and structure of places she will be encountering, and the normative behaviors that will be expected by other people.

   Instruction of various types is the main technique for showing clients how to perform tasks and includes imparting information, giving training in skills, and furnishing direction.

   Didactic instruction is systematic imparting of information a client needs to act in the most effective manner. For example,

> "I can see from what has already happened that you need a lot of information about how to deal with your husband's anger. We have decided already that you will start a conversation with him as soon as he comes home in the evening. The conversation will be about what was good and bad in his day at the shop. Let me go over the kinds of things you could say and what would be important to him. You already know that there is a lot of talk about the plant's closing down or moving South. That worry is on his mind all the time. You could start out with, 'I'm glad you're home. What's the news today about what they are going to do with the plant? Any new gossip?' Since it will be a novelty for your husband to hear that from you, you could expect a grumpy response."

This kind of instruction will be interspersed with the client's reactions and further instructions to handle those reactions.

   Another type of instruction is role playing and simulation. The practitioner can set up a stage where the client rehearses actions to carry out the tasks. The practitioner, for example, can act the husband while the wife tries out the tasks. Role playing provides a vivid means to learn skills and also to find out obstacles to task performance. Role playing is easy with children. With adults it is possible but should be avoided if either the client or practitioner is embarrassed.

   Guided practice can occur in an interview where the problem is played out in the session. Practitioners can guide the client by modeling, for example, preferred behavior toward a child, spouse, or relative. Family quarrels often occur in an interview. The practitioner can intervene with suggestions and create discussions to clear up misunderstandings and wrongdoing. Practitioners can accompany clients to see landlords, lawyers, judges, and relatives to show and teach clients how to handle troublesome affairs. Guidance of this kind should be partial; that is, it should concentrate on a few key actions. Clients should not be hindered from following their own bent and style, nor should their confidence be undermined. They should never be denied advice available.

Accompanying the client. When necessary the practitioner can accompany the client and directly help her in performances that are difficult or where the practitioner has expert knowledge that can come immediately to the client's aid.

Other ways to support task performance

1. Work toward task achievement in increments. Break tasks down into parts and attend to the easiest first and the more difficult ones later. Care should be taken not to underestimate the client. However, it is easier to raise the demand from simple to more complex so as to generate success than to go backward after failure.
2. Devise any necessary plans to help clients perform tasks. Plans can be detailed or simple, entirely depending on what the client needs. If a client's fear, inexperience, or lack of knowledge is substantial, plans should be as detailed as needed.
3. Summarize the plans for task performance often, especially whenever there is a new phase.
4. Review task performance regularly in a systematic way. Keep understandable and simple notes on task performance. Agency resources can be developed to keep uniform records (measurements) of task performance.

    Task review begins with an inquiry about what the client has been able or unable to do since the last session. Complete, substantial, or satisfactory performance should be credited and put aside. Then proceed to the circumstances that stood in the way of performance and the identification and analysis of barriers.
5. Review time limits and number of sessions remaining, a simple and straightforward matter that causes difficulties only if it is not done.
6. What to do in an unexpected difficulty. Strongly advise the client how to slow down, stay cool, temporize, procrastinate, evade, and avoid unexpected difficulties. Advise her to take time to think, and to consult the practitioner or others. Persuade her that if she feels relatively sure, she can and should act.

Obstacles to Task Performance: What to Do If Tasks Do Not Get Done

There is no way to ensure that all clients will work on all tasks and be successful. It is, however, a reasonable expectation that most clients will work and that most, but not all, will be successful. There is enough evidence in the numerous trials of the task-centered model to be optimistic about outcomes. Generally satisfactory performance on tasks is correlated with satisfactory problem alleviation, although this relationship is not perfect. Obstacles to task performance arise in three overlapping areas:

☐ In the social environment. Obstacles in the social environment will appear as lack of resources, stress precipitated by external pressures (such as sudden illness, job loss, failure at some undertaking, loss of loved one, attack), pervasive discrimination, or dysfunctional structural problems in the social environment (such as epidemic, failures of the economic system to provide employment, poor schools, and the like).

☐ In interpersonal transactions. Personal relationships may lack necessary intimacy, security, reinforcements, and cooperation. There may be not only deficits in these necessary relationships but also substantial conflict among the persons most important the client.

☐ In the psychological state. Obstacles to task performance may reside within the mind or reflect the inner psychological state of the individual. Prominent among such obstacles are unwarranted fears and suspicions of others that nevertheless have a strong influence on how the client perceives herself in the world.

Reasons for a good deal of low task performance

1. *The client lacks concrete resources to facilitate task work.* Examples of necessary sustaining resources are money, medical and psychiatric care, adequate housing, adequate work and school, or adequate child care provided by relatives, homemakers, or day care.

2. *The client lacks necessary reinforcements from other persons such as family members, peers, or authorities.* Those other important persons may be estranged, uncaring, hostile, oppressive, or exploitative, or they may be unable to help the client because of their own problems.

3. *The client lacks skills, and does not know how to do the task work.* She may be painfully awkward or may have only enough skill to perform incompletely or erratically.

4. *The client has adverse beliefs.* Her beliefs may lead her to thinking that the tasks have little value or will have negative consequences. She may be afraid of taking the task actions.

5. *The client lacks capacity for task performance.* There may be some incapacity to make attempts. She may misunderstand the task.

6. *The practitioner may be biased and unskilled.*

Guidelines for overcoming obstacles

Removing, reducing, or altering obstacles demands that a systematic plan be developed to remedy the practical barriers to task performance, e.g., lacks of skills, lack of cooperation and support from others, or lack of resources. The plan should include alleviating cognitive barriers to task performance through discussion and counseling regarding fears, suspicions, lack of knowledge, and adverse beliefs.

Listed here are some specific explanations for clients' low task performance as well as some specific guidelines that are frequently applicable for alleviating these obstacles to performance. The practitioner will need to exercise judgment in particular circumstances.

Lack of concrete resources   The practitioner procures the resources at once by ordering them, if that is possible, or by using the referral techniques discussed earlier. If necessary resources are not immediately available or accessible, the client should be instructed to withstand delay. Alternative resources should also be developed. At worst, the client should be helped, as best one can, to tolerate and relinquish expectation of the resource. However, if a genuinely necessary resource is totally unavailable and if no satisfactory substitute can be made, then task performance is not within the control of the client and probably will not occur.

Lack of reinforcements   The practitioner discusses and guides the client, showing her how to communicate and behave toward important other people, show others how to respond, communicate what actions others should take, and let others know that what they do will be reciprocated. The practitioner can undertake facilitating tasks to approach the important other people (teacher, spouse, parent, child, relative, etc.). The practitioner should interpret the client's actions; learn what the other persons could do to help the client; discuss what the others might gain; and plan a program with them. The practitioner can confer, refer, request, instruct, negotiate, or accompany the client, and, if necessary, advocate on the client's behalf.

Lack of skill   In the sessions the practitioner carries out work with the client to help her acquire skills. The techniques of instruction have already been described. The practitioner can refer the client to available experts to augment this learning of social skills.

Adverse beliefs   The client's own experience may have induced beliefs, convictions, or opinions that hamper or inhibit task performance. Examples are low self-esteem; awareness of cultural and economic oppression and discrimination; well-established ideas that others view him as lowly; and a genuine disregard and disapproval of dominant customs, folkways, ethics, or social conventions. Unrealistically low self-evaluations are learned attitudes; they decrease with factual, realistic discussion of their inappropriateness. This is particularly so if these discussions are supported by real experience with some others who like, respect, and appreciate the client. Few people cling to low self-esteem if it can be transformed into a more satisfying self-appraisal. Some people might not be able to make this switch, but they are few indeed.

Beliefs based on a negative attitude toward dominant customs, on the other hand, may be intransigent. Possibly an appeal to basic self-interest and an open discussion of the pros and cons of a particular view may succeed in changing the person's opinion or may not. In any case, the client can at least understand how to be protected from clashes with convention.

Lack of capacity   First, caution is called for to avoid underestimating clients, be they young, antagonistic, old, or mentally handicapped. Obviously, children too young to have developed sophisticated verbal and cognitive skills and persons seriously deteriorated and ill represent a floor of incapacity for many acts. Those clients should be cared for and protected. However, the actions usually called for are to scale down the tasks to be within the person's capacity and to involve others in doing the tasks for and with the client.

Practitioner bias and lack of skills   Practitioners should restrain their biases. Ideally lack of skills should be remedied by in-service training and professional education. However, experience is a masterful teacher. Experience and access to a library or a good resource person are excellent ways to improve skills. If tasks do not get done, here is a checklist of what to look at.

1. Are you working on a problem of high interest to the client?
2. If working on a mandated problem, does the client understand the consequences of ignoring, avoiding, or failing to change?
3. Does the client understand the tasks? Has she been shown how to do them and given help in getting them done?
4. Is the goal specific?
5. Have you reviewed the target problems and task sufficiently, and adjusted the tasks often enough to fit the client and the situation?
6. Have all the available resources been fully provided?

Planning and Stating Practitioner Tasks

Practitioner tasks are actions to be taken by the practitioner on behalf of the client and between the in-person sessions. These actions are intended to support the client's task performance. There are three types of practitioner tasks.

1. Getting information the client needs in order to perform her tasks.
2. Conferring with other agencies to interpret the client's needs, develop a positive attitude toward her, and arrange for commitments to deliver services.

3. Conferring with relatives, friends, and officials to negotiate actions they will take on the client's behalf.

Practitioners are obligated to report to clients what they did, what they found, and, when they fail to accomplish a specific task, the reason for nonperformance.

Verification and Monitoring: Checking on Progress or Difficulties

To verify their effectiveness in a simple manner, the interventions and their results are monitored periodically to test, confirm, and substantiate the effects of the intervention. Such periodic monitoring is not the same as scientific research into effectiveness. On a case-by-case basis, however, periodic verification as part of practice is both common sense and makes for accountable practice.

Monitoring guidelines

At each interview, check the following: Task performance, problem status and change, and new or revised problems.

Caution   Do not expect spectacular improvements. Do not be surprised by no movement. Do not be surprised by real or supposed new or revised problems. These are all ordinary happenings in the intervals between contacts. Monitoring problem status leads to clear pictures of alterations in problems.

There are many ways to track or monitor cases. Some methods need sophisticated research techniques and are practical only if an agency provides staff with the necessary training, time, and consultation. Simple monitoring devices can be used, however, and though they will not satisfy the demands of research, they will satisfy minimum accountability demands. They will provide concrete information to guide practice in particular cases toward productive efforts. Figure 7–2 is an example of a simple monitoring chart. Case circumstances and the preferences of the practitioner and agency will influence what kind of records are used to pin down the facts uncovered in a verification process. Many types of structured notations, charts, graphs, and brief narratives are used (Epstein, 1985).

What to do with the verification checks

When monitoring task performance, complete or substantial achievement is an excellent result. Partial or minimal achievement is a signal to study what obstacles there are. Obstacles can often be resolved by following the guidelines already given. Another way is to revise the tasks. Study of task-centered practice suggests that if a task is not done after three attempts, that task should be changed. Observing that the client had no opportunity to carry out the tasks provides information to interpret failure objectively.

INSTRUCTION: **Put check mark indicating the rating**

1. Task performance	Complete	Substantial	Partial	Minimal	No opportunity
T_1	☐	☐	☐	☐	☐
T_2	☐	☐	☐	☐	☐
T_3	☐	☐	☐	☐	☐
2. Problem status	No longer present	Considerably alleviated	Slightly alleviated	No change	Worse
P_1	☐	☐	☐	☐	☐
P_2	☐	☐	☐	☐	☐
P_3	☐	☐	☐	☐	☐
3. Problem altered		Explain			
P_1					
P_2					
P_3					

FIGURE 7–2 Example of a simple monitoring chart

Interpreting performance ratings

When monitoring problem status, making a rating of "considerably alleviated" indicates a success. Under adverse conditions, "slightly alleviated," is not a failure. However, when ratings are in the "slightly alleviated" or the "no change" categories, the intervention strategy perhaps needs revision. Ratings of "worse" might or might not mean that the interventions are responsible; such ratings might also be the result of stresses in the environment. In any case, "worse" signals a need for thorough reevaluation starting with the client's health; deterioration in the environment; hostile actions from relatives, friends, and authorities; and adverse effects of an agency program. At the very least, any conditions that jeopardize the client should be attended to. It is always possible that we cannot find out or understand the cause of deterioration. It stands to reason, however, that if a client's problem becomes worse, more of the same interventions are not called for. At present, not much is known about the cause of deterioration in the course of intervention.

———— REVISING THE INTERVENTION STRATEGY ————

During intervention a problem can change its appearance enough to warrant redefinition of the problem and a revised contract. Contract revision should follow the monitoring checkup if progress is unsatisfactory or exceeds what was expected, if new problems emerge, or if old problems take on different characteristics.

Contract revisions can be made at any time during the established time limits. They do not necessarily call for an extension of the time limits. The new contract can facilitate the achievement of goals already set. Anytime an extension is justified, it should be provided. Without necessitating formal revision, anytime that task performance is poor, the contract should be revised. If the support services already in place do not work or if the resources supplied are ineffective, remedial planning should take place. This means that the negotiations with other agencies should be reviewed and changes made. Understandings arrived at earlier with relatives and officials should be revised. When it turns out that the practitioner-supported tasks are not feasible or are ineffective, they should be revised.

The whole purpose of verifying the effects of the intervention is to make midcourse corrections while the case is active. These corrections will temporarily destabilize the structure of the task-centered model. However, as soon as a revised intervention strategy is decided on, the regular procedures can be put back into place.

EXAMPLES OF
TASK-CENTERED INTERVENTION ————

Eleanor

Prior to Task-centered Intervention
Eleanor, a 15-year-old black girl, was referred by the juvenile court for foster home placement. She had been living since early childhood with her widowed grandmother, a recipient of social security. Her grandmother had complained to the police that Eleanor was out of control. She was pregnant, refused to attend school, and was argumentative and disobedient. The grandmother feared that Eleanor's future was in jeopardy and wanted her to be "straightened out." The police took Eleanor to the detention home with her grandmother's consent.

Eleanor was in good health with no evidence of mental handicap or disturbance. Her grandmother was elderly, infirm, and poor, a decent, caring person, worried and concerned about Eleanor's bad conduct. The grandmother's home was plain and comfortable, located in an insecure public housing high rise.

Eleanor's father left when she was an infant. She was an only child. Her mother was an excitable woman given to bouts of public drunkenness, lonely, often receiving public aid, and sometimes working as a day housecleaner.

Eleanor was given over to her maternal grandmother to be reared. For short periods she lived with her mother to give her grandmother a respite. Eleanor and her mother fought because the mother was excessively demanding that Eleanor be perfect.

The grandmother cooperated fully in planning Eleanor's placement. The court's reason for placement was to see Eleanor through her pregnancy, arrange for child care for the baby and continued schooling for Eleanor, and provide supervision to control her sexual behavior and argumentativeness.

Eleanor stayed in the foster home two years with her baby girl. She attended school erratically and eventually dropped out altogether. Infant care was left to the foster mother. The infant was healthy and normal. Eleanor fought with the foster mother. She continued to be argumentative, disobedient, and undisciplined. Then she ran away and left her baby in the foster home.

Months later, Eleanor reappeared and went to live with her grandmother again. She came back with a second baby girl. The father was a 22-year-old unemployed youth who was also the father of the first child. Their relationship was a continuing one. He was the only boy Eleanor dated. Both her grandmother and her foster mother disapproved of him because they thought he was a "layabout" without prospects. When Eleanor became pregnant for the second time her boyfriend took her to his relatives in the South until after the baby was born. The grandmother was stretching her social security to provide for herself, Eleanor, and the second baby.

Task-centered Intervention

Application
Eleanor applied to the agency for return of her first child.

Client Target Problems

1. Eleanor does not have custody of her child.
2. Eleanor is herself still a ward of the court.
3. Eleanor does not know what the agency requires of her in order to be freed of their control.

Mandated Problems

> *Court:* Minor in need of supervision, referring to both Eleanor and her first child (legal mandate)
>
> *Agency:* Eleanor lacks adequate parenting skills, education for becoming self-supporting, income for self-care, probably emotionally disturbed (professional opinion)

Client Priorities

1. Get custody of her first child.
2. Find out the law and agency requirements preventing her from getting her child back.

Negotiating Strategy

1. Intra-agency conferences to support work on the client's priorities.
2. Conferences with the court to provide evidence of Eleanor's ability to care for her child.

Assessment

Eleanor became a ward of the court because of having become pregnant out of marriage, and her own family's lack of resources and skills to cope with this problem. She did not behave maternally toward her first child because of youth and inexperience. Her anger was due to being kept away from her stable relationship with her boyfriend and her feeling of being denied satisfactory work and life opportunities. Now only a few months away from being 18 years old and automatically freed of court supervision, Eleanor wants to be independent and get what belongs to her—the child in foster care. Eleanor is capable even though she lacks social skills. She has a basically good relationship with her mother, grandmother, and boyfriend. She lacks confidence in herself and is fearful of the power of the court and agency.

Contract

Target Problems
1. Lack of child custody
2. Lack of skills and resources for independent living

Goals and General Tasks
1. Obtain child custody
2. Enroll in continuation school
3. Obtain public assistance grant
   Time Limit: Eight weeks

Major Interventions

1. Eleanor was fully informed about legal and administrative requirements to explain her status as ward of the court and her child's status.
2. Specific tasks were planned to help her acquire basic child care information, to follow procedures for reenrolling in school and obtaining public assistance, to share household duties with her grandmother.

Client's Response

Eleanor became extremely agitated when she found that she could not be freed of court supervision unless she changed her child care behavior. Once this was clear, Eleanor was committed to doing what was required in order to win her independence.

Practitioner Tasks

1. Teaching basic child care in interviews
2. Mediating with grandmother about housework planning and implementation
3. Instructing Eleanor in legal and agency administrative requirements
4. Negotiating on Eleanor's behalf with the agency, court, public assistance, and school

Obstacles to Task Achievement and Interventions

1. *Eleanor's rage at authorities.* The rules of the agency were explained. Their rationale was discussed. What seemed unfair was openly confronted.
2. *Eleanor's inconsiderateness of her grandmother.* Joint sessions with the grandmother were held. Reciprocal tasks were developed so that the grandmother could get some benefit from keeping Eleanor.
3. *Foster mother's resentment of plan to return child to Eleanor.* The practitioner taught Eleanor how to refrain from provoking the foster mother on visits to her child. She was not to visit in the home but to take the child out and return her clean, cared for, and comfortable. The foster mother was offered an opportunity to express her opinion through agency channels and in court. She did not do so.
4. *Eleanor's delayed contact with school for reenrollment.* The practitioner gave repeated drill in how to talk to school officials so as to diminish Eleanor's fear of them. It was that fear that made her delay contacts.

Outcome
Eleanor became adept at feeding and clothing both children, keeping them clean, and responding to them. The grandmother helped generously. Eleanor completed all steps to obtain public assistance for herself. Last, she finally completed reenrollment procedures for school. The court was pleased but cautious. Hence, although they ordered the child in placement to be returned, they set up a six-month continuance for the agency to monitor and help maintain Eleanor's gains.

Elaine

Referral
Elaine, a 5-year-old white child, was referred by a public assistance worker because of "bizarre" behavior.

Social Context
Elaine lived with her widowed maternal grandmother (age 73) and her maternal unmarried uncle (age 45). She could not be cared for by her parents. Her mother most of the time was either in the state hospital or under its supervision in semi-independent living. Her father lived alone in bachelor housing. He was

a seasonal farm laborer with meager earnings. The grandmother reported to the public assistance worker that Elaine stayed in bed under the covers in cold weather. She had tantrums, could not talk in sentences, and could not be toilet trained. The grandmother feared Elaine will be "mad" like her mother. The grandmother and uncle were both illiterate. Both were responsible and concerned persons, kept a clean home, and were decent and considerate to neighbors and authorities. They were supported by public assistance.

Target Problems
Grandmother: (1) She was unable to provide proper developmental conditions for Elaine. (2) She was afraid Elaine is crazy.

Mandated Problems
Mental Health Agency, Public Health Agency, Community Services Agency: All agree Elaine is "developmentally disturbed." The mental health agency diagnosis is mental retardation; their recommendation is special education.

Client Priorities
Grandmother: Proper training resources for Elaine.

Negotiating Strategy
Questions were raised in the interagency conferences about the propriety of this grandmother, at 73, being the chief person responsible for Elaine's rearing. Since she might be short-lived and become infirm, some agency officials thought that Elaine should be placed in an institution. Consensus was achieved that the agencies would respect the caring qualities in the grandmother's home and her cooperativeness. This meant that for the time being no plans for placement away from the grandmother would be made.

Assessment
Elaine is a mentally retarded child being reared by relatives of limited intellectual capacity. Elaine's eccentric behavior is due to lack of training in speech and social skills. The home climate is excellent.

Contract
Target Problem: Lack of child training resources
Goal and General Task: Secure child training
Time Limit: Eight weeks

Major Interventions

1. Psychological and psychiatric evaluation was secured.
2. The results of these evaluations were explained to the grandmother and uncle.
3. The grandmother agreed to apply for Elaine's admittance to a local day-care facility. Transportation was arranged for the grandmother to attend parent education sessions.

4. Resources were obtained as follows:
   a. The day-care center officials were influenced to admit Elaine alternate half-days despite her developmental deficits. The primary agency assured the day-care center that services would be provided to augment the regular day-care program.
   b. Individual speech therapy was obtained in a clinic located in another city. Transportation for several times each week was arranged.
   c. Elaine's admittance to a local special education class in the public school was secured for alternate half-days. She was to learn motor coordination. Transportation was arranged.
   d. A schedule for Elaine's attendance at all these resources was made up. The schedule was distributed to all agencies and explained fully to the grandmother and uncle.
   e. Regular reporting and coordinating conferences were set up between all the involved agencies.
   f. It was arranged for the grandmother to join and participate in a parent group at the day-care center.

Client Response
Positive

Practitioner Tasks

1. Arranging for evaluations
2. Locating and developing child training resources in a sparsely populated rural area

Obstacles to Task Achievement and Intervention

1. *Some of the local agencies opposed Elaine's remaining with her aged and limited grandmother.* This was resolved through numerous conference discussions.
2. *There was a lack of readily available resources for child training in the locality.* The practitioner organized and packaged the resource by combining various existing services.
3. *The grandmother was sometimes late to pick up Elaine from the various places she was attending.* This was overcome by planned, regular reminders.

Outcome
The "crazy" behaviors stopped. Elaine began learning to talk and play with others. She liked music and water play. She started to use scissors, modeling clay, and cookie cutters. She was clearly a happier child.

☐ ☐ ☐

John

Prior to Task-centered Intervention
John, 15, a black teenager, lived with his grandparents who were his legal

guardians. At age 13 he began running away. He was finally made a ward of the court and referred to the agency for supervision. After two more runaways, John was placed in detention and thereafter in a foster home.

Task-centered Intervention

Client Target Problems

Grandparents:	(1) John does not want to go to school.
	(2) He stays out too late at night.
John:	(1) Too many people are trying to raise me.
	(2) My grandmother pays too much attention to my aunts' advice.

Mandated Problems

Court:	Minor is in need of supervision (legal mandate)
Agency:	Grandparents are too strict (professional opinion)
Foster Mother:	Too many people are involved in supervising John (individual opinion)

Client Priorities
Grandparents and John: John to return home

Negotiating Strategy
Intra-agency conferences reached agreement on goals; conferences with the court provided information about what evidence was needed to order John returned to his grandparents' home.

Social Context
John was friendly and willing to talk. He had a realistic appraisal of the bad consequences of not attending school. He stated that his truancy, staying out late, and running away were a "disease." The grandmother was cooperative but anxious. The grandfather left all decisions up to his wife. The housing is a single dwelling in an old and rundown public housing project. There was no evidence of health or psychiatric problems. The natural parents were not in the picture. The father had been absent for years. The mother was in a state hospital. The grandparents were on social security.

   According to John, the grandmother discussed every bit of his behavior with his aunts. The aunts were "all over him" and his grandmother, telling him and his grandmother what he must do. John stayed away from home frequently overnight. This is the runaway behavior. He went to a friend's house. He did not call home because he was afraid his grandmother would holler. He did not have any safe way to get home late at night. So he stayed overnight with whatever friend he was visiting. John ditched school because that was more "fun" than staying at school. John and his friends were not into drugs or any other antisocial behavior. They "played around" with girls. This worries the grandparents.

Assessment
This problem is one of unskillful handling by anxious grandparents and an expectable rebellious attitude in a normal teenager.

Contract

Target Problems
1. Separation of family
2. John's staying out late
3. John's not attending school

Goals and General Tasks
1. Reunite the family.
2. Arrange for safe transportation and phone calls home to cut down staying out late.
3. Cut down truancy from school.
4. Stop the aunts' interference.
   Time Limit: Eight weeks

Major Interventions

1. Negotiations with the school resulted in their agreement to readmit John.
2. Negotiated agreements between John and his grandmother set rules for his staying out and getting transportation home.
3. Negotiated rules with the aunts regulated their contacts. They are to talk directly to John, rather than go through the grandmother.
4. John went home on a trial basis.

Client Response
Moderately positive, with reservations.

Practitioner Tasks

1. Explored possibilities of school's accepting John and of alternative schools
2. Interpreted situation to court

Obstacles to Task Achievement and Interventions

1. *The grandmother was afraid to tackle the aunts about their interference.* Rehearsal and guided practice were repeated several times. The practitioner conferred with the aunts.
2. *John could not tolerate going back to school.* The problem was retargeted to lack of job training. Referrals were made to explore job training opportunities for teenagers.
3. *John was erratic in following the rules of staying out late.* There was review and repetition of the contract, explaining the effect of nonperformance on the court: the court would be reluctant to let John go home.

Outcome
John agreed to the necessity for seeking job training instead of reenrolling in school. The plan to stop the aunts' interference was fully performed. Staying out late was cut down 80%. The court released John to his grandparents.

======================= **SUMMARY** =======================

The basic essential actions to implement the task-centered approach are:

1. Define and specify target problems to a maximum of three.
2. Assess the target problem, the social context, and the cognitive-affective circumstances of the problem(s).
3. Generate alternatives.
4. Negotiate supportive and collaborative actions of other persons and agencies.
5. Confirm goals, select what will be done, and design the details of the intervention strategy (decision making).
6. Carry out the strategy, relying upon developing tasks, supporting task performance, finding out obstacles to task performance, planning actions to remove, reduce, or alter obstacles, remedying practical barriers, alleviating cognitive barriers, and planning and stating practitioner tasks.
7. Verify and monitor progress.
8. Revise plan as needed.

======================= **REFERENCES** =======================

American Psychiatric Association. (1980). *Diagnostic and statistical manual of mental disorders* (3rd ed.). Washington, DC: Author.

Anderson, R. E., & Carter, I. (1984). *Human behavior and the social environment: A social systems approach*. New York: Aldine.

Basso, R. (1986). *Teacher and student problem-solving activities in educational supervisory sessions*. Unpublished manuscript, Wilfrid Laurier University, Faculty of Social Work, Waterloo, Ontario, Canada.

Berger, R. L. and Federico, R. C. (1982). *Human behavior: A social work perspective*. New York: Longman.

Brown, L. B. (1977). Client problem solving learning in task centered social treatment. (Doctoral dissertation, School of Social Service Administration University of Chicago).

D'Zurilla, T. J., & Goldfried, M. R. (1971). Problem solving and behavior modification. *Journal of Abnormal Psychology, 78*(1), 107–126.

Epstein, L. (1985). *Talking and listening: A guide to the helping interview*. Columbus, OH: Merrill.

Gambrill, E. D. (1983). *Casework: A competency-based approach.* Englewood Cliffs, NJ: Prentice-Hall.

Jahoda, M. (1953). The meaning of psychological health. *Social Casework, 34,* 349–354.

Johnson, H. C. (1980). *Human behavior and social environment: New perspectives.* New York: Curriculum Concepts.

Kirk, S. A., & Greenley, J. R. (1974). Denying or delivering services? *Social Work, 19*(4), 439–447.

Lidz, C. W., Meisel, A., Zerubavel, E., Carter, M., Sestak, R. M., & Roth, L. H. (1984). *Informed consent: A study of decision making in psychiatry.* New York: Guilford Press.

Reid, W. J. (1978). *The task-centered system.* New York: Columbia University Press.

Reid, W. J., & Epstein, L. (Eds). (1977). *Task-centered practice.* New York: Columbia University Press.

Rzepnicki, T. (1982). Task-centered intervention: An adaptation and test of effectiveness in foster care services. (Doctoral dissertation, School of Social Service Administration, University of Chicago).

Spivack, G., Platt, J., & Shure, M. B. (1976). *The problem solving approach to adjustment.* San Francisco: Jossey-Bass.

Weissman, A. (1976). Industrial social services: Linkage technology. *Social Casework, 57*(1), 50–54.

CHAPTER
8

FOURTH STEP

Termination, Extension, Monitoring

Terminating by Plan
Unplanned Discontinuance
Extensions by Plan
Unplanned Extensions
Monitoring
Maintaining Gains
Reopenings
Crises, Emergencies, and Ultimatums
Summary: Basic Actions

_____ TERMINATING BY PLAN _____

The subject of terminating of treatment has not been much studied. It has been thought of as part of the whole process of intervention and hard to consider separately. In practice, the criteria for termination are judgments about clients' mental states and predictions about their future actions.

There is considerable variation among practitioners as to what are the exact criteria that indicate treatment is completed. And it is admittedly difficult to make accurate predictions about what a person can and will do in the future. Despite these difficulties, for practical reasons, we make these predictions all the time, based in part on empirical information and in part on intuition and experience to supplement or substitute for hard information.

Rules in some agencies put a limit on length of service so that the termination time is prescribed by agency policy or established practice. These rules are laid down to economize on resources, to hold down waiting lists, to make use of the motivating pressure of deadlines or cutoff dates, and to conform to the reimbursement policies of third party payers or insurance companies.

A consensus in the field of practice maintains that terminations should not just be stumbled into but should be planned (Levinson, 1977; Siporin, 1975). Yet the little empirical evidence that exists suggests considerable diversity among practitioners in how they go about planning and implementing termination (Fortune, 1985). There is also increasing attention to the built-in termination planning in brief treatment because of its being technologically advanced in its specificity, differentiation, and evaluation of results (Pardes and Pincus, 1981).

Terminating because goals have been met is one of the common criteria suggested for ending treatment. The practice problem with this criterion is the uncertainty about whose goals drive the decision to terminate and whether the goals are feasible under all the circumstances. In the task-centered model it is expected that goals will be reasonably definite, reasonably specific and concrete, and hence capable of being identified and measured when they have been achieved. Many clients will approximate rather than completely achieve goals. Time limits set within the first few interviews provide structure for setting an end

Step 4	Termination
Chapter 8	**End** **Extend** on evidence of client commitment **Monitor** when mandated by law, court order, or formal agency requirements

FIGURE 8–1 Detail of map

to the treatment sequence. Time limits enable clients to exercise control over their participation. It is a rare client indeed who truly becomes unhappy or is set adrift when termination occurs. Practitioners tend to overestimate the value they have for a client's well-being. The rewards of termination to a client are great: more money in the pocket (if the client is paying a fee), more time, freedom from the practitioner's influence and surveillance, and greater independence.

A practitioner may provoke a client's unhappiness about termination if she has overvalued the relationship and if she has communicated that belief to the client by word or deed.

The duration of the sequence will have been established in the contract. (See Chapter 6.) In order to effect an orderly and appropriate termination, the following guidelines are suggested:

1. *Reminders.* At each interview there should be a reminder to the client about which interview is being currently conducted. The fact that the next to last or last interview is occurring should not come as a surprise or a shock to either the practitioner or the client.
2. *End at next to last interview.* The next to last interview is the last in which actual work on the problem is handled.
3. *Reviewing and pointing to the future.* The last interview, the termination interview, should be a review of what has taken place. The purpose is to fix events in mind so they may be recalled to guide future problem solving.
4. There are five comunications in a termination interview:

   ☐ "This is what we accomplished."
   ☐ "This is what we did not accomplish."
   ☐ "This is what you did."
   ☐ "This is what I did."
   ☐ "Come back if you need to."

A number of things have been noted as problems in terminating, but it is difficult to know how frequently these problems occur or how important they are. A large professional folklore views termination problems as potentially difficult and defeating to the treatment aims. Hence, many practitioners are reluctant to adhere to termination decisions made in a contract, fearing that the termination will adversely affect the gains made.

Observations of practice with the task-centered approach have shown that some clients do not come for the final or termination interview. The explanation for this finding is not known; but it is possible that some clients perceive the work to be over and have no interest in a summary; a few may develop separation anxiety and feel upset by the ending, preferring to avoid it. Practitioners may feel distress over ending a sequence of interviews; on the one hand they may criticize themselves for things they now wish they had done differently; or they may have become genuinely fond of certain clients and hate to see them go. Sometimes a practitioner is proud of a client's accomplishments and of her own work and does not want the experience to end.

Other termination problems have been perceived and described generally by Levinson (1977). Those problems are summarized here.

1. The client may cling to the treatment experience and to the relationship with the practitioner.
2. The practitioner who sees termination as traumatic may unintentionally postpone the termination or support the unrealistic wishes of the client to hold onto the experience.
3. The problems may suddenly emerge all over again or in an aggreviated form.
4. Entirely new problems may emerge in the last interview.
5. The client may make rushed efforts to create intimate friends to substitute for the practitioner.
6. The client may react defensively toward the feelings aroused by termination: he may be unmoved by the ending, begin complaining, and become critical, or act out (for example, become angry or fail appointments).
7. If the practitioner reacts defensively, the client may become convinced that he cannot get along without the practitioner, setting off an angry, threatenend, fatigued reaction in the practitioner and starting a set of circular behaviors in which both client and practitioner reinforce each other's problems.

It is wise not to anticipate that these complicated problems will necessarily occur in implementing a planned termination. Their likelihood is diminished by the relative brevity of the time used in task-centered intervention, by the businesslike arrangements resulting from the explicitness of the contract, and by the congruence between practitioner and client on target problem focus, goals, and priorities.

However, should untoward difficulties arise, it is necessary to analyze and reorganize the client's thoughts and attitudes toward a practitioner to whom the client has become emotionally attached. This is time-consuming but only in extreme circumstances should an extension be given to work through these feelings. Rather, the time for such work should be obtained by putting aside any planned discussion about the problems and concentrating on the feelings aroused by the termination. That process often involves intimate discussions about feelings. It is better to place a businesslike constraint on the working relationship than face the separation troubles accompanying the loss of a practitioner who has become too important to a client.

There is a normal and natural degree of dependency many clients experience. The practitioner may in reality be a vital source of resources, advice, and affection. There is nothing at all wrong with clients' being dependent when they lack resources in themselves or in the environment. Practitioners should make sure that clients are fully informed about alternative resources and rewards and grasp the fact that they have managed and can manage on their own.

Clients can also touch base with the agency and the practitioner from time to time if they really need to, including returning for the same or another problem. If the provision of service was businesslike in the first place, termination will probably be the same.

UNPLANNED DISCONTINUANCE

Clients who drop out of treatment without a termination plan or contrary to the termination plan pose a problem. For one thing, substantial irregularity in appointment keeping causes expensive problems in scheduling staff and is a real waste of agency resources. The only way an agency can protect itself from substantial loss of resources from no-shows is to overbook, which causes other problems.

It is assumed that if the client were to continue treatment he would receive benefits that are lost if he drops out. On the other hand, evidence suggests that clients often discontinue treatment because they have received the help they want and need at the moment. Some clients may be dissatisfied with the terms, conditions, and content of the help they are being offered (Reid and Epstein, 1972).

It has been suggested that unplanned discontinuance may be minimized by congruence between practitioner and client on target problems, contract agreements, and keeping the contact short (Parad & Parad, 1968; Reid & Shyne, 1969).

EXTENSIONS BY PLAN

The issue of extending the sequence comes up when the client is dissatisfied with termination, when the practitioner wishes for more time to increase the effectiveness of the treatment, or when there are some known conditions or events forthcoming in the immediate future that can be helped by continuing the contact. Extensions should be mutually agreed to between practitioner and client with the number of additional interviews made definite in a revised contract.

Extending when the original contract has failed to meet expectations on the assumption that the practitioner and the client will try a little harder is unwise. Some problems are intractable because of client characteristics, excess deficits in the environment, lack of knowledge in the field, agency limitations, and lack of practitioner skill. Most social and personal problems are long-lived and recur repeatedly. Expectations of "big cures" are unrealistic. If everything possible has been done and has failed, extending treatment makes no sense. After a lapse of time, if the client returns and the case is reopened, the outcome may be better.

Studies in the task-centered model show that most clients appeared satisfied with the amount of time in brief treatment but some would have liked more contact, meaning one or two more interviews. Other research in brief treatment has shown similar results. Women want additional contact more often than men. A recent study of these issues concludes that clients who react negatively to termination do so because their expected goals have not been attained, or because they have developed a dependency upon the practitioner which may not be resolved (O'Connor & Reid, 1986). Since both these reactions are legitimate it might be appropriate under particular circumstances to extend to the extent necessary to clarify expectations, substantially revise the treatment plan if possible, and work through the treatment-induced dependency.

Extensions are warranted if the target problem is self-limiting (that is, the target problem will dissipate in the near future) and the client can use additional help to complete tasks. For example, a marital separation will occur in a few days or weeks, a discharge from a hospital is scheduled, or a move from one apartment to another is scheduled for a few weeks in the future. Extensions are also warranted when the client asks for an extension and can state what work is to be done. An example might be when a family has moved and is settled in a new apartment and the parents want to work on a parent-child conflict.

UNPLANNED EXTENSIONS

The practitioner should be vigilant about the tendency to drift into long-term, open-ended treatment (driven perhaps by desires to attain elusive goals) without a clear contract. These could be called unplanned extensions and are full of problems. For instance, the interpersonal practitioner-client relationship can become overly important. Clients may be misled into expecting results that are not likely to occur. Caseloads become filled with cases that show little or no movement. All the while, waiting lists may accumulate, and new clients may go without help because there is not enough room for them in the caseload.

MONITORING

Monitoring takes place because the practitioner and the agency initiate it. Clients do not initiate this process. Monitoring means to watch, observe, or check for a particular purpose and to keep track, regulate, or control. The circumstances that call for monitoring in social welfare are of two types: those required by court orders, and those advocated for professional reasons.

In numerous instances a court orders supervision, for example, foster care, probation and parole, or legal protective guardianship. This type of monitoring can be structured by informing the client of the legal requirements clearly and accurately, and a schedule for episodic client reporting or practitioner visiting can be established.

Monitoring for professional reasons, mainly to enable the practitioner to check regularly on maintenance or deterioration of gains, requires discussion with the client. The intention of professional monitoring is to detect early problems and provide early interventions. This type of monitoring ought to be set up only if the client is willing. There should be some reason to believe that early detection can actually be performed and that if performed, a remedy is known and available. Most professional monitoring tends to become surveillance.

In some settings, oversight of clients is standard procedure. Effective preventive interventions on an individual case basis are needed and wanted, but our understanding of early warning signs of problems is limited. Ideas about early warning signals are heavily weighted by ideology and intuitions. It would seem more efficient to avoid cluttering up case loads with long-term, inactive cases by reserving monitoring for cases where surveillance or supervision is court ordered or where eligibility has to be reviewed due to legal or administrative requirements. Short-term monitoring is reasonable if it has a clear-cut objective. Ordinarily, ongoing monitoring in the absence of a mandate should be avoided. Instead, clients should be encouraged to return when and if they need further service.

MAINTAINING GAINS

A great deal remains to be understood about how best to maintain gains that occur in treatment. Behavior modification practitioners and researchers have given the most attention to this subject (Gambrill, 1983). The following guidelines, suggested by Gambrill, have merit for assisting in maintaining gains.

1. Significant other persons should provide ongoing support for new behaviors.
2. The improvements should be continuously useful and be perceived by the client as useful; otherwise they will not be continued.
3. Natural reinforcers in the real environment should substitute for reinforcers used during the treatment experience such as therapist approval, token, points, and so forth.
4. Reinforcement should be on an intermittent, real-life schedule to replace the planned regularized reinforcement provided in treatment sessions.
5. Help clients learn to perform actions they can carry out independently after the sequence is finished.
6. Help clients attribute their gains to their own effort and perceive themselves to be in control.
7. Help clients understand the rationale for maintaining change.
8. Help clients anticipate and recover from relapses.
9. Provide plans for booster sessions with the therapist.
10. Arrange follow-up contacts, with the client's agreement, to check on progress and problems.

_____ REOPENINGS _____

Reopening a case at the client's request is often frowned upon as an undesirable "revolving door." Yet it should be noted that something of interest keeps a client returning to a place where there may be reluctance to work again on the same problem. This kind of a situation is difficult to understand but is worth the effort if time can be made available. Reopenings have productive possibilities in that they can provide the client another chance to make improvements. Most important, reopenings provide the setting for "booster shots" that can be of very short duration but may make a difference in helping a client who has temporarily lost ground to regain it and to avoid further relapse or deterioration.

_____ CRISES, EMERGENCIES, AND ULTIMATUMS _____

Cases on a monitoring status are often subject to crises, emergencies, and ultimatums. A crisis is a particular state of affairs that is life threatening or threatens basic habits of conducting oneself. Crises are believed to occur when there is a severe threat, loss, or challenge (Dixon, 1986; Golan, 1978). Crises are sudden discontinuities in the life arrangements, for example, the sudden death of someone close to the client, the onset of a critical illness, extreme or mutilating surgery, having been criminally assaulted or burglarized, having been burned out, and so forth.

Emergencies are situations where prompt action will remove or retard a threatening crisis: for example, making a phone call can stave off an eviction, influencing a school can stop or slow up a suspension, calling the police may stop an assault, finding temporary accommodations may keep a person from living on the street, or getting clothing can help a person who has none.

Ultimatums occur when there is pressure on an agency to act. There may be pressure to get a patient out of the hospital immediately, for example, or to remove a child from his home immediately. Ultimatums result from a variety of complex pressures on a delivery system. They are rarely true emergencies, although they may produce a crisis state for clients unless they are buffered.

Because crises, emergencies, and ultimatums may occur while a case is being monitored, practitioners must allow leeway in their schedules to meet urgent problems. These unexpected events should be managed by rapid problem specification, high practitioner activity to arrange for stress abatement, termination of the episode, and return to the planned work as soon as possible.

================ SUMMARY: BASIC ACTIONS ================

1. A plan should be made for termination from the inception of the case. The plan should be put into effect by regular reminders of the number of interviews left and reserving the last interview for a review of progress and a look to the future.

2. Unplanned discontinuance can be variously understood. It may be that the client has actually received what he needed, or it may be that the client is dissatisfied in some important way.
3. Cases may be extended by contract when there is a clear and mutually understood and agreed upon purpose. Unplanned extensions should be scrupulously avoided.
4. Monitoring may occur as a result of a court order or a professional interest.
5. Maintaining of gains should be planned for by attempting to construct reinforcers in the natural environment and influencing the client's thinking so he perceives changes as continuously useful.

REFERENCES

Dixon, S. L. (1986). *Working with people in crisis.* Columbus, OH: Merrill.

Fortune, A. E. (1985). Planning duration and termination of treatment. *Social Service Review, 59*(4), 647–661.

Gambrill, E. (1983). *Casework: A competency-based approach.* Englewood Cliffs, NJ: Prentice-Hall.

Golan, N. (1978). *Treatment in crisis situations.* New York: The Free Press.

Levinson, H. L. (1977). Termination of psychotherapy: Some salient issues. *Social Casework, 58*(8), 480–489.

O'Connor, R., & Reid, W. J. (1986). Dissatisfaction with brief treatment. *Social Service Review, 60*(4), 526–537.

Parad, L. G., & Parad, H. J. (1968). A study of crisis-oriented planned short-term treatment, Part II. *Social Casework, 49*(July) II.

Pardes, H., & Pincus, H. A. (1981). Brief therapy in the context of national mental health issues. In S. H. Budman (Ed.), *Forms of brief therapy.* New York: The Guilford Press.

Reid, W. J., & Epstein, L. (1972). *Task-centered casework.* New York: Columbia University Press.

Reid, W. J., & Shyne, A. W. (1969). *Brief and extended casework.* New York: Columbia University Press.

Siporin, M. (1975). *Introduction to social work practice.* New York: Macmillan.

CHAPTER
9

USING THE TASK-CENTERED MODEL FLEXIBLY

ADAPTING THE TASK-CENTERED APPROACH TO
___ SETTINGS, CLIENT GROUPS, AND PROBLEMS ___

The task-centered model is not a universal, all-purpose problem solver. Firmly based on general problem-solving principles, the task-centered approach is able to take advantage of the relevance of problem solving to the control of problems in living. It also readily fits a concentration on the client's own motivation. These characteristics, together with its systematic processes and empirical base, give the model general applicability. Nevertheless, it is always necessary in applying this model to adapt it to better fit particular settings, particular client groups, different problems, and the comfort and convenience of the practitioner.

Unsystematic adaptations of the task-centered approach (and, incidentally, of other approaches) are carried out constantly as practitioners select parts of various approaches, try them out on a case-by-case basis and invent novel procedures. The idea that adaptations should be systematically done and carefully studied and evaluated is a recent development, coming about in the course of the current emphasis on the legitimacy and necessity of planned eclecticism (Norcross, 1986).

Ideal, Systematic Adaptation

An ideal, systematic adaptation process would

1. *Consider risks and benefits.*

    ☐ Taking a broad general look at the task-centered model, what would your hunches and beliefs be about its risks and benefits for the types of cases that comprise your practice?
    ☐ What kinds of changes would you think would reduce the risks? Increase the benefits?

2. *Consider adaptation possibilities.* Still taking a broad general look, what changes would you make to increase the fit between the task-centered model and your own cases?
3. *Select three experimental cases.* Select cases to minimize bias: for example, the first three cases on Monday; or the first case on Monday, Wednesday, and Friday; or in any other manner that prevents making prejudgments on the suitability or nonsuitability of the case.
4. *Use the existing guidelines to handle the case.* It is advisable to use the guidelines as already in existence before making changes to check whether the expectation of a poor fit is actually the case. The guidelines may be found to work satisfactorily and need no alterations. The exception would be in settings where administrative requirements contra-indicate one or more of the guidelines.
5. *Log the instances of gaps and misfits.* A sample log would include

- ☐ Case identification
- ☐ Date of occurrence
- ☐ Guidelines used
- ☐ What was missing (gap)
- ☐ What was unsuitable (misfit)
- ☐ Other relevant information

6. *Design a revised guideline.* Referring to the adaptation possibilities considered in item two, and also to hypotheses generated in trying out the guidelines in item four and five, consider a range of alterations that could fill in gaps and improve the fit of the guidelines. Information on which to base the revision can be found in experience, in relevant research findings and in the theory and guidelines of other models of practica. The source of the information should be stated.
7. *Try out the revised guidelines and log the results.* Repeat the revision process until the most satisfactory condition is obtained.

Informal Adaptation

Informal adaptation is bound to occur in the course of handling a case. Clinical judgment supersedes formal guidelines, except when that judgment leads to abandoning of the model or turning it into some distinctly different entity. Records should be kept of important informal adaptations so practitioners and their colleagues can study and replicate them.

Frequent Types of Adaptations

Altering the order of the model

The start-up and the first two steps of the task-centered model (that is, the referral or application and the identification of target problems and the making of the contract), can be carried out in some other order when the circumstances would make it overly mechanical to comply fully with the order in the guidelines. In fact, experienced practitioners nearly always merge these steps. What is important to preserve the model's distinctive features is to be certain that the initial phases, that is, start-up and steps 1 and 2, get done, regardless of order.

Of particular importance in rearranging the order are circumstances that come up in psychiatric clinics and in child welfare protective services. In psychiatric clinics the administrative regulations nearly always necessitate that the first order of business is diagnosis. This convention requires the assessment portion of step 3, designed as part of the problem solving effort, to be the first type of activity undertaken. However, in the course of securing the assessment information, the start-up, identification of target problems, and general features of the contract can be discussed and reviewed. Not many psychiatric clinics use a written contract, so that the proposed verbal contract can readily be woven into the full-bodied exploration that will constitute the assessment.

In child welfare protective services the first order of business, according to prevailing interpretations of applicable laws and agency practices, is investigating the possibility of child abuse and making a decision on placement or home services. In these instances the investigation, which has its own rules and guidelines, takes precedence over all of the steps of the task-centered model. However, the task-centered model can be put into effect parallel to the investigation. Much of the information obtained from the client in the course of the investigation fulfills the requirements of the task-centered model's initial phases and so serves double duty. The addition of the contract may be helpful in such involuntary cases because it offers the client a measure of independence and respect that might otherwise be lacking in an authoritative process.

Making substitutions

It is always possible to substitute a procedure that serves the same or a similar purpose from another model. The caution that should be observed, however, is to avoid substituting an action that opposes the model. For example, one could not substitute open-ended, long-term treatment for a timed, goal-specific contract!

However, one could interpret the task development guidelines of the task-centered model as reflective discussion. The task-supporting procedures could be interpreted as sustainment, direct influence, exploration, and description. The provision of resources is environmental modification work. A good deal of the supporting of task performance can be seen as provision of interpersonal competencies.

Providing two or more sequences

Sometimes termination is controlled not by the practitioner but by a court order or by a powerful administrative rule. For example, a client may be on probation for a time determined by the judge. A client may be in a court-ordered placement that she cannot leave without a formal release from a court. Aged persons may be held in long-term care because they cannot take care of themselves and have to live under institutional conditions. Such clients may have repeated episodes of service, usually for different problems because their living situation changes.

Adjusting the Model to Personal Style, Preferences, and Custom

Human service professionals have preferences for how to behave, how to sound, and what to emphasize in their work. They can become extremely uncomfortable if they are required to adopt a way of acting that grates against those preferences. Agencies also have customs, preferred terms, and ways of doing that they understand easily. There is no reason why practitioners or agencies must change their styles to use the task-centered model. However, it must be noted that among the therapy disciplines old ideological struggles often take the form of conflict over terminology. The present period is seeing a diminution of these battles. The task-centered model, having been generated out of the revisionist trend of the 70s, may sometimes speak in a language that offends the sensitivities of those who prefer another language. Although the language of the task-centered model conveys particular meanings, the various therapy languages tend to use different terms to convey the same or similar meanings. Therefore, it is not of prime importance to adhere to one language style rather than another, unless a language change alters the model's substance.

COMBINING THE TASK-CENTERED MODEL
—————————— AND OTHER MODELS ——————————

Involving Families and Other Important Persons

The contemporary family treatment movement is dated from the 1950s and has developed as an influential stream of thought and practice, relevant particularly for problems in which several family members, if not the whole family, are considered to be involved. Research in family treatment is a difficult undertaking and is not yet far advanced.

Adaptations of the task-centered approach to family problem solving are being developed (Fortune, 1985; Reid, 1985; Rathbone-McCuan, 1985; Mills, 1985; Tolson, 1977). The essential strategy of family treatment within the task-centered approach emphasizes the identification of target problems and their subsequent reduction in accordance with the general guidelines already detailed in this book. Published reports on these developments show that practitioners who adopt the task-centered approach do so in an eclectic manner, influenced by communication and problem solving training models, and ideas about home tasks, in-session tasks, and environmental tasks. Reid (1985) and Mills (1985) are developing thinking about ways to expand the focus of the target problem to encompass issues in the problem context, thus to enhance the effect of the interventions, and possibly to have some influence on precipitating and maintaining factors. Rathbone-McCuan (1985) and Mills (1985) perceive a merging of crisis intervention with the task-centered approach under specific crisis conditions. The task-centered approach has been found to have a major strength in working with older families because it fosters their participation rather than submerges their autonomy.

Levels of family involvement.

In using the task-centered model with families, the practitioner does not need to follow strict rules about who participates. Two levels of family involvement may pertain.

Minimal or episodic involvement   Occasional and collateral involvement of families is possible. There should be no prejudice or penalty to a client if relatives participate minimally or episodically. Family members may find it difficult to participate for various realistic reasons, aside from a reluctance to face issues and deal with problems. Working people often cannot take time from the job to attend treatment sessions. Fatigue and urgent interests may consume their off-work hours.

Substantial involvement Some families want and agree to attend sessions regularly. Family involvement can be instrumental in providing services, practical problem solving skills, and therapy. Family members may also be seen individually either for a series of sessions or intermittently. Married couples may be seen together in conjoint treatment.

Family interviews can be used to assess, to decide on priorities and duration, to divide up problem-solving activities (i.e., tasks) among family members, to increase the impact of the interventions, and to create flexibility in achieving desired goals.

Target problem identifications in dealing with families

If feasible, target problem identification should be obtained from individuals, possibly in private, before issues are opened up to the group in the family meeting. Family members will often disagree about target problems. The practitioner can help members organize the array of target problems into clusters of those that seem reasonably related. When problems are clustered, disagreements are usually found to reflect contradictory or opposite perceptions of the same problems. These contradictory problem statements can be dealt with as if they are the same problem, only different sides to it.

The target problems should be reduced to three for work on the present contract. Additional problems should be put aside and may be taken up later. However, the processes of problem solving are such that these additional problems diminish and no longer need work after the work on the first three priorities has been accomplished. If there is an excess of urgent problems, they can be handled in parallel individual sessions or in any other manner that takes care of them expeditiously.

Important others

From time to time it will be desirable to include with a family significant other persons with whom the client and family is on intimate terms or closely involved. Caretakers would come under this category, for example, as would homemakers, landlords, or landladies. Still other important people might be aunts and uncles, cousins, neighbors, and spouse-companions.

Groups

Adaptations of the task-centered model for use with groups began with the original inception of the task-centered model. Fortune (1985) has summarized the nature of these adaptations.

1. Forming groups so that the members' target problems and tasks are similar.
2. Using tasks that are the same or similar for each member.
3. Using visual aids (small charts or wall charts, for example) to clarify tasks and track them.
4. Interviewing some group members individually as well as in the group sessions.
5. Using specialized meeting formats to serve a purpose similar to that served by visual aids.

Fortune concludes that task-centered group treatment is adaptable for diverse populations in a range of institutional and community settings.

Child Welfare Practice

Rooney (1981) and Rzepnicki (1985) conducted practice research to generate systematically an adaptation of task-centered intervention applicable to work in child welfare. Rooneys' model is developed for work with families separated because of child placement who have shown definite interest in being reunited. The model is considered to be a reunification process. Its unique adaptations include

1. *Limiting the permissible scope of target problems.*
   The target problems are defined only in connection with conditions blocking the child's return home to the natural parent or parents.
2. *Limiting the possibilities for interagency conflicts.*
   The practitioner maintains at least biweekly contact with all other agencies involved in the case to reduce adversary relationships and enhance cooperation.
3. *Emphasizing parental visits.*
   Many parental visits with the child in placement are arranged, and on-the-spot counsel is made available.
4. *Monitoring regular task performance.*
   Visual aids and regular reviews in interviews are provided so that task performance can be monitored readily and kept on track with as little deviation as possible.
5. *Making access to practitioners easy.*
   Practitioners are available to help clients complete tasks to the maximum.
6. *Maintaining a high level of interaction among family members and attending to goals.*
   Tasks are formulated to maximize the family members sharing work and engaging in reciprocal tasks to achieve goals. In case of conflict between family members on strategy or targets, a reciprocal strategy should be used: that is, clients help one another but receive help directly in return for their focus or priority.

Rzepnicki (1985) developed a model that confined the target problem to expected barriers to achieving permanency for the child. This makes for an extremely closely focused practice. Case goals are addressed to reunifying the family (maintaining the child in the home or returning the child to the home) or achieving an alternative permanency plan. The Rzepnicki model resulted from a partial replication and further development of Rooney's work. The basic elements of the child welfare models as developed by Rooney and Rzepnicki are

1. *Target problems.* Target problems are limited to those conditions that, if not resolved, are harmful or likely to be harmful to the child.
2. *Social context assessment.* There is a thorough assessment of environmental deficiencies and personal and environmental strengths so that maximum effort may be given to remediable conditions that will ease the process of reunification.
3. *Joint case planning.* Coordination of effort of all agencies typically involved in foster care to maximize the service to the client.
4. *Clarification of responsibilities.* Accurate information should be provided to all the participants regarding what is expected of them by the agency, court, foster and/or natural parents, and each other. Legal sanctions, agency roles, and regulations should be communicated clearly and freely.
5. *Time limits.* Child welfare cases may last longer than other cases because problems may be very complex and courts make major decisions about time in care. Practitioners can monitor these cases and create several short contracts rather than enter into an unplanned, open-ended encounter.

Mental Health Settings

Law, custom, and history determine that the treatment of problems defined as mental illness is the domain of the medical profession, particularly psychiatry. A particular adaptation of the task-centered model can be made that should fit with this type of required practice (Brown, 1977).

Start-up

The nature of mental health clinics is well-known and their purpose firmly understood in the human services system. There is little need to find out the referral source's goals or to negotiate an agreement on goals and resource availability. Except for most unusual circumstances, clients are referred to mental health clinics for pretty much what mental health clinics do—diagnosis and treatment of mental illness or emotional disorder thought to resemble mental illness. For practical purposes, the start-up can be dispensed with.

Step 1: client target problems identified

Having been classified already as an actual or potential case of mental illness or disorder, the client may limit her attention to target problems such as personal traits, dysfunctional behaviors, moods, or cognitive confusion. However, she should not be discouraged or limited in the freedom to identify important problems of real life circumstances. The problems the practitioner will be able to undertake will be constrained to those acceptable to the administration of the agency. These constraints on acceptable target problems have to be clarified and explained to the client if not readily understood.

In mental health clinics, the rapid early assessment needs to be expanded to permit the official psychiatric diagnosis according to the rules contained in the DSM III, which covers clinical psychopathology, personality and developmental disorders, physical disorders, stressors, and appraisal of the client's highest adaptive capacity in past year.

Step 2: contract

The contract should be expanded to include drug therapy, psychotherapy, and any other type of therapy that will be provided by the clinic with the patient's agreement.

Step 3: problem solving

An additional component, namely, provision of or support for a specifically psychiatric treatment plan having to do with drug therapy, psychotherapy, or other specified therapy is necessary in a mental health clinic setting. Large areas of overlap occur between what is customarily regarded as clinical therapy and what is called for in the guidelines of the task-centered model. The overlap is so great that in many instances the actual processes will be the same. When the processes are or appear to be different, they can be fitted into the problem-solving guidelines of the model, with those guidelines being rearranged and substitutions made to avoid unnecessary duplication of efforts.

Step 4: termination

Nothing in the task-centered termination guidelines is at variance with most mental health clinic practices.

Health Settings

As in the other settings discussed previously problems being treated in health settings (hospitals or clinics) must be defined in a circumscribed fashion. Problems in health settings are confined to issues about the struggle to control the disease, the patients, the caretakers, and the environment, family, and work. Although these settings require no regular omissions or additions to the task-centered model, the particular adaptation process is one of focusing. The sequences have to be focused on the patient's illness and medical recommendations for treatment. There is no escaping this focus in view of the all-embracing influence of the medical care institution (Epstein, 1983).

SUMMARY

It is always necessary to adapt the task-centered model to improve its fit in particular settings, with particular client groups, and with regard to different kinds of problems, and the comfort and convenience of the practitioner. Formal, systematic adaptations offer the best route to creating effective adaptations consistent with maintaining the necessary essentials of the model. However, informal adaptations are constantly being made and should be recorded for later study and communication to colleagues. A number of studies are reviewed that are directed toward developing model adaptations in child welfare, family treatment, groups, health, and mental health clinics.

REFERENCES

American Psychiatric Association. (1980). *Diagnostic and Statistical Manual of Mental Disorders* (3rd ed.), Washington, DC: Author.

Brown, L. B. (1977). Treating problems of psychiatric outpatients. In W. J. Reid & L. Epstein (Eds.) *Task-centered practice*. New York: Columbia University Press.

Epstein, L. (1983). Short-term treatment in health settings: Issues, concepts, dilemmas. In G. Rosenberg & H. Rehr (Eds.), *Advancing social work practice in the health care field*. New York: Haworth.

Fortune, A. E. (1985). Families and family treatment. In A. E. Fortune (Ed.), *Task-centered practice with families and groups*. New York: Springer.

Fortune, A. E. (1985). Treatment Groups. In A. E. Fortune (Ed.), *Task-centered practice with families and groups*. New York: Springer.

Mills, P. R. (1985). Conjoint treatment within the task-centered model. In A. E. Fortune (Ed.), *Task-centered practice with families and groups*. New York: Springer.

Norcross, J. C. (1986). Eclectic psychotherapy: An introduction and overview. In J. C. Norcross (Ed.), *Handbook of eclectic psychotherapy*. New York: Brunner/Mazel.

Rathbone-McCuan, E. (1985). Intergenerational practice with older families. In A. E. Fortune (Ed.), *Task-centered practice with families and groups*. New York: Springer.

Reid, W. J. (1985). *Family problem solving*. New York: Columbia University Press.

Reid, W. J., & Epstein, L. (Eds.). (1977). *Task-centered practice*. New York: Columbia University Press.

Rzepnicki, T. (1982). Task-centered intervention: An adaptation and test of effectiveness in foster care services. (Doctoral dissertation, School of Social Service Administration, University of Chicago).

Tolson, E. R. (1977). Alleviating marital communication problems. In W. J. Reid & L. Epstein (Eds.), *Task-centered practice*. New York: Columbia University Press.

INDEX